Garland
Studies
in

AMERICAN INDIAN LINGUISTICS

A series of ten monographs containing the results of some of the most significant recent research in the field.

Navajo Verb Prefix Phonology

James M. Kari

Garland Publishing, Inc., New York & London

1976

Copyright © 1976

by James M. Kari

All Rights Reserved

Library of Congress Cataloging in Publication Data

Kari, James M
   Navajo verb prefix phonology.

   (Garland studies in American Indian linguistics)
   Originally presented as the author's thesis, University of New Mexico, 1973.
   Bibliography: p.
   1. Navaho language--Phonology. 2. Navaho language--Verb. 3. Navahi language--Suffixes and prefixes.
I. Title. II. Series.
PM2007.K3 1976   497'.2   75-25117
ISBN 0-8240-1968-7

Printed in the United States of America

NAVAJO VERB PREFIX PHONOLOGY

BY

James M. Kari

B.A., University of California at Los Angeles, 1966

M.A.T., Reed College, 1969

DISSERTATION

Submitted in Partial Fulfillment of the
Requirements for the Degree of

Doctor of Philosophy in Education: Curriculum and Instruction
in the Graduate School of
The University of New Mexico
Albuquerque, New Mexico

August, 1973

ACKNOWLEDGMENTS

Many people have aided and encouraged me in the preparation of this dissertation.

I will always be grateful to the many Navajos who have contributed to this study. In particular, I thank Eddie Begay, Louise Benally, Marlene Benally, Clarence Charley, Rose Fasthorse, Benny Hale, Larry King, Judy Martin, Alice Neundorf, Agnes Ortiz, Irene Silentman, Roseann Willink, John Wilson, and Paul Wilson. Also I extend special thanks to Dr. William Morgan both for his outstanding contribution to Navajo linguistics and for the commentary he provided me on Navajo linguistic diversity. More generally, I am indebted to all of the Navajos who, in recent years, have made Navajo bilingual education a reality and who have made Navajo linguistics a field of both theoretical and practical importance.

I acknowledge the aid of many persons at the University of New Mexico who have provided a stimulating and congenial environment for my graduate studies. In particular, I thank Professor Bruce Rigsby who first introduced me to linguistics and who has given encouragement and friendship throughout the preparation of this work. I am indebted to Professor Bernard Spolsky for the education he has given me in the social relevance of linguistics and in many other things. It has been a rare privilege to work with Dr. Robert Young for the past two years. This dissertation owes much to his kindness and patience as well as to his profound knowledge of the Navajo language. I express my gratitude to a teacher of classical linguistics, Professor Stanley Newman, who, although not on my dissertation committee, gave generously of his time at all stages of this work and read the manuscript with care. And credit is due Ms. Judy Benedetti who has endeavored to make me a better organized scholar.

I state my obligation to Professor Michael Krauss for his writings on comparative Athapaskan, his encouraging correspondence over the past two years, his assistance in orienting me to Athapaskan and Tanaina in the summer of 1972, and, more generally, for his commitment to making linguistics of practical use to Indian people.

I will always be grateful to the person who has contributed so much to Navajo linguistics in recent years, Professor Ken Hale. This dissertation began with a reading of his "Navajo Linguistics, Part I" and was fundamentally affected by personal correspondence and two visits with Professor Hale. I, like many other, deeply respect Professor Hale for his creative and humane approach to linguistics.

I express my continuing gratitude to my parents who have given me their constant love and encouragement in all the years of my education.

Lastly, I give my thanks to my wife, Priscilla, who has made this possible.

TABLE OF CONTENTS

CHAPTER		PAGE
I	Introduction	1
II	Introduction To Navajo Phonology and Morphology	5
	2.1 Review of Previous Research	5
	2.2 Phonetics and Distinctive Features	10
	2.3 A Sketch of the Navajo Verb System	16
	2.4 Position and Function of the Verb Prefixes	19
	2.5 Approaches to the Organization of the Verb Prefixes	28
	2.6 A Reconsideration of Verb Internal Boundaries	36
	2.7 General Phonological Rules	45
	2.71 Subject Pronoun-Classifier-Stem Initial Consonant	45
	2.72 Tone Assimilation	58
	2.73 Vowel Assimilation	61
	2.74 Some Problematic Prefix Vowels	79
	2.75 Strident Assimilation	83
	2.76 Vowel Elision and J- Deletion	86
	2.77 Syllabic N-	92
	2.8 Rule Summary	95
III	Verb Mode Phonology	101
	3.1 Imperfective	103
	3.11 Ø Imperfective	104
	3.12 Ni- Imperfective	120
	3.2 Iterative	131
	3.3 Optative	138
	3.4 Progressive	146

TABLE OF CONTENTS - continued

CHAPTER		PAGE
	3.5 Perfective	167
	3.51 Ghi- Perfective	171
	3.52 Ni- Perfective	185
	3.53 Si- Perfective	196
	3.54 Perfective Summary	216
	3.55 Perfective Choice and Perfective Da- Shift	219
	3.6 Phonology of Hi- 'Seriative' and Si- 'Destruct'	229
	3.7 Mode Phonology Summary	240
	3.8 Rule Summary	245
IV	Morphophonemic Variation	252
	4.0 Introduction	252
	4.10 Types of Variation	255
	4.101 Oh- Reduction	255
	4.102 Ni- Replacement	260
	4.103 Aspect+Si	262
	4.104 Perfective Da- Shift	266
	4.105 Progressive Da- Shift	269
	4.106 Semelfactive Optative 1sg	271
	4.107 Iterative Classifier Shift	272
	4.108 Hi- 'Seriative'	274
	4.109 Si- 'Destruct'	
	4.110 Yi- Doubling	281
	4.111 Sh/Shi- 'Scold'	283
	4.112 Irregular Stem Initial Consonants	285
	4.20 Variation Summary	296

TABLE OF CONTENTS - continued

CHAPTER		PAGE
	4.30 Rule Summary	299
V	Conclusion	302
REFERENCES		307

LIST OF TABLES

TABLE		PAGE
1	Obstruents	13
2	Sonorants and Laryngeals	14
3	Vowels	15
4	Perfective Rule Summary	217

LIST OF ABBREVIATIONS

1, 1sg	first person singular
2, 2sg	second person singular
3	third person
3i	third person indefinite
4	fourth person
1d	first person dual
2d	second person dual
1p	first person plural
1-3	first person singular direct object and third person subject
I	imperfective mode
P	perfective mode
Pg	progressive mode
F	future mode
R	iterative mode
O	optative mode
U	usitative mode
P1	perfective mode, first person singular
F2d	future mode, second person dual plural
dpl	dual plural
pl	plural
pos.	position
PA	proto-Athapaskan
PAE	proto-Athapaskan-Eyak
[...]	phonetic or intermediate representation
/.../	underlying representation

LIST OF ABBREVIATIONS - continued

C	any consonant including '-, y-, and h-
V	vowel
⌐	classifier+stem
___+⌐	zero environment
+	conjunct or formative boundary
#	disjunct boundary
##	word boundary
(#)	disjunct or conjunct boundary
/.../*	modified underlying representation
*...	ungrammatical, proto-form
X	non-null
##MODE+(X)+⌐	primary mode variant or word boundary-mode-(subject pronoun)-classifier-stem
+MODE+(X)+⌐	conjunct mode variant
#MODE+(X)+⌐	disjunct mode variant

CHAPTER ONE

INTRODUCTION

Over the years the Navajo verb has acquired a reputation for being complex. It is well known that Navajo is an extremely difficult language to learn to speak as a second language. This is dramatically illustrated in Werner's 1963 study of "trader Navajo," the Navajo spoken by four white traders on the Reservation. Verb morphology was by far the traders' weakest area of linguistic accomplishment. Two of the traders studied were reasonably good speakers of Navajo but used verbs with abandon. When they attempted to render the subtle paradigmatic changes, Werner noted that their verbs were in "structureless disarray." The other two traders, who were less accomplished speakers, used verbs conservatively, generally holding to one invariant, unmarked form. Ironically, the verbs of the two poorer speakers presented fewer ambiguities than those of the better speakers, despite the fact that the latter were in closer approximation to the correct verb forms (Werner, 1963:105-134).

Although Navajo has received considerable attention by language scholars since the latter part of the nineteenth century and quite intensive study since the 1930's, many basic issues about the structure of the verb remain unresolved. The most formidable problem is posed by the verb prefixes, which appear before the stem in ten or so positions and which perform a dazzling array of derivational and paradigmatic functions. What underlies the prefix system, the position, shape, and function of the fifty or so elements that can appear there is a linguistic problem of considerable magnitude.

Navajo specialists have frequently commented on the unanalyzability of portions of the verb prefix system. In an early draft of her *Navaho Grammar* Reichard remarked, "Even in reducing the verbs to their simplest possible forms we demonstrated the necessity of considering many of them [the prefixes] as compounds . . . One reason for this situation is the great instability of Navajo prefixes and their consequent tendency to contract with other prefixes . . . A second reason is the fact that prefixes of the same kind do not by any means retain the same position in a complex" (Reichard, n.d.:1-2).

In concluding his review of Hoijer's *Navaho Phonology* (1945), the first systematic attempt to list and analyze the verb prefix morphophonemics, Zellig Harris commented, "In addition to all the regular or partially regular alternations, there are so many individual replacements that a set of general rules for deriving phonemic forms, like those devised for Tubatulabal by Swadesh and Voegelin and for Menominee by Bloomfield, seems impossible here" (Harris, 1945:246).

In his review of Sapir and Hoijer's *The Phonology and Morphology of the Navaho Language* (1967) Krauss notes, "It [SH, 1967] is, moreover, not without its shortcomings in certain areas for the analysis of even single words. These are the areas, proportionately quite large in Navaho, the analyzability of which is, from a conventional or purely synchronic point of view, very partial or marginal (where the concept of synchronic morpheme becomes quite arbitrary)" (Krauss, 1970:221).

The major objective of this study is to clarify the structure of the prefix system in the Navajo verb by doing a thorough generative phonological analysis of the morphophonemic alternations that occur in the prefix complex. I treat the most intricate paradigmatic alternations in the verb, that of the modal prefixes, in particular detail since this contributes to a clearer notion of the basic verbal paradigms. It will be demonstrated that, with the help of an important boundary distinction within the verb, the majority of Navajo verb forms can be derived by well-motivated phonological rules. However, my analysis also vindicates the claim of Harris and Krauss that certain areas of the verb resist straightforward synchronic analysis.

A second and minor objective of this study is to isolate a number of verbal structures that have been found to be used with variation. It is of considerable significance that these variations, for the most part, occur in the more obscure areas of the verb, areas that are explainable only by arbitrary or unnatural synchronic rules. The variations provide perspective to the analysis of the mode phonology and reveal insights into the processes of linguistic change in Navajo.

This study is organized as follows: Chapter Two reviews previous Navajo phonology research, introduces the sound system and the verb system, surveys several approaches to the structure of the verb prefixes and develops a statement of the verb internal boundary system, and includes extensive discussion of a number of pervasive phonological rules. Chapter Three contains a lengthy analysis of the phonology of the eight structurally distinct, regular verb modes. Each mode is discussed in a full range of environments. Other topics such as the derivational relationships that hold between certain prefixes and the phonology of two highly unstable derivational prefixes are also discussed in Chapter Three. In Chapter Four twelve types of morphophonemic variation in the verb prefix complex are presented with some empirical evidence of their use and a discussion of their significance for future study of Navajo linguistic diversity. In Chapter Five I summarize the implications of this study for Navajo linguistics and for Navajo bilingual education.

CHAPTER TWO

INTRODUCTION TO NAVAJO PHONOLOGY AND MORPHOLOGY

2.0 Introduction

This chapter contains a review of the previous research on Navajo phonology (2.1), a brief discussion of Navajo phonetics and the distinctive feature system employed in this work (2.2), a sketch of the derivational and paradigmatic systems in the Navajo verb and an introduction to the terminology and theoretical concepts used in this study (2.3), a survey of the verb prefix positions and functions (2.4), a discussion of previous approaches to the structure of the prefix system (including Stanley's boundary system) (2.5), and a reconsideration of the verb internal boundaries based on phonological evidence (2.6). After defining a new approach to the verb prefix boundaries, I present in 2.7 a discussion of a number of general phonological rules. These are rules that refer to processes that are largely independent of alternations in particular verb modes. By introducing these rules prior to the analysis of the verb mode phonology in Chapter Three, we will be able to concentrate in that chapter on the phonological rules that are unique to the mode system. This chapter concludes with a summary of the phonological rules presented herewith (2.8).

2.1 Review of Previous Research

Navajo is the most thoroughly documented of all American Indian languages (Kari, 1973). The research on or relevant to Navajo phonology can be divided into five groups that cover a full spectrum of American Indian linguistic research, from descriptivism to structuralism and generative grammar.[1]

The Franciscan Mission at St. Michaels, Arizona has been a center for Navajo language study throughout this century. The three early dictionaries by the Franciscan Fathers (1910, 1912a, 1912b) are remarkable achievements for that date; with some retranscribing they are useful sources of lexical material. The most significant work of the Franciscans is that of Fr. Berard Haile, who compiled an enormous amount of Navajo textual material. His <u>Learning Navaho</u> (1941, 1942, 1947, 1948) is an early attempt at a pedagogical grammar of Navajo. It is rather ponderously organized but contains a wealth of accurate sentence-level and lexical data and much useful grammatical information. Haile's <u>A Stem Vocabulary of the Navaho Language</u> (1950, 1951) is the most complete Navajo lexicon in print. This work is an excellent source of information on verb stems but provides less paradigmatic material and is less convenient to use in phonological study than are the Young and Morgan dictionaries.

The extended collaboration of Robert Young and William Morgan on the Navajo language is one of the outstanding achievements of American Indian linguistics. Their most important work is <u>The Navaho Language</u> (1943), which contains a useful sketch of the language that includes fairly complete lists of the postpositions and verb prefixes and the best presentation of the verb paradigms in print (henceforth YM, 1943a). The second part of the book is a well-organized Navajo-English, English-Navajo stem dictionary with full paradigmatic forms for each verb (henceforth YM, 1943b). Their later dictionary, <u>A Vocabulary of Colloquial Navaho</u> (1951), and their study of Navajo particles (1948) are valuable supplements to their 1943 work. In terms of attention to detail and ease of reference the work of Young and Morgan is unsurpassed and is the best source of information on the Navajo verb and on the phonology. Their work has served as the primary data source for Stanley 1969a and for this study.

Edward Sapir began his studies of Navajo in 1929. He amassed a great amount of data on the language but was able to prepare only a few short articles on Navajo before his death in 1939. His student, Harry Hoijer, inherited his Navajo and Athapaskan materials. Hoijer has published extensively on Navajo grammar since the 1940's. His Navaho Phonology (1945a) contains a thorough phonetic description and the first attempt to describe the complex morphophonemics in a systematic manner. A significant review of this work by Zellig Harris (1945) added several refinements to the study of the phonology. Hoijer's classic Apachean verb monograph (1945b, 1946a, 1946b, 1948, 1949) remains the best analysis of the Navajo (and Apachean) verb prefix functions. More recently, as co-author with Sapir, Hoijer has published The Phonology and Morphology of the Navaho Language (1967) (henceforth SH), which is largely a recapitulation of his earlier articles with some changes in the verb prefix system and a valuable statistical study of verb stem variation. Hoijer's approach to Navajo morphophonemics is, from the point of view of generative grammar, less than adequate because of his loosely defined use of base forms, his mixture of phonological and morphological criteria, and his tendency to repeat lists of forms rather than to seek the phonological generalization (Stanley, 1969b). These are purely theoretical limitations, however. Sapir-Hoijer 1967 contains the most complete listing of Navajo morphophonemic processes yet in print and will remain as a valuable reference work (Krauss, 1970).

The Navajo language work of Gladys Reichard stands apart from the mainstream of Navajo linguistic research. Reichard took issue with the

"Sapir School" of Athapaskan (Sapir, Hoijer, and Fang-Kuei Li) for its overconcern with structural analysis and its only incidental concern for language as a "living, cultural phenomenon" (1951:4). Her principle work on Navajo, <u>Navaho Grammar</u> (1951), purports to simplify the structure of the language by paying heed to the true meanings of the prefixes and stems. However, this work contains a conception of the verb system that is quite incomprehensible and suffers from Reichard's penchant for defining absolutely everything that shows up in verb prefix complexes (Hoijer, 1953). Occasionally, as Stanley has observed, Reichard has interesting insights into the phonology that are considerably more abstract than those of Hoijer. For example, her analysis of the perfectives as a compound prefix with an underlying perfective morpheme has been incorporated into Stanley's study and this study. Reichard's grammar is a useful source of information on Navajo linguistic diversity, to which she paid close attention, and her chapter on the verb prefixes contains much important data on derivational and aspectual properties of the verb.

Finally, in recent years there have been two dissertations and some important unpublished work on Navajo phonology from a generative perspective. Muriel Saville's 1968 study is largely based on Sapir-Hoijer 1967. Saville does not attempt to present the phonological rules in the context of any thorough analysis of the constituent structure of the verb, and the result is a rather brief and unsystematic picture of the phonology.

A far more ambitious study of Navajo phonology is that of Richard Stanley (1969a). Stanley attempts an analysis of both the complex variations in the verb stems and of the phonology of the more internal verb prefixes and stem initial consonants. His treatment of the prefixes is bold in a number of respects. He proposes that there is a complex hierarchy of seven boundaries between the verb prefixes which he uses in his treatment of the verb mode phonology. (Further discussion of Stanley's boundary system is in 2.5.) I take issue with Stanley's study of the prefixes on a number of points: 1) he limited his study of the modes to environments in which the mode prefix is word initial, and this does not provide a full structural statement of the modes; 2) his boundary system offers a stimulating approach, but it merely adds complexity to his rules and obscures a generalization about the organization of the prefixes; 3) his underlying forms for the prefixes frequently suffer from certain a priori assumptions, such as that all tones are derived (when in fact certain inherently high tones must be posited) and that all pronouns are of the shape CV (when some must be of the shape C and VC), a formulation that is too abstract and diacritic. Nevertheless, Stanley 1969a is a major contribution to Navajo linguistics in its attempt to explain stem variation as a suffixing process and in its attempt at a comprehensive statement of the mode phonology.

Lastly, I should mention the significant advances in Navajo phonology that have been made by Ken Hale. Some of his phonology work is embedded in his remarkable unpublished studies on Navajo grammar that are oriented toward the Navajo speaker (1970, 1971, 1972c; Hale and Honie, 1972), but most of his analyses are not yet written. Two personal communications from Hale to this writer are footnoted in this study (1972a, 1972b) because they contain a wealth of guiding insights into Navajo phonology.

2.2 Phonetics and Distinctive Features

The orthography used in this study follows that of Young and Morgan 1943, and not the "revised Young and Morgan" orthography (Ohannessian, 1969) which omits word initial glottal stops. We always mark word initial glottal stops, 'ani'aah, 'íilyaa. The Young and Morgan orthography was chosen over the linguistically more traditional orthographies of Haile and Hoijer because it is the system used and accepted by Navajos who are literate in their language.

I make no attempt here to discuss the phonetic details of the Navajo sound system. The reader is referred to the extensive discussion of phonetics in Hoijer, 1945a:7-31, SH:3-12, and Hale and Honie, 1972. However, a few remarks are in order. I follow Young and Morgan's practice of using only h- for both the voiceless dorso-velar fricative [x] and the laryngeal [h]. The voiceless dorso-velar continuant appears in word and syllable initial position and is weakened to a voiceless laryngeal on-glide, [h], when non-word initial, [xai] 'winter' (which is written in YM as hai), [nahashniih] 'I am trading it'. The voiceless laryngeal off-glide, [h], appears in syllable final position, [dah] 'up', [nahashniih].

The status of the phoneme y- is somewhat unclear in the literature. Both Reichard and Hoijer describe it as an unrounded front palatal semi-vowel that is produced with more friction than the English y- (Hoijer, 1945a:15; Reichard, 1951:17). Hoijer adds, "That is to say, in pronouncing Navaho y the front of the tongue is held close enough to the palate to produce a slight but audible 'rubbiness' or friction. For this reason it is very similar, especially before e and i, to the [ɣ] variant of γ" (ibid.). Thus, there is no clear phonetic distinction between y- and gh- before front vowels (although this merits closer phonetic study).

In his 1967 work Hoijer adopts the convention of writing gh- before e- and i- in stem initial position and y- before e- and i- in prefix initial position. Hoijer claims, "this convention fits the phonetic facts in most instances although the two sounds, in the case of some speakers, have apparently fallen together. The convention also points up the fact that the two phonemes have different historical origins" (SH:10). Krauss has criticized the arbitrariness of this solution since the convention obscures the fact that both gh- and y- can occur before front vowels in prefix initials and in stem initials (1970:221-222). In this study considerable morphophonemic evidence is presented which shows that y- and gh- can be distinguished in both prefix initial and stem initial positions. To summarize: 1) Both prefix initial gh- and y- delete intervocalically, but it can be shown that the environments of the deletions are not identical; gh- deletes much earlier than y- (see especially the discussion of vowel assimilation in 2.73); 2) underlying gh- is dipthongized to y- before front vowels and to w- before back vowels, while underlying y- remains unchanged before both front and back vowels (see 3.112); 3) stem initial gh- devoices to h- (x-) when it follows a voiceless segment and becomes g- (or g^{gh}-) when next to d- (2.71); on the other hand, it appears that there are in fact two separate stem initial y-'s, one that preglottalizes to 'y- when next to d- (2.71) and one which changes to dz- when next to d- (4.112).

In this study I generally follow the distinctive feature system that has been developed by Hale and Honie (1972). With four additions, the distinctive feature charts from that work are given here as Tables

1, 2, and 3. The orthography at the top of the charts is that of Young and Morgan; that at the bottom is the conventional phonetic notation.

This distinctive feature system differs from that proposed by Stanley (1969a:32-34) in a few minor details. Stanley uses the feature [vocalic] instead of [syllabic]. He treats the unaspirated stops, b, d, dz, j, dl, and g as [+voiced], a practice which is counter to the Athapaskan tradition of treating these segments as voiceless. He also treats the sonorant y- as though it is in velar position, $\begin{bmatrix} -cor \\ -ant \end{bmatrix}$, while Hale and Honie put it in palato-alveolar position, $\begin{bmatrix} +cor \\ -ant \end{bmatrix}$.

Following Harris (1945) prefixal long vowels (with one or two exceptions) are analyzed as clusters of two underlying short vowels, e.g. yah 'ooh'aah 'you dpl carry it in' derives from /'i-oh-'aah/, where i- becomes o- by vowel assimilation. However, in Table 3 a length feature has been added to account for the one inherently long vowel that occurs in underlying forms in the prefix complex, ii- in the first person dual pronoun, iid-. It is also possible that another prefix, the +i+ aspect, contains an inherently long vowel. Although I ignore stem vowels in this study, a length feature is often necessary for them.

Other additions to the feature system are in Table 1 where I have added an unaspirated dorso-palatal stop, g^y-, a marginal innovation at present, and an obstruent y- that is separate from the sonorant y- in Table 2. The obstruent y- is actually a front dorso-velar fricative that would be written phonetically as [γ̝]. In 4.112 the phonological evidence is given for these additional obstruents. Note that I have listed both of these sounds as $\begin{bmatrix} +coronal \\ -anterior \end{bmatrix}$, i.e. in palato-alveolar position. It is probably more precise to treat these sounds in palatal position with the addition of tongue body features, $\begin{bmatrix} -cor \\ -ant \\ +hi \\ -bck \end{bmatrix}$. However,

Table 1

Obstruents

	b	d	t	t'	dz	ts	ts'	z	s	j	ch	ch'	zh	sh	dl	tl	tl'	l	ł	gʸ	y	g	k	k'	gh	x,h
syllabic	−	−	−	−	−	−	−	−	−	−	−	−	−	−	−	−	−	−	−	−	−	−	−	−	−	−
consonantal	+	+	+	+	+	+	+	+	+	+	+	+	+	+	+	+	+	+	+	+	+	+	+	+	+	+
sonorant	−	−	−	−	−	−	−	−	−	−	−	−	−	−	−	−	−	−	−	−	−	−	−	−	−	−
coronal	−	+	+	+	+	+	+	+	+	+	+	+	+	+	+	+	+	+	+	+	+	−	−	−	−	−
anterior	+	+	+	+	+	+	+	+	+	−	−	−	−	−	+	+	+	+	+	−	−	−	−	−	−	−
continuant	−	−	−	−	−	−	−	+	+	−	−	−	+	+	−	−	−	+	+	+	+	−	−	−	+	+
nasal	−	−	−	−	−	−	−	−	−	−	−	−	−	−	−	−	−	−	−	−	−	−	−	−	−	−
lateral	−	−	−	−	−	−	−	−	−	−	−	−	−	−	+	+	+	+	+	−	−	−	−	−	−	−
strident	−	−	−	−	+	+	+	+	+	+	+	+	+	+	−	−	−	−	−	−	−	−	−	−	−	−
aspirated	−	−	+	−	−	−	−	−	−	−	+	−	−	−	−	+	−	−	−	−	−	−	+	−	−	−
glottalized	−	−	−	+	−	−	+	−	−	−	−	+	−	−	−	−	+	−	−	−	−	−	−	+	−	−
voiced	−	+	−	−	+	−	−	+	−	+	−	−	+	−	+	−	−	+	−	+	+	+	−	−	+	−
	b	d	t	t̓	ʒ	c	c̓	z	s	ǰ	č	č̓	ž	š	λ	ƛ	ƛ̓	l	ł	gʸ	ɣ	g	k	k̓	ɣ	x

Table 2

Sonorants and Laryngeals

	m	'm	n	'n	w	'w	y	'y	'	h
syllabic	−	−	−	−	−	−	−	−	−	−
consonantal	+	+	+	+	−	−	−	−	−	−
sonorant	+	+	+	+	+	+	+	+	−	−
coronal	−	−	+	+	−	−	+	+	−	−
anterior	+	+	+	+	−	−	−	−	−	−
continuant	+	−	+	−	+	−	+	−	−	+
nasal	+	+	+	+	−	−	−	−	−	−
lateral	−	−	−	−	−	−	−	−	−	−
strident	−	−	−	−	−	−	−	−	−	−
aspirated	−	−	−	−	−	−	−	−	−	−
glottalized	−	+	−	+	−	+	−	+	−	−
voiced	+	+	+	+	+	+	+	+	−	−
	m	m̓	n	n̓	w	w̓	y	y̓	ʔ	h

Table 3

Vowels

	i	e	a	o	į	ę	ą	ǫ	í	é	á	ó	ii
syllabic	+	+	+	+	+	+	+	+	+	+	+	+	+
consonantal	−	−	−	−	−	−	−	−	−	−	−	−	−
nasal	−	−	−	−	+	+	+	+	−	−	−	−	−
high tone	−	−	−	−	−	−	−	−	+	+	+	+	−
high	+	−	−	−	+	−	−	−	+	−	−	−	+
low	−	−	+	−	−	−	+	−	−	−	+	−	−
back	−	−	+	+	−	−	+	+	−	−	+	+	−
rounded	−	−	−	+	−	−	−	+	−	−	−	+	−
long	−	−	−	−	−	−	−	−	−	−	−	−	+
	i	e	a	o	į	ę	ą	ǫ	í	é	á	ó	i·

Hale and Honie's feature system seems to be adequate.

Finally, I have added one sound to Table 2, a preglottalized back glide, 'w-, a marginal innovation to be discussed in 4.112.

2.3 A Sketch of the Navajo Verb System

In this section I present a brief sketch of the organization of the Navajo verb system as it is traditionally characterized in the Navajo literature. This conception of the verb can rightly be called the 'Sapir-Hoijer verb'. This description is intended primarily as an introduction to the key terminology and theoretical concepts used in this study. The reader is referred to Hoijer, 1945b, 1946a, 1946b, 1948, 1949, 1964; SH:85-103; YM, 1943a:41ff; and Stanley, 1969a:27-94 for further discussion of the verb system.

All Navajo verbal constructions consist of a <u>verb stem</u> and, minimally, a paradigmatic prefix.[2] Verbs can contain several paradigmatic prefixes to indicate person, number, mode, tense, and aspect. In addition, the majority of verbs contain one or more derivational prefixes that are mainly adverbial in function. The derivational prefixes combine with the stem to obtain the particular lexical meaning of the verb. The <u>verb base</u> is the dictionary entry for a Navajo verb. It consists of a stem, a classifier (one of four morphemes that occur immediately in front of the stem), and the derivational prefixes, if any. For example, the stem -bąąs, which refers to the rolling of a wheel, appears in a variety of bases: ł-bąąs 'arrive (by car)', ha...ł-bąąs 'drive it up', ch'í...ł-bąąs 'drive it out', naa-ná...ł-bąąs 'turn it around'.

A <u>verb form</u>, following Stanley 1969a:40, is a verb base plus one or more paradigmatic prefixes and is a word that functions syntactically as a verb. In this study, following the practice of generative phonology,

I treat the verb forms at two levels: at the level of phonetic representation and at the level of underlying (or systematic phonemic) representation. For example, the verb base ch'í...łbąąs appears in the phonetic verb form [ch'ínísbąąs] 'I am driving it out' which derives from the underlying representation /ch'í#ni+sh+ł+bąąs/, where [...] signals phonetic representation (frequently, where it is clear from context, phonetic forms are written without [...]), and /.../ signals the underlying representation. The principal task of this study is to determine the underlying representations of the Navajo verb forms and to account for their phonetic forms by phonological rules.

Navajo verbs are subdivided into two structural categories, neuter and active. Neuter verbs are mainly adjectival in connotation, defining "eventings solidified" (Hoijer, 1964:145). They are inflected only for person and take no inflection for mode. Neuter verbs comprise about one-sixth of Hoijer's corpus of bases. In this study only occasional reference is made to neuter verbs. Several interesting problems in neuter verb phonology deserve further attention.

The active verbs report "eventings in motion" (ibid.). These are conveyed not in a tense system, but in an elaborate mode system that is marked by prefixes in three positions in the verb prefix complex and by variations in the shape of the verb stem. An active verb base can be expressed in as many as seven mode paradigms: imperfective (I), perfective (P), progressive (Pg), future (F), iterative (R), usitative (U), and optative (O). The meanings of the modes will be discussed briefly in the next section and in more detail in Chapter Three. There are two possible shapes for the imperfective mode, ∅ and ni-, and three possible shapes for the perfective, ghi-, ni-, and si-. Thus there are ten verbal paradigms.[3] A given base appears in one of three <u>conjugation patterns</u> which is, essentially, a lexical listing of its perfective prefix (although perfectives are in part predictable by derivational prefixes). These conjugation patterns are discussed further at the conclusion of Chapter Three in 3.7.

Of the ten verbal paradigms, the usitative, which is a ∅ imperfective with an iterative stem, and the future, which is derived from the progressive, are not phonologically distinctive. Therefore, there are eight distinctive mode forms. The phonological alternations that these eight modes undergo are quite intricate and abstract and are the subject of detailed analysis in Chapter Three.

As we mentioned above, mode distinctions are signalled by prefixes and by changes in the shape of the stem. A verb base is entered in the dictionary with its <u>stem set</u>, e.g. ch'í...-ł-bąąs, bą́ą́z, -bąs, -bąs, -bąąs, which are the imperfective, perfective, future, iterative, and optative stems, respectively, for 'drive it out'. Some stems have as many as five distinct stem shapes, while others have an invariant stem throughout. This stem variation reflects an archaic suffix system. In this study I completely ignore this most complex area of the phonology. Stem variation has received matrix analysis by Pike and Becker (1964), statistical study by Hoijer (SH:56-67), and phonological analysis by Stanley (1969a:Chps.3 & 4). In future studies of Navajo stem variation it will be important to incorporate comparative Athapaskan data as well.

The Navajo mode system is even more complex. Verb bases built upon a single verb stem often take more than one set of stem allomorphs, cf. na-bí...-ghil, -ghil, -ghił, -gił, -ghil 'push it about' and ni-bí...-ghííł, -ghil, -ghił, gił, -ghííł 'push it to a point'. The distinctive stems most often appear in the imperfective and the perfective. This variation in stem sets is a vestigial aspectual system that crosscuts the mode system and is marked by obscure stem suffixes and by adverbial and aspectual prefixes. Hoijer has calculated that about one-third of the verb bases in his corpus take two or more aspectual stem sets, and he has isolated nine aspectual stem configurations, the most transparent of which is momentaneous-continuative. In the two 'push' verb bases given above the na- 'about' prefix in the first verb selects the continuative imperfective stem, -ghil, while the second verb contains the momentaneous imperfective stem, -ghííɬ.

In this study I make occasional reference to the phonology of some of the aspect prefixes. (See 3.114). In particular, I analyze (with marginal success) the mysterious +i+ aspect prefix. However, I make no attempt to handle the influence of aspect on prefix and stem phonology in a systematic way.

2.4 The Position and Function of the Verb Prefixes

To further introduce the verb it is instructive to survey briefly the relative position and function of the prefixes that appear in front of the verb stem. The prefix position slots represent the full surface structure of the verb. They should not be equated with the deep structure of the verb which, though not completely worked out as of yet, is devoid of certain prefixes such as subject and object pronoun, deictic, and plural which are syntactically predictable.

In Hoijer's first treatment of the verb prefixes, thirteen positions in front of the verb stem were posited (1945b).

```
IndObj-Postpos-Adv-Theme-It-Pl-DirObj-Deic-Adv-Tense-Mode-Subj-Cl-Stem
   1       2     3    4   5  6    7     8   9   10    11   12  13
```

In his 1967 study Hoijer made several simplifications in this system.

Since indirect object-postposition are only occasionally thematized to a verb base and are more frequently free forms, positions 1 and 2 were removed. Thematic prefixes were grouped with the adverbial prefixes in pos. 3 since the distinction between them is largely degree of productivity rather than position. The tense prefix which was used for the di- of future verbs was collapsed with the pos. 9 adverbial prefixes into an aspect category. Hoijer's revised verb has nine positions in front of the stem.

Adv-It-Pl-Obj-Deic-Asp-Mode-Subj-Cl-Stem
 1   2 3 4   5   6   7   8   9

In this study I follow essentially the same scheme. However, following Hale 1972a, I add a separate perfective prefix after the mode prefix. (The phonological explanation for this addition is presented in 3.5.)

Adv-It-Pl-Obj-Deic-Asp-Mode-Perf-Subj-Cl-Stem
 1   2 3 4   5   6   7   8   9   10

We survey the functions of the prefixes from right to left beginning with the classifier in position 10. The reader is directed to Hoijer (1945b, 1946a, 1946b, 1948, 1949; SH:85ff) and Young (1973) for further discussion of the prefix functions. Abbreviations are given in parentheses for prefixes cited frequently in this work.

Position 10--Classifier (Cl)--There are four classifier prefixes, ∅, ł-, d-, and l-. Since every verb must have a classifier, all verbs are labelled as ∅, ł-, d-, or l- class verbs. Hoijer has calculated that 43% of Navajo verb bases have a ∅ classifier and that the other three classifiers each appear in 19% of the bases.

The functions of the classifiers are still not well understood. Primarily, the classifiers have a voice function marking transitivity and passivity. ∅ is often an intransitive (but not always). Ł- is most

usually a causativizer-transitivizer and d- a passivizer. L- is most
frequently a passive of a causative and can be shown to be phonologically
secondary much of the time. In the formation of passives classifiers
alternate in a regular pattern known as a <u>classifier shift</u>: ∅ becomes
d- as in yi'aał 'he chews it' and yi<u>t</u>'aał 'it is chewed', and ł- becomes
l- as in yiyííłts'ee' 'he ate mush' and yi<u>l</u>ts'ee' 'mush was eaten'.
Certain prefixes and postpositions such as 'ádi- 'reflexive', 'ahi-
'reciprocal', and bi-'i-di- 'agentive passive' also require a shift to
the passive classifier.

Secondarily, classifiers have a derivational function. For reasons
that are obscured in time, certain verbs are associated with a classifier
to which no clear function can be assigned. For example, yáłti' 'he
speaks' contains a ł- classifier yet it is in no way a   causative.
We refer to these as thematic classifiers.

Position 9--Subject Pronoun (Subj)--Five prefixes mark the subject
of verbs. Sh- is the first person singular (1 or 1sg), yi<u>sh</u>dleesh 'I am
painting it'. Ni- is second person singular (2 or 2sg), <u>ni</u>dleesh 'you
are painting it'. The first person dual is iid- (1d), 'iidą́ 'we are
eating', and oh- is second person dual (2d), '<u>ohs</u>ą́ 'you dpl are eating'.
Third person (3) is always marked by zero, yidleesh (yi-∅-dleesh) 'he
is painting it'.

Position 8--Perfective (Perf)--The perfective mode is formed by one
of three mode prefixes and a perfective prefix, í-, y<u>í</u>cha 'I cried'.
The synchronic and diachronic arguments for this prefix are in 3.5.

Position 7--Mode--Prefixes in position 7 mark mode distinctions.
The imperfective mode, a general present tense, is marked by ∅ and ni-.
The progressive mode, for actions performed while going along, is

marked by a ghi- modal prefix. The optative mode connotes wish or intention and is marked by ó-. The three perfectives signal completed action and are marked by si-, ni- and ghi- modal prefixes plus the í-perfective prefix in pos. 8. Full discussion of each mode is in Chapter Three.

Position 6--Aspect (Asp)--Functionally, aspect is the least understood prefix slot. Sapir called this a 'mixed relational' position (SH:97) since these prefixes are both aspectual, in that they modify the mode system, and thematic-adverbial like prefixes of pos. 1. They range in productivity from di- 'inceptive', which appears in all future constructions and in scores of bases, to si- 'destruct', which is found in just one base.

a) Di- 'inceptive' is an aspectual prefix that combines with ghi- progressive in pos. 7 to form the future mode, deeshghał 'I'll eat meat'. Di- also appears as an inceptive aspect, disbąąs 'I am starting to drive'

b) Di- 'fire' is a thematic prefix that occurs in a few bases relating to fire, yidiłid 'he is burning it'.

c) Di- 'oral' is a thematic prefix that appears in a number of verbs that make reference to the mouth, yádíshtih 'I am chattering'.

d) Di- 'elongated object' may be a reflex of Athapaskan shape classifying prefixes found in Carrier and Tanaina (Young, 1973), dah doolnih 'he is holding his arm up'.

e) Di- 'adjectival' occurs in a variety of neuter verbs, diłhił 'it is dark'.

f) Hi- 'seriative' is an aspectual prefix that marks action performed one time after another, hishtííh 'I am breaking them off one after another'. This prefix undergoes very striking phonological changes. Discussion of it is reserved until the end of Chapter Three (3.6). There may in fact be more than one pos. 6 hi-.

g) Łi- 'inherent quality' occurs in neuter verbs and historically appears to be a classifier, łichíí' 'it is red'. It undergoes unusual phonological alternations (See 3.125).

h) Yí- 'tentative' may be historically related to the incorporated postposition, bí- 'against' that occurs in pos. 1. It occurs in verbs denoting indirect perception or indefinite destination. Reichard glossed this prefix as 'doubtful destination', yínishdon 'I am shooting at it', yínibé 'you are picking fruit', yínishíh 'I am calling him, naming him'. There may in fact be more than one yí- or í- prefix in pos. 6. Yí- 'tentative' undergoes very radical phonological alternations. It seems to occur with a ni- modal prefix, but, unlike the ni- imperfective, takes an unexplained ó- in zero environment, yínishbé 'I am picking fruit', yóbé 'he is picking fruit'. See Krauss, 1970:225-226 for an interesting discussion of yí- 'tentative'.

i) Ni- 'have the quality of' is an adjectival prefix that appears in neuter verbs, nidaaz 'he is heavy'.

j) Ni- 'terminative' is an aspectual prefix that indicates motion to a point, nidaah 'he sits down'.

k) Ni- 'inchoative' appears in inchoative aspect constructions, bi'niiłbéézh 'I started to boil it'.

l) Ni- 'roundish object' like di- 'elongated object' may be a vestigial shape classifying prefix such as is found in some Northern Athapaskan languages, dah <u>n</u>eesht'ááį 'I am proud' (I am holding up a spherical object--my head) (Young, 1973).

m) Dzi- 'streak' is an aspectual prefix that in active verbs always appears in compounds with a pos. 1 adverbial prefix, 'adzíítááł 'I gave it a kick'.

n) I- (uncertain meaning) appears in a number of aspectual subsystems, yiitaɬ 'you are kicking it'. We refer to this prefix (or prefixes) as '+i+ aspect'. This prefix poses numerous phonological difficulties. (See 3.114.)

o) Jii- 'emotion' is a phonologically aberrant thematic prefix that is found in two or three bases, jiinishɬá 'I hate it'.

p) Si- 'destruct' occurs in one base, 'kill it', sisxé 'I kill it', and is highly unusual phonologically (3.6).

Position 5--Deictic (Deic)--The three pos. 5 prefixes have extremely complex syntactic functions that are only partially understood at present. These prefixes undergo an array of interesting phonological rules as well (see 2.74 and 2.76).

The 'i- (or 'a-) 'third person indefinite' (3i) prefix seems to have an ergative function. It marks an unspecified object in transitive verbs, 'asdiz 'I am weaving (something)', 'ayą́ 'he is eating (something)'. It also functions as an unspecified subject in intransitives, 'azį́ 'someone stands', 'anitééh 'someone habitually lies down'. 3i also appears in agentive passive constructions as an indefinite subject, ch'íbidi'neelchą́ą́' 'he was chased out'.

Ji- 'fourth person' (4) can only refer to human (or personified animal) subjects and is often introduced into the verb in coreference constructions. It is also used as an honorific. See Akmajian and Anderson, 1970 for syntactic analysis of ji-, jibizh 'he is braiding it'.

The hwi- (or ho-) 'area' prefix has at least three functions. Like ji-, it is syntactically introduced in coreference constructions and functions as a human object, hweeshtééɬ 'I am carrying him along' (Akmajian and Anderson, 1970). Hwi- also functions as a locative agreement marker, Bill bikooh hoołtsą́ 'Bill saw the canyon' (Kaufman, 1972). And in certain verbs hwi- acts as a thematic derivational prefix (often of vague meaning), hótaał 'you are singing'.

Position 4--Direct Object (Obj)--Six direct object prefixes appear in pos. 4: shi- first person singular, shijoołtééł 'he is carrying me along'; ni- second person singular, niiłtsą́ 'he saw you'; nihi- first person and second person dual, nihiiłtsą́ 'he saw you/us'; yi∿bi, third person singular, yiztał 'he kicked it', biztał 'it was kicked by him'.[4] Yi∿bi- are particularly interesting syntactically. Yi- is obligatorily inserted into the third person of all transitive verbs (unless there is an 'i- 3i object). It alternates with bi- in obviative-proximative constructions (Parrish, Anderson, Akmajian, and Hale, 1968; Hale, 1973a). Yi∿bi- can also occur as a thematic object prefix in the so-called 'transitivized' verbs, bidishní 'I say it to him', yidííniid 'he said it to him'.

Two other pos. 4 prefixes are 'ahi- 'reciprocal', 'ahoot'į́ 'they see each other', and 'ádi- 'reflexive' ('á- is a pos. 1 prefix), 'ádiishghé 'I am killing myself'. These two prefixes trigger a shift to the passive classifier.

Position 3--Plural (Pl)--One prefix, da- occurs in pos. 3. It is generally a distributive (rather than collective) plural. It can pluralize the subject or the object of verbs, dayiiłtsą́ 'they pl saw it', 'ádaniłééh 'you sg are making them'. Plural formation is an extremely complex syntactic process in Navajo, da- being only one of the pluralizers. Hale 1972c contains some stimulating analysis of plural formation. Plurality is also discussed by Witherspoon (1971), Haile (1941:124-128), and Sapir-Hoijer (1967:89-90).

Position 2--Iterative (It)--One prefix, ná-, occurs in pos. 2. It appears in iterative mode constructions with no prefix in pos. 7, náshdlish 'I repeatedly paint it'. It optionally causes a classifier shift.

Position 1--Adverbial (Adv)--The prefixes in pos. 1 are derivational in function. They co-occur with the stem and with other prefixes from pos. 5 or 6 to provide the lexical meaning of a verb base. There are five subdivisions in the pos. 1 prefixes. Below is an abbreviated list of pos. 1 prefixes which are 25-30 in number.

a) Some prefixes in pos. 1 are very productive derivational prefixes. Some of these are: na- 'about', naabé 'he swims about'; ch'í- 'out', ch'íiníłbą́ą́z 'he drove it out'; 'i- 'away', yah 'ani'aah 'you carry it inside'; na- 'down', náálne' 'I dropped it'; ha- 'up and out', háínígeed 'you dug it up'.

b) Other adverbial prefixes are quite unproductive and are thematic with certain stems, yá- 'talk', yáshti' 'I am speaking'; so- 'pray', sodiszin 'I am praying'; hasht'e- 'ready', hasht'eiilnééh 'we are preparing it'; cho- 'use', choyooł'į́ 'he is using it'.

c) A few pos. 1 prefixes are postpositional in origin and are actually compound prefixes consisting of a direct object and a postposition. (Postpositions are discussed in the following section.) These include bi- 'against' (bi+í), nabínighil 'you are pushing it around', and bik'í 'on it' (bi+k'í), bik'íołtih 'you dpl cover it up'.

d) Two pos. 1 prefixes are aspectual in connotation, ná- 'back', nááshtééł 'I am carrying an animate object back'; náá- 'semeliterative, once again', náánááshtééł 'I am carrying an animate object once again'.

e) Young has recently demonstrated that a set of object pronoun prefixes may occur in pos. 1 under the following conditions: 1) a

transitive verb base containing no postposition but has an indirect
object, shiidiitsih 'he pointed it at me', shideidiitsih 'they pl
pointed it at me' (where shi- object is to the left of da- plural);
2) a transitive verb in which the direct object is thematic hwi-, or
'i- in pos. 5 and which includes an indirect object, as bihodiiłt'i' 'they
got him into trouble', bidahodiilt'i' 'we pl got him into trouble'; and
3) certain transitivized passive verbs as yinoodzin 'he hexed him',
yidanoodzin 'they hexed him' (Young, 1973).

Position 0-00--Prepounded particles--In the prefix position system
now being used for the Navajo verb by Hoijer, Hale, and Young and Morgan,
postpositions and adverbial particles that occur in front of verbs are
treated as free forms. It is sometimes the case that these particles
are thematized or prepounded to the verb base. For example, in 'áyaa
'iish'nííł 'I subjugate them', the adverbial 'áyaa 'under self' must be
listed in the lexicon as part of the verb base. In biih yítłizh 'I fell
into it', the indirect object bi- and the postposition -iih 'into' are
part of the verb base. Young has proposed that such indirect object-
postpositions be given the position numbers 0-00 (1973).

It is clear that Navajo is still undergoing what Sapir termed the
characteristic Athapaskan process of 'polysynthesis', a trend toward
the incorporation of free elements into the verb complex as prefixes of
fixed position. This trend is most graphically illustrated by the
postpositions which are, at times, completely free forms, while at other
times, as in the above examples, are independent words that are thematized
to bases. Still other postpositions are found within the prefix complex
in pos. 1 such as bí- 'against' and bik'í- 'on it' described above.

2.5 Approaches to the Organization of the Verb Prefixes

The general conception of the Navajo verb and functions of the verb prefixes sketched in the two previous sections are reported in the literature with considerable consistency. However, we find that due to theoretical differences among the students of Navajo and to certain discrepancies in terminology, details of the structure of the prefix system have been reported quite variously. In this section I will survey the different ways in which the prefix system has been structured. I will argue (in this chapter and in Chapter Three) that a thorough phonological analysis of the verb will resolve many of these inconsistencies and will contribute to a clearer notion of the regularities within the verb and, in particular, to the organization of the verb mode paradigms.

Young and Morgan define two types of paradigm: <u>conjunct</u>, when derivational prefixes occur to the left of the mode prefix and <u>disjunct</u>, when there are no derivational prefixes to the left of mode (1943a:77). In YM's paradigm section each mode is listed in terms of these two categories. There is one set of disjunct forms for each mode, but usually several types of conjunct forms are given. For example, in the imperfective mode section we find listed as conjunct I (verb 2, p. 79) a paradigm for pos. 5 'a- 3i.

(1) 'asdiz 'I am spinning'

(2) 'ídiz 'you are spinning'

Another conjunctive paradigm, conjunct IV (verb 4, p. 80), is given for pos. 1 adverbial prefix 'a- 'away, out of sight'.

(3) yah 'iish'aah 'I carry it out of sight'

(4) yah 'ani'aah 'you carry it out of sight'

Clearly, a distinction beyond this conjunct-disjunct definition is needed to explain why these two "conjoined" prefixes that are apparently phonetically identical undergo different phonological processes, i.e., in (1) the vowel of 'a- is unchanged but in (3) it is realized as 'ii-; in (2) ni- has been absorbed by the preceding prefix and has raised its tone but (4) retains ni-.[5]

Hale follows the Young and Morgan conjunct-disjunct distinction in his 1956 presentation of ten model verb paradigms (pp. 30-38). However, most of his model paradigms include a list of allomorphs for one or more of the pronominal forms. For example his P1 lists two second person singular pronouns, ni- and í- and would thus include both (2) and (4).

In his Apachean verb monograph Hoijer identifies three functional categories of prefixes: themes (invariable derivational prefixes), prefix complexes (variable derivational prefixes), and paradigmatic prefixes (classifiers, mode prefixes, deictic prefixes, and subject, object, and indirect object pronouns). Paradigm classes are defined by the prefix in pos. 7 mode (or, in the case of future, by pos. 6 aspect and pos. 7 mode) (1946a). Phonological alternations for the paradigms are noted only for mode-subject pronoun-classifier-stem. The adverbial and aspectual prefixes receive little phonological study and are assumed not to affect paradigm classes.

Although Hoijer does not set up conjunct and disjunct paradigm types as do Young and Morgan, he makes use of these terms in his description of the imperfective mode. "Apachean has three imperfective paradigms: the regular (or conjunct) imperfective, the h- (or disjunct) imperfective, and the n- (or completive) imperfective" (1946a:1). In a footnote he adds, "The terms conjunct and disjunct were used by Sapir and also by the author in previous publications" (Ibid.). No other definition is provided, but we learn from his presentation that the regular conjunct imperfective takes "subject pronoun set 1" which is defined as having high toned V̂ for 2sg pronoun, and that h- disjunct imperfective takes "subject pronoun set 2" which has ni- for 2sg (1945b:202). Thus, (2) 'ídiz, is an imperfective conjunct and (4) 'ani'aah, is an imperfective disjunct. Note the conflict in terminology: according to YM, both of these verbs are conjunct. Furthermore, Hoijer's pronoun set criterion says nothing about (1) and (3) where there are differences in the vowel quality and length of the 3i and adverbial prefixes.

It will be shown (below and in Chapter Three in the treatment of the imperfectives) that Hoijer's disjunct-conjunct distinction is essentially the correct one. However, the classification of 2sg pronouns is only one of several important alternations that can be clarified by disjunct-conjunct.

In Hoijer's 1967 study, the disjunct-conjunct distinction is dropped entirely. Instead he divides the verb prefixes into two groups, derivational prefixes (DPr) and paradigmatic prefixes (PPr) (SH:13). No phonological rationale is given for this categorization, and, as such, it serves only to mark the morphological-semantic relations amongst the prefixes. The morphological character of DPr-PPr is illustrated by SH's treatment of the absorption of ni-. In one case a DPr, pos. 6 ni- 'possessed of a certain quality', goes to high tone when preceded by a PPr, e.g. jídaaz (ji-ni-daaz) 'he is heavy'. In another case a PPr, ni- 2sg goes to high tone when preceded by a PPr or a DPr, e.g. shíł'á (shi-ni-i-'á) 'you ask me to do an errand' and díbááh (di-ni-bááh) 'you start to war' (SH:22). Recall that in (4) ni- is preceded by a DPr which does not absorb it. It should be obvious that the morphological DPr-PPr distinction cannot handle the ni:í alternations.

Reichard's conception of the verb is most difficult to understand due to her bold semantic analysis and to her insistence on coining her own terminology. She groups the modes in essentially the same way as do Hoijer and Young and Morgan despite terminological differences. Most innovative is her notion of a verb "system" which is a grouping of "temporal, aspective, and modal distinctions, all of which are made by similar processes" (1951:129). Reichard defines four systems: the progressive-continuative, the inceptive, the cessative, and the repetitive. The progressive-continuative system includes what other scholars call the progressive, future, yi- perfective and the continuous imperfective modes, all of which have a yi- modal prefix and a meaning of unrestricted motion. (However, the yi- of the imperfective will later be shown to be separate from the other three.) Reichard's criterion that a system group modes and aspects made by similar processes is relaxed for the inceptive system. Inceptives include momentaneous imperfectives with di- 'start from', ni- imperfectives and perfectives with ni- 'start for', and momentaneous yi- imperfectives. The cessative system groups all verbs with +i+ aspect prefixes which are rather dubiously glossed as "pause while . . ." Cessative crosscuts other systems, e.g. di+i- is called an inceptive cessative, "starts to pause". Interestingly, Reichard was critical of Hoijer's and Young and Morgan's use of the term 'disjunctive' calling it "misleading" and "inaccurate" (Reichard and Bittany, 1940:13). Without further explanation, she notes that "the cessative as treated in this analysis, particularly as determining the inceptive and perfective cessative conjugations and as accounting for some distinctive principal parts, enables us to eliminate the 'conjunct' and 'disjunct' categories of Hoijer and Young-Morgan" (1951:133). The repetitive system groups verbs that take hi- 'seriative' and its allomorph, yi-. Thus, all modes are viewed as being affliated with one of these systems.

There are serious limitations to Reichard's system distinction. The inceptive mixes aspectual prefix di- and modal prefix ni-. Since there is no clearly defined structural principle for grouping the modes and aspects, Reichard resorts to semantic intuitions that result in modes with the same prefix complexes appearing in different systems (yi-imperfective) and systems crosscutting other systems (inceptive cessatative). Hoijer has criticized Reichard's system distinction as a confusion of the mode-aspect and derivational prefix systems, a confusion brought about by her vaguely defined use of semantics as an organizing principle (Hoijer, 1953:82).

The system distinction is disregarded in Reichard's paradigm chapter where verb prefixes are arranged alphabetically with modes and lists of bases given for each prefix (1951:154-293). Verbs (1) and (2) would be classed as paradigmatic forms for 'a- 3i in the imperfective and (3) and (4) as forms for 'a- 'away, out of sight' in the imperfective (pp. 177-179). The paradigm chapter is noteworthy because of the extensive information it contains on derivational prefixes. The paradigms convey far more about patterns in the verb prefixes than do the systems.

Stanley's treatment of the verb prefix boundaries is the most elaborate attempt to set up structural categories within the prefix complex to account for phonological alternations. He argues that a language of Navajo's morphological complexity requires a system of morpheme boundaries that is far more involved than the word boundary (#), formative boundary (+), affix boundary (=) system used in Chomsky and Halle's analysis of English phonology. He posits a strong-to-weak hierarchy of six "positional" boundaries, #, =, *, !, ", +, plus a formative boundary, -, that occurs when two or more prefixes fall between a pair of stronger boundaries. Stanley claims that, "As a general rule, affixes close to the stem undergo more collapsing, with each other and with the stem, than formatives far from the stem" (1969a:99). He offers a grouping of the prefixes that contains five boundaries internal to the verb:

```
#OPP-ADV-IT*PL-OBJ-DEIC!ASP"MODE+SUBJ-PERF-PAS-CAUS=STEM#.
  1   2   3  4  5    6     7   8     9   10   11   12
 ‾‾‾‾‾‾‾‾‾‾‾ ‾‾‾‾‾‾‾‾ ‾‾‾‾‾ ‾ ‾‾‾‾‾‾‾‾‾‾‾‾‾‾‾‾‾‾‾‾‾‾‾‾
      A           B      C  D              E
```

Each section of the verb prefix system that is surrounded by a pair of boundaries from the hierarchy is labelled A through E. The boundaries to the right of # become increasingly weak until = stem boundary which is the strongest verb internal boundary. PAS and CAUS stand for the passive classifier d- and the causative classifier ł- which Stanley treats as being in two separate positions.

To demonstrate the utility of the boundary hierarchy, Stanley cites the alternations for 2sg, $\hat{V}$:ni-. He would account for (2) by noting that underlying ni- is preceded by a type B prefix ('a- in pos. 5), while (4) is preceded by a type A prefix ('a- in pos. 1). In terms of the boundary hierarchy, each would have a different underlying representation: (2) /#*! 'a "+ni=STEM/ and (4) /# 'a *!"+ni=STEM/. He contends that the full set of positional boundaries (i.e., excluding - formative boundary) must be listed with the lexical representation for each verb, claiming that the information is needed for many phonological rules.

He establishes a convention that phonological rules apply to a section of lexical representation delineated by positional boundaries. He can then explain (2) by two rules.

(5) $i \rightarrow \emptyset$ / *CVn___...=

(6) CVn $\rightarrow$ CV̂ / #...___C...#

Rule (5) can only apply to (2) because 'a- is to the right of *, the boundary between A and B. In (4) 'a- is to the left of * so neither (5) nor (6), which feeds into (5), can apply. The three boundaries to the right of A*B, !, ", and +, need not be mentioned in (5) because they are weaker than the boundary that triggers the rule (1969a:105-6).

Stanley has made some revisions in his first system of boundaries in an unpublished article (1971). He points out that his earlier formulation, which he terms a "positional approach", is limited in that it treats word internal boundaries and surface structure boundaries of the syntactic component as separate systems (pp. 16-17). He goes on to outline a new approach that once again lists a hierarchy of boundaries in the lexicon for each verb. All external and internal boundaries are then assigned by rules based on the surface structure. Within the verb the surface structure assigns # to each of the major boundary divisions.[6] At this point he states: "An elaborate set of principles apply to weaken various occurences of #. These principles would first involve setting up a hierarchy of classes of affixes, where class membership is determined by how closely the affix combines with adjacent material" (p. 27). He then groups the Navajo verb into nine affix classes. (This grouping reflects a change in his 1969 position. No longer does = stem boundary rank higher that A*B. In fact, it ranks next to weakest, allowing the boundaries to increase in strength consistently to the left of stem.) With these conventions the hierarchal nature of the positional boundaries is retained, and the system is made sensitive to the surface constituent groupings.

Kiparsky, in a brief comment, has gone even further to formalize the Navajo boundary hierarchy. He suggests that the boundaries be abandoned in favor of a system of bracketing that predicts boundary strength and that blocks or triggers rules at the same time. Kiparsky then suggests that the richness of the morphology will reflect the number of potential boundaries that are operative in a language (1971:644).

Despite the fact that the Navajo internal boundary hierarchy has been formalized so that it can be incorporated into the syntactic component, and despite Kiparsky's suggestion of the utility of the hierarchy for cross-linguistic research, there is very little evidence that there is any need at all for a hierarchy of boundaries in the Navajo verb. In Stanley 1969a the only clearly phonological evidence for an internal boundary stronger than formative boundary centers around the behavior of 2sg ni- (as discussed above). However, Stanley rejects the notion that there is a simple strong-weak division in the prefixes, claiming that further distinctions to the right of A*B boundary are needed to differentiate phonological rules.

The empirical nature of Stanley's boundary hierarchy is suspect. He notes: "It is intuitively clear that languages like Navajo with complex morphologies must have several phonologically distinguishable boundary types, but deciding precisely how many types are needed and how they are distributed is exceedingly difficult" (1971:12). Nowhere do we find justification for either of the two A-E prefix divisions. The recent claim that the grouping reflects "how closely the affix combines with adjacent material" is unsupported. It will be demonstrated that there are only two boundaries within the verb that block and trigger phonological processes. One is something akin to the A*B boundary, and the other is a formative boundary. All other internal boundaries, !, ", +, and =, are not provably of different strength, and, in Stanley 1969a, function only to mark prefix position. They can be more graphically represented by either prefix numbers (pos. 6, 7, etc.) or by morphological labels (aspect, stem, etc.). Furthermore, Stanley's formulation of boundaries is seriously limited due to the fact that he did not treat the phonology of prefixes to the left of pos. 6 aspect to any extent. The important boundary related processes, such as ni- absorption versus ni- preservation, are keyed to a boundary several positions to the left of aspect.

By briefly reviewing the major studies of the organization of the verb prefix system, we find numerous discrepancies. Certain terms, such as conjunct-disjunct, are being used in virtually antithetical ways whereas other terms, such as Reichard's system, are not generally understood. Although semantic, morphological, and, most recently, suspiciously complex and diacritic phonological approaches have been used to describe verb prefix patterns, the Young and Morgan verb paradigms remain the most secure statements about the structure of the verb.

In the next section I will attempt to resolve a number of these issues by reviewing the question of verb internal boundaries.

2.6 A Reconsideration of Verb Internal Boundaries

First we will look at the alternations for ni- 2sg. As seen in (2) and (4), ni- alternates between $\hat{V}$- on the preceding prefix and ni-. In (7) I place ni- next to a wide range of left hand environments.[7] In parenthesis is the prefix position number. Note that all but the first three forms are ∅ imperfectives (with pos. 7 empty).

(7)

a. (7) ghi Pg   yílghoł 'you are running along'
b. (7) ni I   nílgheed 'you are in the act of arriving running'
c. (7) si imp[8]   dah sí'aah 'you are putting it up'
d. (6) si destruct   síłxé 'you are killing it'
e. (6) di inceptive   díbááh 'you are starting to war'
f. (6) di fire   díłid 'you're burning it'
g. (6) hi seriative   hítííh 'you break them off one after another'
h. (6) dzi streak   'abídzíłhaał 'you bat it off'
i. (6) ni terminative   nídaah 'you sit down'
j. (5) 'i 3i   'ídiz 'you are spinning'
k. (5) hwi area   hótaał 'you are singing'
l. (4) shi obj   łeeh shíłteeh 'you're burying me'
m. (4) nihi obj   łeeh nihíłnííł 'you are burying us'
n. (3) da pl   'ádaníééh 'you are making them'
o. (2) ná iterative   nánídlish 'you repeatedly paint it'
p. (1) 'i away   yah 'ani'aah 'you carry it out of sight'
q. (1) na about   nanilnish 'you are working'
r. (1) ha up   hanigééd 'you are digging it up'
s. (1) da die   danitsaah 'you are dying'
t. (1) yá speak   yáníłti' 'you are speaking'
v.   ∅   nicha 'you are crying'

The generalization from (7) is that ni- goes to high tone on the vowel of the preceding prefix when the prefix belongs in pos. 4, 5, 6, or 7. Ni- is retained if it is preceded by nothing or by a prefix in pos. 1, 2, or 3. Stanley's rules 5 and 6 predict all forms in (7) except 7n. The A*B boundary in rule 5 limits the deletion of i- to cases where ni- is preceded by prefixes in B, C, or D. Note above that Stanley's A*B boundary is placed between pos. 2 and pos. 3. This implies that 7n, da- pl, will group with the object pronoun, etc. to absorb ni-, e.g. *'ádálé. Thus, it is more precise to set the A*B boundary between pos. 3 and pos. 4. A reformulation of Stanley's rules 5 and 6 will follow the presentation of the data in (8) and (9).

In (8) we see that when a vowel initial pronoun, oh- 2d, is preceded by a CV prefix, two alternations are realized.

(8)
- a. (7) ghi Pg   woh'nah 'you dpl are crawling along'
- b. (7) ni I   noht'ááh 'you dpl arrive flying'
- c. (7) si imp   dah soh'aah 'you dpl are putting it up'
- d. (6) si destruct soɫxé[9] 'you dpl kill it'
- e. (6) di inceptive dohbááh 'you dpl start to war'
- f. (6) di fire   dohɫid 'you dpl burn it'
- g. (6) hi seriative hohtííh 'you dpl break them off'
- h. (6) dzi streak 'abídzóɫhaaɫ[9] 'you dpl bat it off'
- i. (5) 'i 3i   'ohdiz 'you dpl are spinning'
- j. (5) hwi area   hohtaaɫ 'you dpl sing'
- k. (4) shi obj   ɫeeh shoɫteeh[9] 'you dpl bury me'
- l. (3) da pl   daohcha 'you dpl cry'
- m. (2) ná iterative naóhdlish 'you dpl repeatedly paint it'
- n. (1) 'i out of sight yah 'ooh'aah[10] 'you dpl carry it out of sight'
- o. (1) ha up   haohgééd 'you dpl dig it up'
- p. (1) na about   naohniih 'you dpl are distributing them'
- q. (1) yá speak   yaóɫti'[9] 'you dpl speak'

These forms show that a CV prefix of position 4, 5, 6, or 7 becomes C in front of oh- whereas a prefix of position 1, 2, or 3 retains its vowel (although the prefix vowel may alter in quality as in 8n). Thus the environment for vowel deletion in (8) patterns nicely with the environment for ni- absorption in (7).

Next look at a less common alternation, the behavior of the unusual pos. 6 hi- 'seriative' prefix when it is preceded by nothing and by several types of prefixes.

(9)

a. ∅   hishtííh 'I am breaking them off'
b. (2) ná iterative náhashtííh 'I repeatedly break them off'
c. (3) da pl   dahiitííh 'We pl are breaking them off'
d. (5) ji 4   jiitííh 'he is breaking them off'
e. (1) na about   nahashniih 'I am trading it'
f. (2) ná iterative nináhashniih 'I repeatedly trade it'
g. (3) da pl   ndahiilniih 'we are trading it'
h. (4) yi obj   nayiiłniih 'he is trading it'
i. (5) ji 4   njiiłniih 'he is trading it'

In 9d, h, and i hi- has been reduced to i- when preceded by a prefix from pos. 4 or 5. In the other verbs, where hi- is preceded by prefixes from pos. 1, 2, or 3, the h- is present in the surface forms. To account for this we must have a rule that deletes the h- of the seriative prefix under certain conditions. In (9) as in (7) and (8) the distinction between left and right hand prefixes is essential.

The fact that three processes, ni- absorption, vowel deletion, and seriative h- deletion are triggered when ni-, oh-, and hi- are preceded only by prefixes from pos. 4, 5, 6, or 7 is a strong indication that there is a boundary between positions 3 and 4. Furthermore, it will become apparent in formulating rules for (7), (8), and (9) and elsewhere that there is no need for boundaries of differing strengths to the right of pos. 4. We posit in (10) that the verb has only one strong internal boundary, #.

(10)   ##ADV+IT+PL#OBJ+DEIC+ASP+MODE+PERF+SUBJ+CL+STEM##
         1   2 3   4   5   6   7   8   9 10

The # boundary is analogous to Stanley' A*B boundary, and all other prefixes are separated by + formative boundary. A double occurence of # signifies word boundary.

Phonological rules in Navajo can be conditioned in several ways. Following Hale (1972a, 1972b) I establish several conventions. A number of rules are constrained to apply only before classifier+stem. The symbol [signals classifier+stem. Segments that appear immediately before [are said to be in _zero environment_. C stands for any consonant (including glottal stop and y-). In certain instances C can include elements found in classifier or stem initial consonant position. Some rules are conditioned by [but can be preceded by an optional consonant, C_0[. In a few rules where the stem initial consonant and not the classifier is critical, STEM is listed. These conventions allow us to state the full range of morphological conditions.

Now we can reformulate Stanley's rules 5 and 6 into a single _ni-absorption_ rule:

(11) CV+ni+[→ CV́

Rule 11 will absorb ni- only if it is preceded by + formative boundary and will retain ni- if preceded by # boundary. Furthermore, in order for ni- absorption to operate, ni- must be in zero environment, i.e. if some segment intervenes between ni- and [the rule will not apply.

This is not clear from the data in (7). Forms such as honishteeh 'I carry him to a point', where sh- pronoun intervenes between CV+ni___+C prove that ni- absorption must be constrained to zero environment. This constraint on the rule will be discussed again in 3.123.

                  7g/hi+ni+tííh/   7r/ha#ni+gééd/

ni-absorp: [hí+tííh]

ultimately: [hitííh]   [hanigééd]

Ni-absorption is blocked from 7r by # which appears lexically because ha- is a pos. 1 prefix.[11]

In (8) vowel deletion is also triggered by a + formative boundary:

(12) V → ∅ / C___+V.

                8e/di+oh+bááh/   8p/na#oh+niih/

vowel del: [doh+bááh]

ultimately: [dohbááh]   [naohniih]

Rule 12 deletes the first of two vowels if separated by + but is blocked by a pos. 1 prefix like na- which is followed by #.

The forms in (9) can be accounted for by a <u>seriative h-deletion</u> rule:

(13) h → ∅ / CV+___i.

Rule 13 preserves h- when it is preceded by # or ## and deletes it when it is preceded by +.[12]

                9e/na#hi+sh+i+niih/   9i/na#ji+hi+i+niih/

ser. h-del: [na#ji+i+i+niih]

ultimately: [nahashniih]   [njii+niih]

Note that rule 13 must follow rule 12, vowel deletion, to preserve the long vowel.

Rules 11, 12, and 13 apply only if the + formative boundary is present. They are blocked by the presence of a strong # boundary. This type of rule has been called a "ranked" rule by McCawley (quoted in Stanley, 1971:3), in that the rule is ranked by the weakest boundary that blocks its application. However, there is no need to assume that rule ranking in Navajo requires a full hierarchy of boundaries as Stanley has claimed (1971:6). Further differentiation between the prefixes separated by + can be handled by marking the morpheme class, e.g. [+Aspect], which states the non-phonological nature of such restrictions better than boundaries that are not provably of one strength or another.

Fang Kuei Li, in his masterful 1933 study of Chipewyan phonology writes,

> An examination of the prefix system in Chipewyan reveals to us some very interesting facts that give us certain indications as to the conditions under which certain weakening, loss or coalescence may take place. We find that prefixes in Chipewyan can be divided into two main groups, the primary prefixes and the secondary prefixes. Belonging to the primary prefixes are . . . the modal, aspectual, pronominal subject prefixes and the classifiers of the verb. Belonging to the secondary prefixes are the local, adverbial prefixes and the incorporated nouns and postpositions of the verb. In another word, the primary prefixes stand nearest to the stem and adhere more closely together than the secondary prefixes which stand further away from the stem, e.g. before the third person pronominal objective and subjective prefixes of the verb and have less coalescence between the stem . . .
> Another interesting fact that is thus revealed is that the consonants of the primary prefixes are few in kind . . . There are no aspirated (with the exception of t-) and glottalized stops and no affricatives of any sort. The secondary prefixes, on the other hand, have as rich a consonantal system as the initial of the stem syllable. It seems clear that the secondary prefixes are probably late incorporations of independent stems, many of which, however, do exist as such in Chipewyan (1933:459-60).

Li goes on to cite numerous phonological processes that are keyed to the primary-secondary prefix distinction. For example, he notes the following 2sg behavior: θįdá 'sit down' ← Ath.*se-ne-da; nè'áɬ 'you are chewing it', 'ànèlè 'you are making it so' where ni- absorbs to a nasal (instead of a high tone) on the preceding prefix or is retained exactly as it is in Navajo.

In his 1946 Chipewyan sketch, Li relabels these two prefix classes. The prefixes more closely attached to the stem are called conjunctives, and the prefixes before the pronominal object are called disjunctives. Recall that Hoijer used these same terms in his early Athapaskan work but defined them only with respect to ni- 2sg. I propose that Li's conjunct-disjunct distinction be applied to the Navajo verb. That is, prefixes in pos. 1, 2, or 3 shall be called disjunctive prefixes, and prefixes in pos. 4, 5, 6, 7, 8, 9, or 10 shall be called conjunctives. The # boundary shall be called the "disjunct boundary", connoting the fact that prefixes to its left are "disjoined" from the stem and more loosely attached phonologically. We note that in the Navajo verb, just as Li noted for Chipewyan, the conjunctive prefixes are formed from a very limited set of consonants (only b, d, n, ł, l, s, dz, sh, j, h, hw, gh, and ' appear in lexical representation in pos. 4-10), whereas the disjunctives can take almost the full range of consonants.

In addition, it is of considerable significance that in Eyak, the archaic pre-Athapaskan language and the important link in the Na-Dene hypothesis, the verb begins with the direct object (Krauss, 1965). This confirms Li's speculation on the relatively recent historical origin of the disjunctive prefixes.

This use of disjunct-conjunct contradicts YM's use of the terms. Hopefully, the terminological confusion that has arisen amongst Navajo scholars who have followed YM's usage (Hale, 1956) and Athapaskanists who have followed Li's usage (Krauss, 1970) will be rectified.

There are still unanswered questions about Navajo boundaries, and future research must incorporate syntactic evidence. Sometimes the prepounded particles discussed in 2.4 enter into sandhi with verb prefixes. For example, in shaazhdoo'ááł 'he'll give it to me' ← shaa jidoo'ááł (which is a slow speech variant) and in dash‿doo'ash 'they will start off' ← dah jididoo'ash (also a slow speech variant) shaa and dah have triggered ji- vowel elision and deaffrication (rules to be discussed below in 2.76). This suggests that a boundary weaker than ##, perhaps another #, separates the thematized preverbs and pos. 1.

We have seen that the disjunct boundary is essential for preventing pos. 1, 2, or 3 prefixes from triggering three common phonological rules. We will find this boundary participating in a number of other rules as well. In addition, the alternations in the verb mode paradigms can be accounted for with considerably greater generality with the disjunct boundary than without it. With the disjunct distinction we are able to classify all verb bases in one of three mode variants: 1) the primary mode variant has no derivational prefixes in front of the mode slot, i.e. mode is word initial, ##MODE+(X)+[(where X is subject pronoun); 2) the conjunct mode variant has a derivational conjunct prefix from pos. 4, 5, or 6 prior to mode, +MODE+(X)+[; and 3) a disjunct mode variant has a derivational disjunct prefix from pos. 1, 2, or 3 before mode, #MODE+(X)+[.13 I will use the three mode variants in Chapter Three to present the modes in all of their structural realizations. In sum, the # disjunct boundary is essential for defining the Navajo active verb.

2.70 General Phonological Rules

Before we investigate the phonology of the verb modes, we must introduce a number of phonological rules that occur frequently in Navajo verbs and that are independent of the mode phonology. I refer to these rules as general phonological rules. I first take up the rules that affect subject pronoun-classifier-stem initial consonant which are fundamental to the derivation of any verb (2.71). Then I look at the tone assimilation rule (2.72) and at the very intricate set of processes that are involved with the assimilation of vowels (2.73). I will demonstrate that this analysis of vowel assimilation helps to determine the underlying form of certain verb prefixes (2.74). I also take up several rules that alter prefixes further to the left of the stem such as strident assimilation (2.75), vowel elision and j- deletion (2.76), and syllabic n- (2.77).

2.71 Subject Pronoun-Classifier-Stem Initial Consonant

Subject pronoun-classifier-stem initial consonant phonology has received extensive treatment. Useful summaries of the alternations appear in Hoijer, (1945a:41-48), Sapir-Hoijer (1967:49-56), Young-Morgan (1943b:IV-VI), and Reichard (1951:31-43). Stanley (1969a:Chps. 5 and 6) and Higgins (1971) have done generative analyses of these positions. In addition, Hale (1972c) and Hale and Honie (1972) treat some of these processes. Higgins' study, "A dialogue on the Navajo classifier", is the most thorough formal analysis of this area of the verb and, at the same time is an interesting experiment in linguistic writing, being written for Navajo speakers in the form of a Socratic dialogue.

I will employ the following lexical representations for the prefixes that appear in pos. 9 subject pronoun and pos. 10 classifier:

$$\begin{Bmatrix} /\ \emptyset\ / \\ /\ sh\ / \\ /\ ni\ / \\ /\ iid\ / \\ /\ oh\ / \end{Bmatrix} + \begin{Bmatrix} /\ \emptyset\ / \\ /\ ł\ / \\ /\ l\ / \\ /\ d\ / \end{Bmatrix} + STEM.$$

A very common alternation in the stem initial consonants of ∅-class verbs is presented in the imperfectives for (14) 'to be ticklish', (15) 'to be burning', (16) 'to spit it out', and (17) 'to spit'.

(14) 1 yish̲hozh   (15) 1 dishł̲id
      2 ni̲g̲hozh   2 díl̲id
      3 yi̲g̲hozh   3 dil̲id
      2d woh̲hozh   2d dohł̲id

(16) 1 hadis̲óóh   (17) 1 dish̲ah
      2 hadíz̲óóh   2 díz̲hah
      3 haidiz̲óóh   3 diz̲hah
      2d hadohs̲óóh   2d dohsh̲ah

We see a voiced continuant (gh, l, z, or zh) in stem initial position when preceded by a vowel but a voiceless continuant (h, ł, s, or sh) when preceded by the voiceless continuants of the 1sg pronoun, sh-, and the 2d pronoun, oh-. A voicing assimilation rule accounts for the alternations in (14)-(17) in a straightforward manner.

(18) $\begin{bmatrix} +cns \\ +cnt \\ +voi \end{bmatrix} \rightarrow [-voi]\ /\ \begin{bmatrix} +cnt \\ -voi \end{bmatrix}$ ____

Of course, rule 18 allows us to view the phonetic voiceless stem initial continuants as non-systematic phonemes derived by voicing assimilation (Stanley, 1969a:218).

Rule 18 can be collapsed with the rule that devoices word initial continuants in noun stems (Hale, 1971:57-64; Hale and Honie, 1972:119).

(19) a. saad 'language'   bizaad 'his language'
     b. shéé 'saliva'   bizhéé 'his saliva'
     c. łį́į́' 'horse'   bilį́į́' 'his horse'
     d. hosh 'cactus'   bighosh 'his cactus'

Therefore, I revise rule 18 as a <u>continuant devoicing</u> rule:

$$(18) \quad \begin{bmatrix} +cns \\ +cnt \\ +voi \end{bmatrix} \rightarrow [-voi] \;/\; \left\{ \begin{matrix} \#\# \\ \begin{bmatrix} +cnt \\ -voi \end{bmatrix} \end{matrix} \right\} \underline{\quad}.$$

The first of the revised rules sub-parts can account for the voiceless initial continuants in (19), preserving the claim that stem initial continuants are always voiced.[14]

Rule 18 operates almost without exception. However, Hale has recently noted that certain neuter verbs with ∅ classifier show a sequence of voiceless+voiced continuants, e.g. nishzhóni 'I'm nice' (cf. nizhóni 'it is nice') and dinishghin 'I am holy' (cf. dighin 'he is holy') (Hale, 1972c:28). At present these verbs must be viewed as exceptions. This is one of the mysteries of neuter verb phonology.

Proto-Athapaskan is reconstructed without voiced fricatives. Krauss suggests that historically stem initial fricatives became voiced intervocalically. Yet there is no case for such a rule being operative in Navajo phonology as Howren (1971) has assumed. Navajo forms presented in Krauss 1969 (p. 56) such as naashzhee' ← nə s łə shee' 'he went hunting' reflect the proto forms, vocalized *łə- (l-) classifier and voiceless stem initial fricative, and should not be regarded as synchronic underlying forms. Howren has formulated a synchronic continuant voicing rule for Dogrib (forthcoming).

Rule 18 should predict that ł-class stems will show devoiced continuants. This is evident in gh- initial stems such as -ł-ghozh 'to tickle it', cf. (14).

(20) 2 niłhozh

3 yiłhozh

21. 2/ni+ł+ghozh/

cont devoic: [ni+ł+hozh]

ultimately: [niłhozh]

The following paradigms for (21) 'to dribble it along' and (22) 'to tame it' at first glance seem to violate the claim that stem initial continuants are voiced. But note the l- classifier appearing in ld.

(21) 1 disááes   (22) 1 yishǫǫh
     2 dísááes   2 nishǫǫh
     3 yidisááes   3 yishǫǫh
     ld diilzááes   ld yiilzhǫǫh
     2d dohsááes   2d wohshǫǫh

Young and Morgan list these verbs under s- in their dictionary and comment, "Many of the s- initial stems insert l- before the stem and change s- to z- in ldpl" (1943b:174). However, I choose to account for the voicelessness of the stems by positing an underlying ł- classifier which has devoiced z- or zh- and then has been deleted. For this a ł- deletion rule is needed.

(23) ł → ∅ / ___ {s, sh}

22. 3/yi+di+ł+záás/

cont devoic: [yi+di+ł+sááes]

ł dele: [yi+di+sááes]

ultimately: [yidisááes]

The ld forms preserve the voiced continuants because ł- classifier has become voiced after the d- of the ld pronoun iid-. This d- is then deleted. I add ł- voicing and d- deletion rules which will be discussed further below.

(24) ł → l / d___

(25) d → ∅ / ___C

22.1d/iid+ł+zhǫǫh/

ł voic:	[iid+l+zhǫǫh]
d dele:	[ii+l+zhǫǫh]
cont devoic:	————
ultimately:	[yiilzhǫǫh]

In addition, a late rule that degeminates a sequence of two identical consonants must be formulated to account for the 1sg forms 21.1, 22.1, as well as 16.1 and 17.1. Consonant degemination is given as (26).

(26) C C → C
    [αF] [αF]

where: F stands for any set of features.

	17.1/di+sh+ł+zhah/	23.1/sh+ł+zhǫǫh/[15]
cont devoic:	[di+sh+ł+shah]	[sh+ł+shǫǫh]
ł dele:	[di+sh+shah]	[sh+shǫǫh]
C degem:	[di+shah]	[shǫǫh]
ultimately:	[dishah]	[yishǫǫh]

A transitivized l- initial stem, such as -ł-lid 'cause it to burn' (cf. (15)) is presented in (27).

(27) 2 dił id

    3 yidił id

If we revise our ł- deletion rule (23) to delete ł- in front of ł- as well as in front of s- or sh-, we can derive the verbs in (27) as follows:

(23) ɬ → ∅ / ___ $\begin{bmatrix} +cnt \\ +cor \\ -voi \end{bmatrix}$

	27.2/di+ni+ɬ+lid/	27.3/yi+di+ɬ+lid/
cont devoic:	[di+ni+ɬ+ɬid]	[yi+di+ɬ+ɬid]
ɬ dele:	[di+ni+ɬid]	[yi+di+ɬid]
ni-abs:	[dí+ɬid]	———
ultimately:	[díɬid]	[yidiɬid][16]

According to the continuant devoicing rule, we would expect l-class continuant initial stems to remain voiced. In (28) I present an l-class verb, 'to hunt'.

(28) 1 haashzheeh
      2 hanilzheeh
      3 haalzheeh
      2d haoɬzheeh

Because of the intervening l- classifier, zh- does not become voiceless in 28.1 or 2d. However, this l- has been deleted in 1sg and has been devoiced in 2d. Other l- and ɬ-class verbs behave like 28.1. The 1sg and the third person of si- perfectives also show a deletion of the classifier. Observe the deleted classifier in the right-hand column of (29).

(29) a. niɬhozh 'you tickle it'   yishhozh 'I tickle it'
     b. nilghaɬ 'eat meat'   yishghaɬ 'you eat meat'
     c. síníɬgan 'you dried it'   yisgan 'he dried it'
     d. hashínílzhee' 'you hunted'   haashzhee' 'he hunted'[17]

To account for 28.1 and the right-hand column in (29) we must assume that l- and ɬ- classifiers are deleted between two consonants. Note that because l- blocks devoicing in 28.1 and 2d and in 29b and d, the new classifier deletion rule must be ordered after devoicing and thus can be written for ł- alone, since all cases of l- will have turned to ł- by devoicing.

(30) ł → ∅ / C__C

	28.1/ha#sh+l+zheeh/	29a/sh+ł+ghozh/
cont devoic:	[ha#sh+ł+zheeh]	[sh+ł+hozh]
cl dele:	[ha#sh+zheeh]	[sh+hozh]
ultimately:	[haashzheeh]	[yishhozh]

In the derivation for 28.1, l- has become ł- and then has been deleted, preserving the zh- stem initial consonant.

We have yet to account for 28.2d, haołzheeh where the usual oh-pronoun has been altered. The forms in (31) show that the h- of the oh-pronoun is lost in front of ł- in certain environments but is retained in others.

(31) a. wołhozh 'you dpl are tickling him'
 b. wołghał 'you dpl eat meat'
 c. dohłid 'you dpl are burning'
 d. wohshǫǫh 'you dpl are taming it'

31a and b pattern with haołzheeh in that h- is deleted. 31c and d are l- initial stems with ∅ and ł- classifier, respectively. If we restrict the h- deletion rule to an environment in which h- is deleted in front of ł+C, we can explain 28.2d and 31a and b where h- is deleted and 31c, d, and e where h- is retained.

(32) h → ∅ / __łC

	28.2d/ha#oh+l+zheeh/	31c/di+oh+lid/
cont devoic:	[ha#oh+ł+zheeh]	[di+oh+łid]
h-dele:	[ha#o+ł+zheeh]	_____
ultimately:	[haołzheeh]	[dohłid]

Rule 32 is blocked from 31c because the ɬC environment is not met.

The causative homonym of 31c, 31d, can also be exempted from h-deletion if certain ordering relationships are observed (Higgins, 1971:63). If ɬ- deletion comes before h- deletion, the ɬC environment is removed and h- is preserved. The final form, 31e, can be handled by the same ordering.

	31d/di+oh+ɬ+lid/	31e/oh+ɬ+zhǫǫh/
cont devoic:	[di+oh+ɬ+ɬid]	[oh+ɬ+shǫǫh]
ɬ dele:	[di+oh+ɬid]	[oh+shǫǫh]
h dele:	_____	_____
ultimately:	[dohɬid]	[wohshǫǫh]

Rule 32, h-deletion, is critically ordered with respect to two rules. As seen in the previous derivations, rule 23, ɬ- deletion, is ordered before h-deletion to account for the cases where h- is retained. This justifies the revised version of ɬ- deletion (see footnote 16), and this allows rule 26, consonant degemination, to be kept late in the ordering. In addition, classifier deletion must follow h-deletion as the following erroneous derivation shows:

28.2d/ha#oh+l+zheeh/

cont devoic:	_____
cl dele:	[ha#oh+zheeh]
h dele:	_____
ultimately:	*[haohzheeh]

So far I have made only brief mention of the ld verbs. I noted that 21.1d and 22.1d contain l- classifier instead of the ɬ- that is present in the other forms of those paradigms. In (33) three types of ld verbs are presented.

(33) a. yiilghozh 'we tickle it'

b. yiilziih 'we miss it'

c. yéiilti' 'we are speaking'

d. haiilzheeh 'we hunt'

e. yiilghał 'we eat meat'

f. yiicha 'we cry'

g. 'iikááh 'we make a sandpainting'

Recall that 21.1d and 22.1d were explained by rule 24, ł- voicing. The underlying d- of the 1d pronoun, iid-, changed ł- to l-. This d- then disappeared by rule 25, d- deletion. 33a, b, and c are underlying ł-class verbs, and they are also derived by ł- voicing and d- deletion.

                33c/yá+iid+ł+ti'/

ł voic: [yá+iid+l+ti']

d dele: [yá+ii+l+ti']

ultimately: [yéiilti']

On the other hand, 33d and e are underlying l-class stems, and ł- voicing is inapplicable. D- deletion removes the d- in 34d, e, f, and g.

           33d/ha#iid+l+zheeh/   33g/'i+iid+kááh/

ł voic: ————————   ————————

d dele: [ha#ii+l+zheeh]   ['i+ii+kááh]

ultimately: [haiilzheeh]   ['iikááh]

The d- of 1d pronoun has a greater role to play. The well known "d- effect" rule was first formulated by Sapir (1949:79) and has been given recent attention by Stanley (1969a:250) Hoijer (1969) and Howren (1971). Note the alternation of the stem initial consonant in the 1d forms (in the right-hand column) of these ∅ class verbs.

(34) a. dizééh 'he belches'   diidzééh
    b. yózhíh 'he names him'   yíníijíh
    c. yiiloh 'he ropes it'   yiidloh
    d. naaghaał 'he looks about'   neiigaał
    e. yímáás 'he arrives rolling'   yii'máás
    f. yiniih 'he hears about it'   yii'niih
    g. 'iiyóół 'he takes a breath'   'ii'yóół[18]
    h. yoo'į́ 'he sees it'   yiit'į́

In 34a-d underlying voiced continuants z-, zh-, l-, and gh- become non-continuant dz-, j-, dl-, and g-. In other words, they have retained their position features but have taken on d-'s non-continuancy. In 34e-g we see that nasals m- and n- and glide y- become glottalized when preceded by the ld pronoun. Finally, in 34h a stem initial glottal stop becomes t'.

To be more phonetically precise, a [-continuant] gh- is actually an affricate, g^{gh}-. This affricate is detected in a distinct rounded release before o-. In nighozh 'you are ticklish', yiig^{w}ozh 'we are ticklish' and in naa'ííghod 'I fell over stiffly', naa'iig^{w}od 'we fell over stiffly' the rounded dorso-velar affricate, g^w- is in clear phonetic contrast with forms such as deeshgoh 'I'll fall down' which comes from underlying /goh/. (Some interesting variation in the g^w- forms will be presented in 4.112.) It appears that a late phonetic rule deaffricates g^{gh}- to g- before i-, e-, and a- although this deserves closer phonetic study. There may be a slight contrast between /d+gh/ and /g/ before vowels other than o-. For example, 'asiig^{y}eh /'i+si+í+iid+gheh/ 'we got married' appears to have a somewhat more strongly palatalized g- than does nígeed /ni+í+geed/ 'I dug a ditch'.

Other than the ':t' alternation, which requires a change in three features and which we simply list, all alternations in (35) can be handled by the following d- effect rule:

(35)
$$d + \left\{ \begin{array}{c} ' \\ C \\ \left[\begin{array}{c} +cnt \\ \langle +son \rangle \end{array} \right] \end{array} \right\} \rightarrow \emptyset \left\{ \begin{array}{c} t' \\ \left[\begin{array}{c} -cnt \\ \langle +glt \rangle \end{array} \right] \end{array} \right\}.$$
$\quad\quad 1 \quad\quad 2 \quad\quad\quad 1 \quad\quad 2$

The first disjunctively ordered sub-part of d- effect applies to glottal initial stems like 34h. If this environment is not met, the portion of the rule in angled brackets applies to sonorant stem initial m-, n-, or y-. If this has not applied, the remaining environment in rule 35 applies to continuant initials. If no environment in 35 has applied, rule 25, d- deletion, removes the d- of the pronoun.

Reichard (1951:21) and Stanley (1969a:234-235) have noted the similarity between the effects of the ld pronoun on stem initials and those of the d- classifier in reflexives, reciprocals, passives, and iteratives. Stanley's solution for this is stimulating. He claims that Navajo has only two classifiers, d- 'passive' and ł- 'causative'. The l- classifier is a result of the combination d+ł, i.e., a passive of a causative. In this way, the same three rules needed for ld verbs, ł- voicing, d- effect and d- deletion can be used to account for the classifier shifts such as these in the right-hand column of (36).

(36) a. yidiyoołhééł 'he'll kill it'   'ádiyoolghééł 'he'll kill himself'
 b. joo'į́ 'he sees it'   'ahijoot'į́ 'they see each other'
 c. yiyiighą́ą́' 'he killed them'   bi'doogą́ą́' 'they were killed'
 d. yishłeeh 'I become'   náshdleeh 'I repeatedly become'

Stanley assumes that the shifted classifiers contain a transformationally introduced d- classifier. Therefore, the underlying representation of the reflexive of 36a contains two classifiers.

36a /'á#di+si+ghi+d+ł+ghééł/

ł voic: ['á#di+si+ghi+d+l+ghééł]

d dele: ['á#di+si+ghi+l+ghééł]

ultimately: ['ádiyoolghééł]

The reciprocal, passive and iterative forms in 36b-d contain just the d- classifier, and d- effect accounts for the alternation in stem initial consonant.

36b /'i+hi+ji+ghi+d+'į́/   36c /bi+'i+di+ghi+í+d+ghą́ą́'/

d eff: ['i+hi+ji+ghi+t'į́]   [bi+'i+di+ghi+í+gą́ą́']

ultimately: ['ahijoot'į́]   [bi'doogą́ą́']

    Stanley also claims that the thematic l- classifiers that we discussed in 2.4 are derived from d+ł. For these he coins the term 'pseudopassive' and adds, "the use of the passive classifier in pseudopassives is quite different from its use elsewhere. In pseudopassives it functions simply as a derivational prefix which, furthermore, need not even have any remnant of passive meaning" (1969a:86). However, the d+ł solution seems to be too deep for the non-alternating thematic l- classifiers. In this study, I will treat l- classifier as derived from d+ł only if it is in alternation with ł-, e.g. 36a. Otherwise, l- classifier will be listed as such in lexical representation.[19]

    The inflectional d+ł passive classifiers seem to be the only productive compound classifier system in Navajo. Krauss has reviewed the evidence for Navajo compound classifiers and has called for further research on the matter (1969:65). Reichard and Bitanny state that l- and d- classifiers can combine in derivative function to mean "be caused (l-) by (d-)" (1940:12). However, this is hardly a productive process.

An example of the l+d combination is kǫ' yilt'ááł 'a torch is being carried along' (Reichard and Bitanny, ibid.; Haile, 1950:118) which derives from /yi+l+d+ááł/. But other -t'ááł bases such as 'áyaa 'i-t'ááł 'to subjugate it', biza ni-t'ááł 'to kiss her', and bigha di'ni-t'ááł 'to persuade him' do not appear to take l- in passive constructions.

Another instance of a compound classifier is in the verb 'loiter' which is derived from the verb 'go' presumably with d+l classifiers. The singular stem of 'go' is vowel initial, -ááł ('go' is one of several stems that take suppletive stems for singular, dual, and plural). The singular stem set for 'loiter' is -dlááł, -dlá, -dláá', -dlaah, -dla', e.g. 'áhodiyíídlááł 'you are loitering along' /'á#hwi+di+hi+ghi+ni+d+l+ááł/ where the vowel initial stem is preceded by two classifiers.

There are rare instances of thematic l- classifiers becoming transitivized, cf. hanilgheed 'you run up and out' and habiyíłgheed 'you cause it to come running out'. The fact that stem initial gh- has remained voiced in the latter form suggests that this verb has been derived from underlying ɨ+l.

/ha#bi+hi+ni+ɨ+l+gheed/

ni absorp: [ha#bi+hí+ɨ+l+gheed]

cont devoic: [ha#bi+hí+ɨ+ɨ+gheed]

ɨ dele: [ha#bi+hí+ɨ+gheed]

ultimately: [habiyíłgheed]

Yilt'ááł, 'áhodiyíídlááł, and habiyíłgheed are best thought of as what Krauss has called 'accidental compound classifiers' (where two classifiers have become lexicalized) rather than as the result of a productive derivational process. This is in contrast to the productive derivational classifier compounding that has been observed in Hupa

(Golla, 1970:86-87) and Mattole (Krauss, ibid.)[20]

To summarize the analysis of subject pronoun-classifier-stem initial consonant positions, the phonological rules discussed in this section are listed in order of application.

(24) ł- voicing

(35) d- effect

(25) d- deletion

(18) continuant devoicing

(23) ł- deletion

(32) h- deletion

(30) classifier deletion

(26) consonant degemination

2.72 Tone Assimilation

In Stanley's analysis of the Navajo verb it is assumed a priori that there are no inherently high tones in lexical representation. High tone vowels in verb stems are derived by the absorption of nasal and glottal increments, and high tone prefix vowels are derived by nasal increments. Saville also assumes that all high tones are secondary upon the absorption of an n- increment (1968:76-78). This approach leads to a number of difficulties. Krauss (forthcoming) has pointed out that in the stem phonology, positing an underlying glottal segment to derive high tones conflicts with the comparative evidence which points to the development of high tone in Navajo in the absence of glottalization. In the prefix system there are some non-inherent high tones such as those derived by rule 11, ni- absorption, but assuming that all high tones are so derived forces improbable lexical representations for certain prefixes. For example, Stanley's representation for optative, /honhi/, will be shown to be simply /ó/.

In his classic study of the three tone levels in Sarcee, Sapir recognized some inherently high tones in nouns and verb prefixes, and he distinguished two types of derived high tone, those in verb stems and those in the prefix system (1925:194). Cook's generative analysis of Sarcee tone makes use of these same three distinctions (1971a:168-170). Inherent or 'lexical tone' is marked in underlying representation for certain noun stems and verb prefixes, e.g. mīł 'snare', mı̀ł 'sleep', míł 'moth'; nà- distributive subject, nā- 'again' (where ` is low tone and ¯ is middle tone). High tone in verb stems, or 'paradigmatic tone', is "assigned by grammatical process and is functional on the morphological level, each tone being a member of a given paradigm" (p. 169). Derived tones in the prefixes, such as those resulting from ni- absorption, are called 'syntagmatic tones'. Both paradigmatic and syntagmatic tone are assignable in the phonological component although paradigmatic tone makes use of grammatical information such as [+perfective].

In Navajo, just as in Sarcee, certain prefixes carry an inherently high tone, e.g. /ch'í/ 'out', /k'í/ 'apart', /bí/ 'against', /ná/ 'iterative, /ó/ 'optative', and /í/ 'perfective'. I will show in the analysis of vowel assimilation rules and in the analysis of the verb modes that these prefixes participate in a number of tone related phonological rules. For example, a tone assimilation rule is needed as is evident in the iteratives of the verbs in (37).

(37)   Imperfective   Iterative
   a. hanołchaad   hanánółcha' 'card it' 2d
   b. hanishchaad   hanánishcha' 'card it' 1
   c. 'adiłbąs   ń'díłbąs 'make a trip' 3
   d. 'azhdiłbąs   nízh'díłbąs 'make a trip' 4

The ná- iterative prefix has assimilated its inherently high tone onto the vowel to its right across one or more intervening consonants.[21]

However, in the following verbs with one inherently high tone prefix we see that if there is more than one CV sequence to the right of the high tone prefix or if the vowel to the right of the intervening consonant is long, tone assimilation does not take place.

(38) a. ch'ínánishchééh R1   but   ch'íninishchééh I1 'drive it out'
    b. náháshbįįh R1   but   náhojiłbįįh R4 'build a hogan'
    c. ninááshniih R1   but   ninahiilniih R1d 'trade'
    d. yádíshtih I1   but   yádiiltih I1d 'chatter'

Therefore, <u>tone assimilation</u> operates on the first syllable before C_o [, provided it contains a short vowel.

(39)   V → v̂ / v̂ (#) C_1___ +C_o [
     [-lng]

Although detailed explanation must wait until the analysis of the verb modes, it is important to point out that in order to derive the forms in (40), tone assimilation must be ordered before two rules that delete consonants, (41) <u>gamma deletion</u> and (42) <u>y- deletion</u>.

(40) a. nááshtééł /ná#ghi+sh+ł+tééł/ Pg1 'carry an animate object'
    b. yínéíłkah /yí+ná#yi+ł+kah/ R3 'track it'

(41) gh → ∅ / V(#)___V

(42) y → ∅ / V#___i

	40a/ná#ghi+sh+ł+tééł/	40b/yí+ná#yi+ł+kah/
<u>tone assim</u>:	[ná#ghí+sh+ł+tééł]	[yí+ná#yí+ł+kah]
<u>gh dele</u>:	[ná#í+sh+ł+tééł]	_____
<u>y dele</u>:	_____	[yí+ná#í+kah]
<u>ultimately</u>:	[nááshtééł]	[yínéíłkah]

In these verbs gh- and y- provide the environment for tone assimilation before they are deleted.

2.730 Vowel assimilation

Previous studies of Navajo phonology have devoted little attention to the analysis of vowel assimilation. The problem is an elusive one since assimilations occur in several different environments and are used with a great deal of variation. In a sense, vowel assimilation is the central problem in Navajo prefix phonology. An understanding of the vowel rules forms the basis for determining the output of certain phonological rules and for setting up underlying representations for a number of prefixes, in particular those that underlie the verb modes.

A check through Sapir-Hoijer, Reichard, and Saville yields few references to vowel assimilation. Only the late assimilation of Ci before velar consonants or '- followed by a- or o- is given direct attention (SH:19; Reichard, 1951:22-23; Saville, 1968:82-83). Other references to vowel assimilation in Sapir-Hoijer and Reichard are incidental to the treatment of the mode paradigms. For example, Hoijer supplies lists of vowels to illustrate vowel assimilation in each of the verb modes.

Stanley handles the vowel assimilation rules as separate processes (1969a:184, 199-200, rules 1a-1e) and, consequently, no general notion of their behavior is conveyed. For example, his rule 1a is a general rule that assimilates to o- all vowels that precede oh- 2d. But rule 1d is an extremely complex and limited rule of almost opposite effect than 1a that assimilates a- or o- of part D prefixes (i.e., mode prefixes) to i- if followed by a part E prefix that contains i- (i.e., shi, ni, or di, Stanley's lexical representations for 1sg, 2sg, and 1d).[22]

Phonetically, Navajo has four vowels, i-, e-, a-, and o- (with o-ranging to u- in certain dialects). These four vowels will be represented here by a two feature matrix, [±high], [±back]. (See SH:10-12 for a discussion of the phonetic detail of the vowels and vowel clusters.) At the systematic phonemic level it is fairly certain that Navajo has a three vowel system, i-, a-, o-. E- almost never appears in underlying representation in the prefix complex, and its presence on the surface is the principal motivation for readjustment rules and exceptional outputs throughout this study. Reichard has also remarked that e- is a derived vowel (1951:30). In addition, Stanley has argued that e- is a secondary vowel in stem variant phonology (1969a:Chp IV). (A discussion of some of the problems of deriving e- is below.)

There are two general types of vowel assimilation: VCV and VV. VCV assimilation occurs in nouns and postpositions as well as in the verb prefix and enclitic systems and can be handled by a single mirror-image rule. Adjacent vowel assimilations occur in certain prefix internal environments and present a much more complex problem. I will formulate two VV assimilation rules that are intricately ordered with a set of rules that delete consonants and alter tones and vowels. All this is complicated by dialect variation. First, in 2.731 we will briefly consider VCV assimilation. Then in 2.732 we will look at the VV processes step by step.

2.731 VCV assimilation

Listed in (43) are nouns and verbs in phonetic and underlying representations that show occurrence and non-occurrence of VCV assimilation. An asterisk following the underlying form indicates an intermediate representation given for sake of clarity.

(43) a. ba̱ghan /bi+ghan/
 b. bo̱hooghan /bi+hoo+ghan/
 c. sha̱gaan /shi+gaan/
 d. bo̱ko̧' /bi+ko̧'/
 e. ba̱má /bi+má/
 f. ba̱'áán /bi+'áán/
 g. bó̱hoosh'aah /bí#hoo+sh+ɨ+'aah/*
 h. bí̱dahooł'aah /bí+da#hoo+ɨ+'aah/*
 i. bi̱taa' /bi+taa'/
 j. shi̱ná /shi+ná/
 k. naha̱shniih /na#hi+sh+ɨ+niih/
 l. ináhá̱shtih /ni+ná#hi+sh+tih/
 m. 'e̱'e'aah /'i+'i+'aah/
 n. 'e̱'essíí̱h /'i#'i+sh+ɨ+zíí̱h/

It should be stressed that all of the vowel changes in (43) are approximate, varying with ə- or, in slow speech, with i-. Based on the fully assimilated forms, we can generalize that the back vowels, a- and o-, assimilate backness and height regressively and progressively (in 43k and l) across intervening velars, '-, or m-. 43h-j show that non-velar consonants block this assimilation. The lowering of 'i#'i to 'e'e in 45m and n is exceptional since both underlying vowels are altered. Reichard has detected a non-assimilating variant in this environment, 'i'i'aah (1951:371).

The intervening consonants hardly form a natural class and m- and '- will simply be listed. The asterisk in the environment of VCV assimilation signals that the environment can be converted to its mirror-image, VC___, in cases of progressive assimilation.

(44) $\begin{bmatrix} +hi \\ -bck \end{bmatrix} \rightarrow \begin{bmatrix} \alpha hi \\ +bck \end{bmatrix} / * \underline{\hspace{1em}} \left\{ \begin{matrix} ' \\ m \\ \begin{bmatrix} -cor \\ -ant \end{bmatrix} \end{matrix} \right\} \begin{bmatrix} \alpha hi \\ +bck \end{bmatrix}$

exception: 'i#'i → 'e'e

VCV assimilation deserves closer phonetic and statistical study. For example, subjectively it appears that g- is a weaker trigger for VCV assimilation than are other velars; i.e., for 43c shigaan can be heard more often than bikǫ' for 43d. Perhaps VCV assimilation is a graded phenomenon that shades into optionality and non-occurrence. Such a solution is more obvious for syllabic n- (see 2.77).

2.73 VV Assimilation

Adjacent vowel assimilation within the verb prefixes is a deeper and more complex process than VCV assimilation. I will formulate two VV assimilation rules: a) vowel assimilation, which will be presented in two versions to accommodate dialect variation, and b) vowel fronting. The ordering relationship between these two rules and processes that delete consonants (rule 41, gamma deletion and rule 42, y- deletion) and alter tones (such as rule 38, tone assimilation) and vowels (such as rule 12, vowel deletion) is critical. In this discussion brief reference will be made to a number of related processes as well as to some rather complex underlying forms for the verb modes. However, a full discussion of these rules and mode representations will be deferred until the analysis of verb mode phonology in Chapter Three. Topics are presented in this order: first, I examine adjacent vowels of like quality to present certain tone, vowel insertion, and degemination rules and to make a preliminary statement of the environment of VV within the verb; second I look at the assimilations that i- and o- undergo (with comment on dialect variation) and at two conditions that must be placed on this process; third, I look at a vowel absorption process; fourth, the vowel fronting rule is examined; and five, the entire solution is summarized and an alternative solution and some unresolved issues are discussed.

1) Rules affecting VV of like quality

When there occurs a sequence of underlying vowels identical in quality, there is no alteration in quality although tones and vowel length may be affected by phonological rules. In (45) I list a variety of adjacent i-'s and their underlying forms.

(45) a. 'iisdziih   /'i#sh+dziih/ I1 'inhale'
     b. yiitał   /i+iid+tał/ I1d 'kick it'
     c. nabíigil   /na+bí#iid+ghil/ I1d 'push it about'
     d. siitał   /si+í+iid+tał/ P1d 'kick it'
     e. 'atíínítįįd   /'atí#ghi+í+ni+tįįd/ P2 'harm it'
     f. yóó' 'íínítne' /'i#ghi+í+ni+ł+ne'/ P2 'throw it away'
     g. yah 'iidoo'ááł /'i#yi+di+ghi+'ááł/ F3 'carry it off'

First, notice that there is only one underlying prefix vowel in 45a. The long surface vowel is the result of a rule that inserts an i- when no vowel appears between the # disjunct boundary and C_o[. This pepet vowel insertion rule plays an important part in the derivation of the verb modes, particularly the imperfective (see 3.11).

(46) ∅ → i / #___C_o[

That the inserted vowel is indeed an i- will become clearer when it is seen next to vowels other than i-.

45a/'i#sh+dziih/

V insert: ['i#ish+dziih]
ultimately: ['iisdziih]

To facilitate presentation of the data, forms that undergo pepet vowel insertion will be listed with [+i̊] in underlying representation in this section.

In 45b, c, and d the underlying sequences of vowels have apparently been degeminated so that they are no longer than two moras. The vowel degemination rule plays an important part throughout the verb mode phonology. I state in informally as follows:

(47) Sequences of prefix vowels identical in quality shall be no more than two moras in length.

Also, 45d has undergone a tone lowering rule which lowers a high tone when it precedes a + boundary and a low tone vowel.

(48) v́ → V / ___ +V

	45b/i+iid+ta*/	45c/na+bí#iid+ghil/	45d/si+í+iid+ta*/
V dele:	_____	_____	[s+í+iid+ta*]
tone lower:	_____	_____	[s+i+iid+ta*]
V degem:	[iidta*]	[na+bí+id+ghil]	[s+iid+ta*]
ultimately:	[yiita*]	[nabíigil]	[siita*]

Note that rule 12, vowel deletion, does not apply to either 45b because there is no CV prefix preceding +iid or to 45c because of the # disjunct boundary.

In addition, 45f has undergone a tone raising rule that raises a low tone vowel immediately before í- or á-. Tone raising must be ordered after vowel deletion and rule 41, gamma deletion.

(49) V → v́ / ___ (#) {í/á}

Rule 49 is not triggered by the optative prefix ó- which we will see participates in a separate tone rule.

The derivation for 45g is presented along with that for 45f to illustrate the ordering relationship between rule 41, gamma deletion, an early rule, and 42, y- deletion, a late rule, which deletes the y- of the direct object prefix in 45g.

	45f/'i#ghi+í+ni+ɬ+ne'/	45g/'i#yi+di+ghi+'ááɬ/
V dele:	['i#gh+í+ni+ɬ+ne']	
gh dele:	['i#í+ni+ɬ+ne']	['i#yi+di+i+'ááɬ]
tone rais:	['í#í+ni+ɬ+ne']	
y dele:		['i#i+di+i+'ááɬ]
ultimately:	['ííníɬne']	['iidoo'ááɬ]

Adjacent o-'s are relatively rare. In the optative paradigm ó- regularly comes in contact with oh- 2d. I know of only one pos. 1 prefix, cho- 'use' that ends in o- and can be placed next to ó- optative.

(50) a. [woohtaɬ]   /ó+oh+taɬ/ O2d 'kick it'
     b. [woohne']   /ó+oh+ne'/ O2d 'happen to one'
     c. [choosh'į́į́']   /cho#ó+sh+'į́į́'/ O1 'use it'

50a and b are derived by rule 48, tone lowering, while 50c requires a new tone rule, optative tone lowering, which lowers the tone of the optative prefix when it is preceded by a disjunct prefix.

(51) ó → o / X#___

	48b/ó+oh+ne'/	48c/cho#ó+sh+'į́į́'/
tone lower:	[o+oh+ne']	
opt tone low:		[cho#o+sh+'į́į́']
ultimately:	[woohne']	[choosh'į́į́']

There are no a- vowels among the conjunctive prefixes. Adjacent a-'s occur in only one environment. Verbs that contain pos. 1 ná- 'encircle' or ná- 'back' (and occasionally pos. 2 ná- 'iterative') plus a preceding pos. 1 prefix, under certain conditions that are still undetermined, delete the n- of the ná- prefix. If the preceding pos. 1 prefix contains a-, the result is áá-, or no assimilation. If the preceding prefix is i-, the result is éé-. Hoijer lists a rather confusing set of environments for this n- deletion rule (SH:43-47). Note the underlined áá- in forms of 'wash it' (52), and 'exhume it' (53). N- deletion paradigms in YM often differ from one another as is illustrated by the I2 forms below in 52c and 53b. Certainly this rule is used variably.

(52) a. tánáosgis O1

b. tanínásgis R1

c. táánígis I2 /tá+ná#ni+gis/

d. táásínígis P2 /tá+ná#si+í+ni+gis/

(53) a. hanásht'e' I1

b. hanáníɬt'e' I2

c. háádeesht'eeɬ F1 /ha+ná#di+ghi+sh+ɨ+t'eeɬ/

The n- deleted form 53c is derived by the tone raising rule.

53c /ha+ná#di+ghi+sh+ɨ+t'eeɬ/

n dele: [ha+á#di+ghi+sh+ɨ+t'eeɬ]

tone rais: [há+á#di+ghi+sh+ɨ+t'eeɬ]

ultimately: [háádeesht'eeɬ]

In reviewing the data in (45), (50), (52) and (53) we find that after vowel, gamma, and y- deletion rules have applied, VV sequences can occur either immediately before C_o[as in 45a-d and 50a-c, or they may occur further to the left in the prefix complex with one or more CV sequences before C_o[, as in 45e-g and 52c and d, and 53c. We will see in the following sections that a distinction in the position of the VV sequences is important for distinguishing the two vowel assimilation rules.

2) i- and o- assimilations

In (54) when i- is adjacent to e-, o-, or a-, it is assimilated.

(54) 1.0 ee

    1.1 i (#) e → ee

       a. hasht'eeshłééh /hasht'e# i sh+łééh/* Il 'get ready'
                              [+vi]

    1.2 e (#) i → ee

       b. deeshghał /di+ghe+sh+l+ghał/* Fl 'eat meat'

       c. yóó' 'eelghod /'i#ghe+l+ghod/* P3 'run away'

    2.0 oo

    2.1 i (#) o → oo

       a. yah 'oołbąąs /'i#oh+ł+bąąs/ I2d 'drive it in'

       b. woohtał /i+oh+tał/ I2d 'kick it'

       c. sootał /si+í+oh+tał/ P2d 'kick it'

       d. baa 'ooshgééd /'i#ó+sh+ł+gééd/ Ol 'stab him'

       e. 'óoshdįįh /'í#ó+sh+dįįh/ Ol 'disappear'

    2.2 o + ii → oo

       f. wootał /ó+iid+tał/ Old 'kick it'

       g. woodloh /ó+iid+loh/ Old 'rope it'

    3.0 aa

    3.1 a # i → aa

       a. daacha /da# i +cha/* I3 'cry'
                    [+vi]

       b. naabé /na# i +bé/* I3 'swim about'
                   [+vi]

       c. nááshtééł /ná#ghi+sh+ł+tééł/ Pgl 'carry an animate object'

       d. nááłne' /na#ghi+í+sh+ł+ne'/ Pl 'drop it'

       e. yaashkaah /ya#i+sh+kaah/ Il 'spill it'

       f. yanáashkááh /ya+ná#i+sh+kááh/ Rl 'spill it'

These data suggest that i- assimilates to the height and/or backness of an adjacent vowel. However, before this rule can be written, consider two cases of vowel fronting.

We see in 54.2f and g the inherently long vowel of iid- has assimilated to o- (and has been shortened by vowel degemination). But note what happens to a#iid.

(55) a. deiicha /da#iid+cha/ I1p 'cry'

   b. neiibé /na#iid+bé/ I1d 'swim about'

Here a- has fronted to e- before the inherently long vowel of the 1d prefix, iid-, suggesting that the i- assimilation rule be constrained to short vowels.

The other case of vowel fronting is more interesting.

(56) a. néíníɬne' /na#ghi+í+ni+ɬ+ne'/ P2 'drop it'

   b. yeideeshkááɬ /ya#i+di+ghi+sh+kááɬ/ F1 'spill it'

In comparing these with the 1sg perfective in 54.3d and the imperfective and iterative in 54.3e and f, we see that i- assimilation has occurred in front of C_o[whereas vowel fronting has occurred before CV+C_o[. This suggests that i- assimilation must be constrained to occur only before C_o[. In other words, the a#i sequences in (56) do not become aa- because of the ni- and di+ghi- prefixes that separate them from C_o[.

All of the assimilations in (54) can be derived by the following i- assimilation rule with the condition that a- plus ii- does not assimilate:

(57) $\begin{bmatrix} +hi \\ -bck \end{bmatrix} \rightarrow \begin{bmatrix} \alpha hi \\ \beta bck \end{bmatrix} / \begin{bmatrix} \alpha hi \\ \beta bck \end{bmatrix} C_o$[.

   condition: ≠ a#ii

The environment slash has been eliminated to indicate that rule 58 is a mirror-image rule.

To derive the verbs in (54) several ordering relationships must be observed. Pepet vowel insertion must be ordered before i- assimilation. (Notice that the case that the inserted vowel is an i- rests on the fact that the vowel assimilates or remains unchanged just as does underlying i-.)

	1a/hasht'e#sh+lééh/	2e/'í#ó+sh+dįįh/	3a/da#cha/
V insert:	[hasht'e#ish+lééh]	_____	[da#i+cha]
i assim:	[hasht'e#esh+lééh]	['ó#o+sh+dįįh]	[da#a+cha]
opt tone low:	_____	['ò#o+sh+dįįh]	_____
ultimately:	[hasht'eeshłééh]	['óoshdįįh]	[daacha]

Vowel deletion, tone assimilation, gamma deletion, and tone raising must be ordered before i- assimilation.

	3c/ná#ghi+sh+ł+tééł/	3d/na#ghi+í+sh+ł+ne'/
V dele:	_____	[na#gh+í+sh+ł+ne']
tone assim:	[ná#ghí+sh+ł+tééł]	_____
gh dele:	[ná#í+sh+ł+tééł]	[na#í+sh+ł+ne']
tone rais:	_____	[ná#í+sh+ł+ne']
i assim:	[ná#á+sh+ł+tééł]	[ná#á+sh+ł+ne']
ultimately:	[nááshtééł]	[náálne']

Yet i- is not the only vowel that assimilates. The sequence ao- becomes aa- in certain dialects. The speech of William Morgan, for example, is characterized by this assimilation. Variants are listed with the data in (58) to indicate the dialect dependent nature of the o- to a- assimilation.

(58) a. daacha ∿ daocha   /da#oh+cha/   I2p 'cry'
     b. haahgééd ∿ haohgééd   /ha#oh+gééd/   I2d 'dig up'
     c. ntsídaahkees ∿ ntsídaohkees   /ntsí+da#oh+kees/   I2p 'think'

The distribution of these vowel assimilation variants constitutes one of the most interesting problems in Navajo dialectology. Robert Young (personal communication) has noted a tendency for aa- speakers to come from the eastern side of the Reservation, perhaps east of the

Chuskas. Reichard noted this same difference in vowel assimilation but made no statement about its regional distribution (1945:164). It is possible that non-assimilating ao-, which is perceived as being more conservative, is encroaching on aa-'s territory.[23]

The distribution and the perception of the aa- dialect suggest that it is an innovation. By adding a parenthesis to the feature [-back] in rule 57, we can formalize the fact that the aa- dialect has generalized i- assimilation to all high vowels. The following i-o assimilation rule contains two subparts:

(57b) $\begin{bmatrix} +hi \\ (-bck) \end{bmatrix} \rightarrow \begin{bmatrix} \alpha hi \\ \beta bck \end{bmatrix} / \begin{bmatrix} \alpha hi \\ \beta bck \end{bmatrix} C_o [.$

By convention, the first subpart applies to $\begin{bmatrix} +hi \\ -bck \end{bmatrix}$, converting it to e-, o-, or a-. If the first subpart is not triggered, the second subpart operates on the other high vowel, o-, converting it to a- if next to a-. (The other possible sequence, ae-, does not occur in underlying forms and would not be affected by 57b since e- is a low vowel.)

A condition must be placed on rule 57b. Note in the following verbs that no assimilation takes place when the ó- optative or the rare o- imperfective (c-e below) prefixes are to the right of a-.[24]

(59) a. naoshnish   /na#ó+sh+l+nish/   Ol 'work'
     b. haooh'neeh   /ha#ó+oh+'neeh/   O2d 'crawl up'
     c. taoshnih   /ta#ó+sh+nih/   Il 'mix it'
     d. náoshką   /na#ó+sh+ką/   Il 'beseech'
     e. náoshtáád   /ná#ó+sh+l+táád/   Il 'unravel it'

Thus, the innovative high tone vowel assimilation rule has not been generalized to assimilate ó-, a fact we will state in a condition on rule 57b.

	58b /ha#oh+gééd/	59a /na#ó+sh+ł+nish/
i-o assim:	[ha#ah+gééd]	
opt tone low:		[na#o+sh+ł+nish]
ultimately:	[haahgééd]	[naoshnish]

Optative tone lowering is ordered after i-o assimilation to facilitate the statement of the ó- condition.

A further condition must be placed on the vowel assimilation rule. Note in the following verbs that i- has not assimilated to o-.

(60) a. bik'iogééd   /bik'i#oh+gééd/ I2d 'cover it'
     b. k'íoshdlaad /k'í#ó+sh+ł+dlaad/ Ol 'pull it in two'
     c. 'atíoshłe'   /'atí#ó+sh+le'/ Ol 'injure him'

I- has the effect of fronting a preceding velar or t- so that it is reinforced, and the regular vowel assimilation process is blocked. T- blocks i- assimilation because of its strongly velarized release. (Recall that Fr. Berard transcribed this sound as t^x-.)

Having considered three conditions and the o- assimilating dialect, vowel assimilation (referring to both i- and i-o assimilation) can be written in its final form.

(57) a. (for ao- dialects) $\begin{bmatrix} +hi \\ -bck \end{bmatrix} \rightarrow \begin{bmatrix} \alpha hi \\ \beta bck \end{bmatrix} / \begin{bmatrix} \alpha hi \\ \beta bck \end{bmatrix} C_o [$

     b. (for aa- dialects) $\begin{bmatrix} +hi \\ (-bck) \end{bmatrix} \rightarrow \begin{bmatrix} \alpha hi \\ \beta bck \end{bmatrix} / \begin{bmatrix} \alpha hi \\ \beta bck \end{bmatrix} C_o [$

conditions: a) ≠ a # ii
             [+lng]
         b) i- is not preceded by $\begin{bmatrix} -cor \\ -ant \end{bmatrix}$ or t-
         c) 58b is blocked if a- is followed by ó-.

3) Vowel absorption

Still another process affects the vowels. After vowel assimilation has operated, a high tone vowel followed by # absorbs a following short, low tone vowel.

(61) a. ch'óh'ash   /ch'í#oh+'ash/ U2d 'go out'
     b. bółk'į́įh   /bí#oh+ł+k'į́įh/ I2d 'peel it'
     c. 'akóshłééh   /'akó#[i,+vi]+sh+łééh/ I1 'make it thus'
     d. náhtł'óóh ~ naohtł'óóh /ná#oh+tł'óóh/ R2d 'weave it'
     e. 'ahiohkad   /'ahí#oh+kad/ I2d 'applaud'
     f. bik'iołtih   /bik'í#oh+ł+tih/ I2d 'cover it'
     g. 'atioh'į́   /'atí#oh+'į́/ I2d 'injure him'
     h. nabéshhil   /na+bí#[i,+vi]+sh+ghil/ I1 'push it about'
     i. ntsékees   /ntsí#[i,+vi]+kees/ I3 'think'

Aside from the é- in 61h and i which must be listed as an exception, all the high tone vowels resulting from absorption conform to the vowel assimilation rule.[25] The variants for 61d reflect the aa- and ao- dialects, the conservative dialect showing a short, high diphthong, ao-. The short, high diphthongs in 61e-g reflect the fronted velar condition on the vowel assimilation rule.

The vowel absorption rule can be written as follows:[26]

(62) V̂ # V   → V̂
         [-lng]

   exception: í # i → é

	61b/bí#oh+ł+k'į́įh/	61i/ntsí#kees/	62d/ná#oh+tł'óóh/
V insert:	_____	[ntsí#i+kees]	_____
V assim:	[bó#oh+ł+k'į́įh]	_____	([ná#ah+tł'óóh])
V absorb:	[bóh+ł+k'į́įh]	[ntsé+kees]	[náhtł'óóh] ~ [naoh+tł'óóh]
ultimately:	[bółk'į́įh]	[ntsékees]	[náhtł'óóh] ~ [naohtł'óóh]

	61g /'atí#oh+'į́/	60b /k'í#ó+sh+ł+dlaad/
V assim:	————————	————————
V absorb:	['atíoh+'į́]	————————
opt tone low:	————————	[k'í#o+sh+ł+dlaad]
ultimately:	['atíoh'į́]	[k'íoshdlaad]

In the derivations for 61g and 60b vowel assimilation is inapplicable because of the velar fronting condition. Vowel absorption does not apply to 60b because of the ó- optative prefix which is subsequently lowered by optative tone lowering.

4) Vowel fronting

The environments which permit vowel fronting suggest that it is ordered later than vowel assimilation.

We have already seen that vowel fronting occurs when a- precedes a long ii-.

(63) a. dei̱icha   /da#iid+cha/   I1p 'cry'
     b. néi̱ishtał   /ná#ii+sh+tał/ R1 'kick it'

We have also seen that a#i sequences that are separated from C₀ [by at least one CV undergo vowel fronting.

(64) a. néíníłne'   /na#ghi+í+ni+ł+ne'/ P2 'drop it'
     b. hadéínigo'   /ha+da#ghi+í+ni+go'/ P2 'fall down'
     c. yeideeshkááł /ya#i+di+ghi+sh+kááł/ F1 'spill it'

In addition, verbs that contain yi- prefixes undergo vowel fronting after y- has been deleted by rule 44, y- deletion.

(65) a. hadeiłgééh   /ha+da#yi+ł+gééh/   I3 'make him fall down/
     b. yínéíłkah   /yí+ná#yi+ł+kah/   R3 'track it'
     c. néineest'ą́   /ná#yi+ni+ɛi+í+t.'ą́/   P3 'raise it'
     d. yádeíníiltééh /yá+da#yí+ní+iid+ł+teeh/ Pglp 'speak'
     e. yádeíłtééh   /yá+da#yí+ł+tééh/   Pg3p 'speak'

However, a condition identical to that placed on i- assimilation must be placed on the vowel fronting rule.

(66) a. hainitá   /ha#yi+ni+tá/   I3 'search for it'
     b. 'ákáiilzis   /'áká#iid+l+zis/   Ild 'gird up'
     c. bitaaiikai   /bitaa#iid+kai/   Ilp 'go among'
     d. táidigéésh   /tá#yi+di+géésh/   I3 'shear it'

When a- is preceded by a velar or t-, vowel fronting is blocked.

From these examples it is apparent that the vowel fronting rule is not constrained to an internal C_o [environment as is the vowel assimilation rule. Note that when vowel fronting does occur in ___C_o [, as in 66a, b, and e, it is after y- has been deleted by rule 42.

We can write <u>vowel fronting</u> as follows:

(67) $\begin{bmatrix} -hi \\ +bck \end{bmatrix}$ → [-bck] / ___ $\begin{bmatrix} +hi \\ -bck \end{bmatrix}$

  condition: a- is not preceded by $\begin{bmatrix} -cor \\ -ant \end{bmatrix}$ or t-.

That vowel fronting is a late rule ordered after y- deletion is confirmed by variants for 65d and e, yádayíníiltééh and yádayíltééh where y- has not deleted and vowel fronting has not taken place.[27]

	63a/da#iid+cha/	64a/na#ghi+í+ni+ł+ne'/	65b/yí+ná#yi+ł+kah/
V dele:	_____	[na#gh+í+ni+ł+ne']	_____
tone assim:	_____	[na#gh+í+ní+ł+ne']	[yí+ná#yí+ł+kah]
gh dele:	_____	[na#í+ní+ł+ne']	_____
tone rais:	_____	[ná#í+ní+ł+ne']	_____
V assim:	_____	_____	_____
ý dele:	_____	_____	[yí+ná#í+ł+kah]
V front:	[de#iid+cha]	[né#í+ní+ł+ne']	[yí+né#í+ł+kah]
ultimately:	[deiicha]	[néíníłne']	[yínéíłkah]

These derivations illustrate the late order of y- deletion and vowel fronting as opposed to the early order of gamma deletion and vowel assimilation. Rule 57, vowel assimilation, does not apply to 63a because of the long vowel ii-; nor to 64a because ni- separates a#i from C_o[; nor to 65b because of the intervening y-.

5) Summary of vowel assimilation analysis

In the preceding analysis I have accounted for adjacent vowel assimilations in the Navajo verb by positing two rules: a) a fairly deep vowel assimilation rule, (57), which alters i-, or alternatively both i- and o-, and is constrained to operate in the internal ___C_o[position; and b) a late vowel fronting rule, (67), that operates on any a#i sequence.

These two rules are in a complex ordering relationship with ten other phonological rules. To summarize:

(46) pepet vowel insertion

(12) vowel deletion

(38) tone assimilation

(48) tone lowering

(41) gamma deletion

(49) tone raising

(57) vowel assimilation

(62) vowel absorption

(51) optative tone lowering

(42) y- deletion

(67) vowel fronting

(47) vowel degemination.

One other approach to Navajo vowel assimilation has been suggested by Hale (1972a). He posits that the vowels assimilate in a hierarchy, weak to strong: i, e, o, a (for the aa- dialect) or i, e, o-a (for the ao- dialect), where the strongest of two adjacent vowels dominates in the assimilation.

However, my attempt to formalize the hierarchy resulted in a dubious rule, or, more precisely, two dubious conjunctively ordered rules for the height and backness changes. What is most suspect about the proposed vowel assimilation hierarchy is the behavior of e-. The hierarchy predicts that e- is stronger than i- and weaker than o-, but this is contrary to the evidence found in the few forms where e- appears in underlying representation: hasht'e̲iilnééh not *hasht'eelnééh for 'we dpl get ready', hasht'e̲ohłééh not *hasht'oohłééh for 'you dpl get ready'. It is more precise to confine vowel assimilation to the high vowels, i- and o-, as in rule 57, and to leave e- out of the process.

The secondary nature of e- is the foremost unresolved issue concerning Navajo vowels. To illustrate the restricted, exceptional, or variable behavior of e-, we present a number of examples:

1) As noted above, both the 'i#i → 'e'e and í#i → é outputs of VCV assimilation and vowel absorption are unexplained exceptions.

2) A number of verbs show i∼e in variation in initial prefixes: he̲shtííh ∼ hi̲shtííh 'I break them off one after another', he̲shnííł ∼ hi̲shnííł 'I bury them one after another' (also noted by Reichard, 1951:376); bé̲náshnił ∼ bí̲náshnił 'I am smoking meat'.

3) Certain e-'s are not derivable by obvious phonological rules: k'é̲hozdoon 'straight' where underlying k'í- has simply lowered its vowel. More mysterious is k'é̲hdoon 'you dpl stand straight' and k'é̲łdoon 'you dpl straighten it' (YM, 1951:308) where é- has replaced the expected

velar fronted íó-. Ę́- is not a typical variant for íó- forms, and this remains an unexplained oddity.

4) Certain perfectives take é- in first person subject pronoun position which must be derived by a readjustment rule, sę́tał 'I kicked it', dę́baa' 'I went to war'. In certain eastern areas these forms are heard as sį́tał and dį́baa'.

5) Most significantly, all e-'s that appear in the modal prefix position in ni- imperfective/perfective, si- perfective, ghi- progressive/perfective are derived by ad hoc readjustment rules. The ee- vowels are another important topic for dialect study. Such forms as deeshłeel 'I'll become' are occasionally heard as deishłeel or even diishłeel, again apparently in eastern areas.

The solution presented here is more comprehensive than any other treatment of Navajo vowel assimilation, but it is far from finished. Future research should focus on documenting dialect variation in the use of vowels and on deriving the anomalous e-'s.

2.74 Some Problematic Prefix Vowels

Determining the lexical representations of several prefixes serves as a test for the vowel assimilation rule. The pos. 5 3i pronoun, the pos. 1 prefix 'away, out of sight', and the pos. 1 prefix 'thus' are usually referred to in the Navajo literature as 'a-, 'a-, and 'á-, respectively. However, in paradigms for the 3i prefix in (68) 'to spin', the 'away' prefix in (69) 'to carry it away', and the 'thus' prefix in (70) 'to make it' we find alternations that contradict the vowel assimilation and vowel fronting rules if an a- is set up in the underlying representations for these prefixes.

(68) 1 'asdiz
2 'ídiz
3 'adiz
1d 'iidiz
2d 'ohdiz

(69) 1 yah 'iish'aah
2 yah 'ani'aah
3 yah 'ii'aah
4 yah 'aji'aah
1d yah 'iit'aah
2d yah 'ooh'aah

(70) 1 'áshłééh
2 'áníłééh
3 'íiłééh
4 'ájíłééh
1d 'íilnééh
2d 'óhłééh

Rule 67, vowel fronting, predicts forms of 'ei- and 'éi- for 69.1d and 52.1d if an a- is in the underlying forms, and in 69.1 and 3 we would expect a#i to become aa- and not ii-. Also, note that 69.2d and 70.2d contain o- and not a- or ao- as predicted by vowel assimilation.[28] Rather than positing an underlying a- and then constraining rules 67 and 57, it is better to view 3i, 'away', and 'thus' as underlying /'i/, /'i/, and /'í/, respectively. Then only a rule converting 'i- to 'a- under certain conditions is needed.

Further evidence for an i- rather than a- representation is found when 'away' and 3i occur next to one another as in the imperfective of 'to burrow'.

(71)   1 'e'eshnííɬ
       2 'i'ínííɬ
       3 'e'enííɬ
       4 'i'jinííɬ
       1d 'i'ii'nííɬ
       2d 'o'ohnííɬ

In this paradigm it is apparent that 1 and 3 reflect the idiosyncratic VCV assimilation (rule 44) output, 'i'i → 'e'e. VCV assimilation does not apply to 71.2 and 4 because of the operation of prior rules (ni-absorption in 2 and a vowel elision rule to be discussed below in 4). What is most significant about 2 and 4 is that the adverbial prefix 'away' is realized as 'i- whereas in 69.2 and 4 it appears as 'a-.

A solution for the alternations in 68-71 is to posit an underlying i- and a rule that changes 'i to 'a in front of [+consonantal], i.e., a rule that does not operate in front of a glottal stop.[29]

(72) 'i → 'a / ___ [+cons]

	68.3/'i+diz/	71.1/'i#'i+sh+nííɬ/	71.4/'i#'i+ji+nííɬ/
V elis:	_____	_____	['i#'+ji+nííɬ]
VCV assim:	_____	['e#'e+sh+nííɬ]	_____
'i to 'a:	['a+diz]	_____	_____
ultimately:	['adiz]	['e'eshnííɬ]	['i'jinííɬ]

A similar solution is tempting for the so called ho- 'area', kó- 'in this way', and 'ákó- 'that way' prefixes. The velars in these three prefixes appear as labio-velars, hw- and kw-, before i, e, a, and y. Note the alternation of velars and labio-velars in (73) 'sing', (74) 'carry an animate object', (75) 'increase in size', (76) 'make it thus', and (77) 'plow'.

(73) a. hashtaał   I1

b. hótaał   I2

c. hataał   I3

d. hojitaał   I4

e. hwiitaał   I1d

f. hwíínítááł   P2

g. hwiitááł   P1d

(74) a. hweeshtééł   Pg1

b. hwííłtééł   Pg2

c. hoołtééł   Pg2d

(75) a. 'ąą kódeeshnííł   F1

b. 'ąą kwááshnííł   Pg1

c. 'ąą kwáánííł   Pg2, 3

d. 'ąą kójoonííł   Pg4

(76) a. 'ákóshlééh   I1

b. 'ákónílééh   I2

c. 'ákwíilnééh   I1d

d. 'ákwíinilaa   P2

e. 'ákwíilyaa   P1d

(77) a. nihodiyeeshdlał   F1 'to plow'

b. nihwiishdlaad   I1

c. nihwiyéłdláád   P1

d. nihwiyíníłdláád ~ nahwisíníłdláád   P2

If we assume that these verbs contain underlying /ho-/, /kó-/ and /'ákó-/, then a rule would be needed that labializes the velars and assimilates o- to i-, e-, or a-. The first two of these vowel assimilations are contrary to the vowel assimilation rule which states that i- assimilates

to e-, o-, or a-. Even more awkward would be the rule that turns o-
to i- next to y- or s- as in the variants in 77d.

One can argue from verbs like 77c and d and from the vowel assimilation
rule which has been formulated that the three prefixes in question are
underlying /hwi-/, /kwí-/ and /'ákwí-/ and that a <u>delabialization</u> rule
operates on the labiovelars when they precede [+consonantal], (i.e. not
y-), or o-. In addition, a rule ordered after delabialization changes
<u>ho-</u> <u>to</u> <u>ha-</u> in front of C_oC as in 54I1 and 3.[30]

(78) $\begin{bmatrix} C \\ -cor \\ -ant \\ +rnd \end{bmatrix} \begin{bmatrix} V \\ +hi \\ -bck \end{bmatrix} \rightarrow [-rnd][+bck] / \underline{\quad} \left\{ \begin{matrix} o \\ [+cons] \end{matrix} \right\}$

(79) ho → ha / ___ C_o [

     73c/hwi+taał/ 76b/'ákwí#ni+lééh/ 77d/ni#hwi+yi+í+ní+ł+dláád/*

delab: [ho+taał] ['ákó#ni+lééh]

ho to ha: [ha+taał]

ultimately: [hataał] ['ákóníllééh] [nihwiyíníłdláád]

Thus, the back vowels that appear in allomorphs of the six prefixes
discussed in this section are secondary. This analysis reinforces the
claim that vowel assimilation is essentially an i- assimilation rule.

2.75 Strident Assimilation

The assimilation of blade and tip fricatives and affricates has
been given extensive treatment by Hoijer (1945a:11-14; SH:15-17).
Alternations for sh- 1sg, shi- 1st pers obj, ji- 4, si- perfective
(which also appears as z-), and dzi- 'into space' are shown in (80) in
phonetic and underlying representations.

(80) a. 'asdiz   /'i+sh+diz/
    b. sik'is   /shi+k'is/
    c. shitéézh   /si+tééezh/
    d. shijool   /si+jool/
    e. yishtash   /yi+s+tash/*
    f. jizhghish   /ji+z+ghish/*
    g. dziztį́   /ji+z+tį́/*
    h. jį́tl'izh   /dzi+ni+tl'izh/
    i. 'abíjíshhaał   /'a+bí#dzi+sh+ł+ghaał/

There is considerable variation in the application of this rule, attesting to its near the surface order. Reichard has noted numerous examples of this variation (1951:379).

Hale and Honie treat these alternations as part of a single regressive strident assimilation rule that makes coronal stridents, s, z, dz, sh, zh, or j, agree in anteriority with a following coronal strident (1972:Chaps. 9 & 10). Strident assimilation is a late rule that is often suppressed in slow speech.

(81) $\begin{bmatrix} +\text{cor} \\ +\text{str} \end{bmatrix} \rightarrow [\alpha\text{ant}] / \_\_\_ X \begin{bmatrix} +\text{cor} \\ \alpha\text{ant} \\ +\text{str} \end{bmatrix}$

    where: X is non-null

Stanley has formulated a progressive strident assimilation rule to account for 1sg forms in the si- perfective mode with d- or l- classifier (which will be discussed in detail in 3.532). Progressive strident assimilation also occurs in 1sg forms of si- 'destruct', ntsi- 'kneel', and ntsí- 'think' verbs.

(82) a. sistin   /si+sh+d+tin/*
    b. hasis'na'   /ha#si+sh+d+na'/*
    c. yisisdlaad   /yi+si+sh+d+dlaad/*
    d. sisxé   /si+sh+ł+ghé/
    e. sósxééł   /si+ó+sh+ł+ghééł/
    f. ntsidósgeeh   /ntsi+di+ó+sh+geeh/
    g. ntséskees   /ntsí#sh+kees/

It is not certain how to account for these cases of progressive strident assimilation. Perhaps a single rule can be stated with a mirror image environment that is triggered by morphological markings for si- perfective, si- 'destruct', etc. It appears that the progressive strident assimilation is weaker than the regressive rule: e.g. nishíshnish /na#si+í+sh+l+nish/, hashéshzhee' /ha#si+í+sh+l+zhee'/ suggest that the [-ant] strident in the stem is dominant over the [+ant] prefix strident that triggered progressive assimilation in a similar environment in 82a-c.

Hale (personal communication) has suggested that progressive and regressive strident assimilation may be governed by a paradigmatic constraint: regressive everywhere except where s- and sh- would alternate in a paradigm. In other words, progressive strident assimilation would apply to 82a because other members of that paradigm contain s-, yistin, siitin, and the regressive output, shishtin, would cause paradigmatic conflict.

A counter-example to Hale's paradigmatic constraint is the si-imperfective dah shish'aah 'I put it up', dah sí'aah 'you put it up', where sh- and s- are allowed in the same paradigm. Alternatively, I present evidence from j- deleting verbs to be discussed in the next section and from one highly interesting verb, neidzizt'i 'he streaked around' to be discussed in 3.534 that <u>progressive strident assimilation</u> is a separate and earlier rule than regressive strident assimilation.

Following this analysis, a condition must be added to the progressive rule that blocks it from s-sh sequences when a [-anterior] strident appears in the stem as in nishíshnish. (Or, equally possible, perhaps rule 81 contains a condition that a [-anterior] stem overrides a s-s sequence.)

(83) $\begin{bmatrix} +\text{cor} \\ +\text{str} \end{bmatrix} \rightarrow [\alpha\text{ant}] ./ \begin{bmatrix} +\text{cor} \\ \alpha\text{ant} \end{bmatrix} X\underline{\quad}$

condition: $\neq \text{si}+\text{sh}+(X)+\begin{bmatrix} -\text{ant} \\ +\text{str} \end{bmatrix}$

2.76 Vowel Elision and J- Deletion

I have formulated one vowel deletion rule, rule 12, that removes the vowel of a conjunctive prefix when it is next to a vowel, [dołghosh] /di+oh+l+ghosh/. In addition, it is apparent that certain prefixes such as 'i- 3i, ji- 4, dzi- 'streak' and a number of nV- prefixes lose their vowels in <u>consonantal</u> environments. In this section we will look at vowel elision in 'i-, ji-, and dzi- prefixes.

Below I present two verbs that take 'i- 3i as a thematic prefix. Note that in (84) 'to spin' 'i- is present in all forms except g where it has been reduced to '- (recall that 'i- becomes 'a- by rule 53). In (85) 'to swim about' which contains a preceding adverbial prefix, 'i- has been reduced to '- in b, c, and d.

(84) a. 'asdiz   I1   (85) a. na'ashkǫ́ǫ́'   I1
     b. 'ajidiz   I4   b. n'ji1kǫ́ǫ́'   I4
     c. 'adeesdis F1   c. n'deeshkǫ́ǫ́1   F1
     d. 'asédiz   P1   d. ni'sé1kǫ́ǫ́'   P1
     e. 'azdiz   P3   e. na'askǫ́ǫ́'   P3
     f. ná'ásdiz   R1
     g. ń'jídiz   R4

'i- has become '- before j-, d-, or s- provided that 'i- is not immediately
before C₀[and that there is a preceding prefix. In comparing 84b and
g we see the importance of the preceding prefix in the vowel elision
process, word initial clusters such as *'jidiz for 84b being inadmissable.
The fact that there must be at least one CV prefix before C₀[for 'i-
to drop its vowel is illustrated by the non-eliding forms, 84f, 85a
and e. Two perfectives, 85d and e, are particularly interesting in this
respect. Both contain underlying si+í and both have undergone certain
readjustment rules (which will be discussed later in 3.53) prior to
the application of 'i- vowel elision.

                                    readjust
85d/na#'i+si+í+sh+1+kǫ́ǫ́'/   →   /na#'i+si+é+1+kǫ́ǫ́'/
85e/na#'i+si+í+1+kǫ́ǫ́'/   →   /na#'i+s+1+kǫ́ǫ́'/

(86) i → ∅ / X'___+CV₁+C₀[

The vowel does not elide in 85e because the si- mode prefix has been
reduced to non-syllabic s-.

                  85d/na#'i+si+é+1+kǫ́ǫ́'/   85e/na#'i+s+1+kǫ́ǫ́'/
V elis: [na#'+si+é+1+kǫ́ǫ́']   _____
'i to 'a: _____   [na#'a+s+1+kǫ́ǫ́']
ultimately: [ni'sé1kǫ́ǫ́']   [na'askǫ́ǫ́']

Two other prefixes lose their vowels in environments similar to 'i- vowel elision. The ji- 4 prefix retains its vowel adjacent to C_o[and next to a CV prefix if nothing precedes it. However, if ji- is preceded <u>and</u> followed by prefixes, it loses its vowel and deaffricates to zh- as in 87d-f. The dzi- 'streak' prefix loses its vowel and deaffricates to z- in an identical environment as in 88d-f.

(87) a. <u>ji</u>dleesh   (88) a. 'ab<u>í</u><u>dzí</u>íɬhaal

   b. 'a<u>ji</u>dleesh   b. 'ab<u>zí</u>ítáál

   c. <u>ji</u>doodlish   c. biɬ nid<u>zí</u>ɬts'in

   d. 'a<u>zh</u>doodlish   d. 'abí<u>zd</u>ííɬhaɬ

   e. k'í<u>zh</u>níɬdla'   e. 'a<u>zd</u>ootaaɬ

   f. ní<u>zh</u>didoodááɬ   f. biɬ ni<u>zn</u>íɬts'in

Thus far, nothing has been said about the CV prefix that follows the vowel eliding prefix. However, if ji- is next to a y- glide, as in [hojiyóɬdlaad] /hwi+ji+hi+ó+ɬ+dlaad/ 'he wishes to plow it', vowel elision and deaffrication do not take place. In this case y- has come from the mysterious hi- 'seriative' prefix by a rule to be discussed in 3.6.

It is natural to extend rule 86 to ji- and dzi- vowel elision. Only one feature need be added to the environment of the collapsed <u>vowel elision</u> rule, [+cons], to exclude y- (as well as glottal stop).

(86)
$$i \to \emptyset \;/\; X \left\{ \begin{matrix} ' \\ \begin{bmatrix} -cnt \\ +cor \\ +str \end{bmatrix} \end{matrix} \right\} \underline{\quad} [+cns]\; V_1 + C_o [$$

It is interesting to note that 'i-, ji- and dzi- are never found next to the h- of the hi- seriative prefix due to rule 13, seriative h- deletion, and to the h → y rule alluded to above, e.g. jiitííh /ji+hi+tííh/ 'he breaks them off'. Furthermore, ji- and dzi- are never found next to sV-. One candidate for such an environment, ji+si perfective, is altered to ji+s by the same readjustment rule noted above for 'i+si perfective, e.g. jistin 'he froze'. The other candidate, ji+si 'destruct', is altered to ji+i by a 'destruct' s- deletion rule that parallels the seriative h- deletion rule, e.g. jiiɬxé /ji+si+ɬ+ghé/ 'he kills it'. (This si- destruct rule will be discussed in 3.6.)

Following rule 86, deaffrication applies to ǰ +C or dz+C.

(89) $\begin{bmatrix} +\text{cor} \\ +\text{str} \\ -\text{cnt} \end{bmatrix} \rightarrow [+\text{cnt}] \,/\, \underline{\quad} C$

	87d/'i#ji+di+ghi+dlish/	88f/ni#dzi+ni+ni+ɬ+ts'in/
V elis:	['i#ǰ+di+ghi+dlish]	[ni#dz+ni+ni+ɬ+ts'in]
deaffric:	['i#zh+di+ghi+dlish]	[ni#z+ni+ni+ɬ+ts'in]
ultimately:	['azhdoodlish]	[nizníɬts'in]

A serious challenge to the collapsed vowel elision rule is presented by verbs with zh'C clusters.

(90) a. dazh'doodis   'they will be spinning'
    b. 'ábizh'niilaa   'he started to make it'
    c. 'idízh'nóoghį́į́ɬ   'he will start to eat'

The problem here is that there has been a metathesis of 'i- and ji- (cf. 87b, 'ajidleesh). If we assume that the metathesis has happened early in the derivation, perhaps by a readjustment rule, we encounter difficulty in applying rule 86, e.g. (after metathesis) /da#ji+'i+di+ghi+dis/*. In order to elide the two vowels simultaneously in ji- and 'i- we might restate vowel elision to apply contiguous to a glottal stop. But this is counterfactual since other vowel elisions are not triggered by '-, cf. 85a na'ashkǫ́ǫ́' and 85b n'jiɬkǫ́ǫ́' where j- and not '- has caused na- to drop its vowel. (This will be taken up in 2.77 in the discussion of syllabic n-.) If glottal stop does not trigger vowel elision, then we can posit that rule 86 is a cyclic rule, the first and only one in this study, that operates on 'd- on its second application, or we can overlook the similarity in 'i- and ji- vowel elision and treat them as separate rules.

If we assume that metathesis is not an early rule, we can apply rule 86, as it stands, simultaneously to both 'i- and ji-. After deaffrication, a <u>glottal -zh metathesis</u> rule operates on 'zhd-:

(91) ' zh C → zh ' C

This is one of the few triliteral clusters in Navajo phonetic representation.

      73a/da#'i+ji+di+ghi+dis/

<u>V elis</u>: [da#'+j+di+ghi+dis]

<u>deaffric</u>: [da#'+zh+di+ghi+dis]

<u>'zh metath</u>: [da#zh+'+di+ghi+dis]

<u>ultimately</u>: [dazh'doodis]

Interestingly, many Navajo speakers accept either or both of these variants for the verbs in (90).

(92) a. da'jidoodis   ∿   da'zhdoodis

  b. 'ábi'jiniilaa   ∿   'ábi'zhniilaa

  c. 'idí'jinóoghííł   ∿   'idí'zhnóoghííł

In the first variant, vowel elision has applied just once, preserving ji-. In the second variant, metathesis has not applied. Speakers rank the forms in (90) as most common with the left-hand variants in (92) more common than those on the right. The forms in (92) are described as 'jerky'. This variation supports the claim that metathesis is a late rule as well as the collapsed version of the vowel elision rule.

Parenthetically, it is appropriate here to mention an interesting rule that affects verbs that contain both ji- 4 and dzi- 'streak', /ji+dzi/. Compare these dzi- verbs in 2sg with the fourth person forms in the right-hand column.

(93) a. bił ndzíłts'in   bił ni<u>ij</u>íłts'in
     b. bił ndzííłts'in   bił ni<u>i</u>zhníłts'in
     c. 'abízdííłhał   'ab<u>ii</u>zhdoołhał
     d. 'adzítaał   '<u>ij</u>itaał

The lamino-alveolar strident in dzi's position and the extra vowel in these fourth person forms suggest that the ji- prefix has altered dzi- by rule 83, progressive strident assimilation, and then has lost the j- by a new rule, j- <u>deletion</u>.

(94) j → ∅ / ___i+j

Note that j- deletion must follow progressive strident assimilation and precede vowel elision and deaffrication. This suggests that progressive strident deletion is a fairly early rule. In 3.534 it will be shown that j- deletion has a somewhat wider role in the phonology.

                  93b/ni#ji+dzi+ni+ni+ł+ts'in/   93d/'i#ji+dzi+taał/

pg <u>strid</u> <u>assim</u>:   [ni#ji+ji+ni+ni+ł+ts'in]   ['i#ji+ji+taał]

<u>j</u> <u>dele</u>:   [ni#i+ji+ni+ni+ł+ts'in]   ['i#i+ji+taał]

<u>V</u> <u>elis</u>:   [ni#i+j+ni+ni+ł+ts'in]   _____

<u>deaffric</u>:   [ni#i+zh+ni+ni+ł+ts'in]   _____

<u>ultimately</u>:   [niizhníłts'in]   ['iijitaał]

Hoijer has noted a rule similar to j- deletion in the Chiricahua forms 'i-béidził-^{n}di (← 'i-bé-ji-dził-^{n}di) 'he knocks it off' and go-tai-dził-^{n}di (← go-taa-ji-dził-^{n}di) 'he knocks them down one after another' (Hoijer, 1946c:71). Here j- does not trigger progressive strident assimilation before it deletes.

2.77 Syllabic N-

The one remaining vowel deletion rule is that which produces syllabic n-. There is some confusion in the literature regarding this process. Hoijer states that syllabic n- is an optional but preferred alternant of nV- in front of a consonant (1945a:11, SH:21-22). His transcription makes liberal use of syllabic n-. But this policy leaves much unaccounted for. For example, najigeeh, a reported optional variant for njigeeh, is almost never heard (SH:21); and nV- prefixes in certain environments, such as before glottal stop are never reduced to a syllabic, ná'ásdiz is never *ń'ásdiz. Young and Morgan use syllabic n- much more sparingly than does Hoijer and are a reliable source for the (relatively) obligatory occurrences of syllabic n-. What is needed is a statement that distinguishes obligatory, optional, and non-occurring environments for syllabic n-. In his review of Sapir-Hoijer, Krauss has pointed out the need for more amplification of this process (1970:222).

Syllabic n- poses an interesting problem for current phonological formalism. It is produced by a late phonetic rule that is used with considerable variation. What is unique about the syllabic n- rule is that the variability of its use is a graded phenomenon, i.e. the rule is relatively obligatory in certain environments, optional in others, and impossible in others.[31]

NV- sequences almost always reduce to n- before non-continuant coronal verb prefixes.

(95) a. njigeeh

b. ńjíɬhis

c. ń'jíɬbąs

d. ndoogoh

e. 'abíndzíɬhaɬ

Before non-continuant coronal noun and verb stems, n- and nV- seem to be equally possible.

(96) a. ntsin ∿ nitsin
 b. ntin ∿ nitin
 c. ndzééh ∿ nidzééh
 d. njoołinjooł ∿ nijooł
 e. nch'ah ∿ nich'ah
 f. ndééh ∿ nidééh

Before continuant coronals the rule is clearly optional.

(97) a. ńsíłhiz ∿ nísíłhiz
 b. n'soołkaad ∿ na'soołkaad
 c. nnábah ∿ ninábah
 d. ńnásxis ∿ ninásxis
 e. nshínílzhee' ∿ nishínílzhee' ∿ nishíńlzhee'
 f. nnishteeh ∿ ninishteeh ∿ nnshteeh
 g. ńsh'į́ ∿ nísh'į́
 h. nłchxǫ' ∿ niłchxǫ'

Before bilabials, velars, glottal stop and y-, i.e. non-coronals, the rule is relatively impossible. However, it appears that the non-coronal non-continuants are more possible with syllabic n- than are the [+continuants] or glottal stop. The syllabic variants listed in (98) are possible but less frequent than those in (97).

(98) a. nibéésh ∿ nbéésh
 b. nabéshhil ∿ nbéshhil
 c. nikéénishdááh ∿ nkéénishdááh
 d. nik'aash ∿ nk'aash

Before non-coronal continuants and glottal stop, the rule is always impossible.

(99) a. nahashniih   *nhashniih

b. nahaɬtin   *nhaɬtin

c. ná'ásdiz   *ń'ásdiz

d. ná'óshkad   *ń'óshkad

e. náyiiɬts'iɬ   *ńyiiɬts'iɬ

f. ní'eesh   *ń'eesh

g. nighozh   *nghozh

h. nímásí   *ńmásí

i. nimá   *nmá

j. niyoo'   * nyoo'

Thus it appears that the syllabic n- rule has target environment, $\begin{bmatrix} +\text{coronal} \\ -\text{continuant} \end{bmatrix}$, where it is relatively obligatory (less so if this consonant is a stem initial syllable). As we move away from this environment, the rule becomes optional, with $\begin{bmatrix} +\text{coronal} \\ +\text{continuant} \end{bmatrix}$ being a stronger environment for the rule than $\begin{bmatrix} -\text{coronal} \\ -\text{continuant} \end{bmatrix}$, which is still a stronger environment than $\begin{bmatrix} -\text{coronal} \\ +\text{continuant} \end{bmatrix}$. Thus coronality is the primary dimension for the rule and continuancy the secondary dimension.

For the present I simply state <u>syllabic n-</u> with three conditions.

(100) $n\binom{\acute{v}}{v} \rightarrow \binom{\acute{n}}{n}$ / ___ $\begin{bmatrix} +\text{cor} \\ -\text{cnt} \end{bmatrix}$

conditions: a) optional if C = STEM

b) optional if C = $\begin{bmatrix} +\text{cor} \\ +\text{cnt} \end{bmatrix}$

c) weakly optional if C = $\begin{bmatrix} +\text{cns} \\ -\text{cor} \\ -\text{cnt} \end{bmatrix}$

Once the degree of variability in the environments for syllabic n- is more precisely determined, the rule might be written in the notation developed by Labov (1972:123):

(100') $n\binom{\acute{v}}{v} \rightarrow \binom{\acute{n}}{n}$ / ___ $\left\langle \begin{matrix} +\text{cor} \\ -\text{cnt} \end{matrix} \middle\rangle \middle\langle \begin{matrix} +\text{cor} \\ -\text{cnt} \\ \text{[STEM]} \end{matrix} \middle\rangle \middle\langle \begin{matrix} +\text{cor} \\ +\text{cnt} \end{matrix} \middle\rangle \middle\langle \begin{matrix} +\text{cns} \\ -\text{cor} \\ -\text{cnt} \end{matrix} \right\rangle$

The angled brackets indicate that syllabic n- is a variable output in four environments, from strong, $\begin{bmatrix}+cor\\-cnt\end{bmatrix}$, to weak, $\begin{bmatrix}+cns\\-cor\\-cnt\end{bmatrix}$.

In 4.20 I discuss how syllabic n- might be incorporated into a Navajo sociolinguistic study.

2.8 Rule Summary

For convenience all phonological rules presented in this chapter are listed here in their order of presentation in their most revised form. Henceforth rules from Chapter Two will be identified by a II, e.g. rule II-12, vowel deletion.

(11) ni- absorption   CV + ni[→ CV́

(12) vowel deletion   V → ∅ / C___+V

(13) seriative h- deletion   h → ∅ / CV+___i

(18) continuant devoicing $\begin{bmatrix}+cns\\+cnt\\+voi\end{bmatrix}$ → [-voi] / $\left\{\begin{matrix}\#\#\\\begin{bmatrix}+cns\\+cnt\\-voi\end{bmatrix}\end{matrix}\right\}$ ___

(23) ł- deletion   ł → ∅ / ___ $\begin{bmatrix}+cnt\\+cor\\-voi\end{bmatrix}$

(24) ł- voicing   ł → l / d___

(25) d- deletion   d → ∅ / ___C

(26) consonant degemination   C   C → C
                                [αF] [αF]

(30) classifier deletion   ł → ∅ / C___C

(32) h- deletion   h → ∅ / ___łC

(35) d- effect   d + $\left\{\begin{matrix}'\\C\\\begin{bmatrix}+cnt\\\langle+son\rangle\end{matrix}\\1\end{matrix}\right\}_2$ → ∅ $\left\{\begin{matrix}t'\\\begin{bmatrix}-cnt\\\langle+glt\rangle\end{bmatrix}\\1\end{matrix}\right\}_2$

(39) tone assimilation   V → V́ / V́(#)C₁___+C₀[
                         [-lng]

(41) gamma deletion gh → ∅ / V(#)___V

(42) y- deletion y → ∅ / V#___i

(44) VCV assimilation $\begin{bmatrix}+hi\\-bck\end{bmatrix}$ → $\begin{bmatrix}\alpha hi\\+bck\end{bmatrix}$ / *___$\left\{\begin{matrix}'\\m\\\begin{bmatrix}-cor\\-ant\end{bmatrix}\end{matrix}\right\}$ $\begin{bmatrix}\alpha hi\\+bck\end{bmatrix}$

   exception: 'i#'i → 'e'e

(46) pepet vowel insertion ∅ → i / #___C_o[

(47) vowel degemination Sequences of prefix vowels identical in quality
         shall be no more than two moras in length.

(48) tone lowering v̂ → V / ___+V

(49) tone raising V → v̂ / ___(#) {í/á}

(51) optative tone lowering ó → o / X#___

(57) vowel assimilation a. $\begin{bmatrix}+hi\\-bck\end{bmatrix}$ → $\begin{bmatrix}\alpha hi\\\beta bck\end{bmatrix}$ / $\begin{bmatrix}\alpha hi\\\beta bck\end{bmatrix}$ C_o[

         b. $\begin{bmatrix}+hi\\(-bck)\end{bmatrix}$ → $\begin{bmatrix}\alpha hi\\\beta bck\end{bmatrix}$ / $\begin{bmatrix}\alpha hi\\\beta bck\end{bmatrix}$ C_o[

   conditions: a) ≠ a#ii
                      [+lng]
              b) i- is not preceded by $\begin{bmatrix}-cor\\-ant\end{bmatrix}$ or t-
              c) 57b not applicable to a#ó

(62) vowel absorption V̂# V → V̂
                            [-lng]

   exception: í#i → é

(67) vowel fronting $\begin{bmatrix}-hi\\+bck\end{bmatrix}$ → [-bck] / ___$\begin{bmatrix}+hi\\-bck\end{bmatrix}$

   condition: a- is not preceded by $\begin{bmatrix}-cor\\-ant\end{bmatrix}$ or t-

(72) 'i to 'a 'i → 'a / ___[+cns]

(78) delabialization $\begin{bmatrix}-cor\\-ant\\+rnd\end{bmatrix}$ $\begin{bmatrix}+hi\\-bck\end{bmatrix}$ → [-rnd] [+bck] / ___$\left\{\begin{matrix}o\\{[+cns]}\end{matrix}\right\}$

(79) ho to ha   ho → ha / ___C_o[

(81) strident assimilation (regressive) $\begin{bmatrix} +cor \\ +str \end{bmatrix}$ → [αant] / ___X $\begin{bmatrix} +cor \\ αant \\ +str \end{bmatrix}$

(83) progressive strident assimilation $\begin{bmatrix} +cor \\ +str \end{bmatrix}$ → [αant]/ $\begin{bmatrix} αant \\ +str \end{bmatrix}$ X___

   condition: ≠ si+sh+(X)+$\begin{bmatrix} -ant \\ +str \end{bmatrix}$

(86) vowel elision   i → ∅ / X $\left\{ \begin{bmatrix} +cor \\ +str \\ -cnt \end{bmatrix} \right\}$ ___[+cns] V_1+C_o[

(87) deaffrication $\begin{bmatrix} +cor \\ +str \\ -cnt \end{bmatrix}$ → [+cnt] / ___C

(91) glottal-zh metathesis   ' + zh + C → zh + ' + C

(94) j- deletion   j → ∅ / ___i+j

(100) syllabic n-   n $\binom{(´)}{V}$ → $\binom{(´)}{n}$ / ___$\begin{bmatrix} +cor \\ -ant \end{bmatrix}$

   conditions: a) optional if C = STEM

   b) optional if C = $\begin{bmatrix} +cnt \\ +cor \end{bmatrix}$

   c) weakly optional if C = $\begin{bmatrix} +cns \\ -cor \\ -cnt \end{bmatrix}$

NOTES TO CHAPTER TWO

[1] In 2.5 I will review the differing approaches taken by Navajo scholars to a particular topic, the organization of the verb prefixes.

[2] The only exception to this is the verb ní 'he says' which is a lone stem with no prefixes.

[3] Hoijer posits that there are eleven paradigms. I will demonstrate in 2.11 that his yi- imperfective is phonologically predictable.

[4] Direct objects (other than yi-) appear only occasionally in this study. I abbreviate them as follows: niiłtsą́ 'saw' 2-3 stands for 'he saw you', niheeshtééł 'carry an animate object along' 2d-1 stands for 'I am carrying you dpl along'.

[5] It will be shown in 2.74 that both the 3i pronoun and 'away, out of sight' are best represented as underlying /'i/.

[6] In his 1971 article Stanley has altered the distribution of the five word internal boundaries so the PERF and SUBJ are grouped with MODE in D, and E contains only the two classifiers. No explanation is given for these changes (p. 28).

[7] The alternations in (7) and (8) are suggested by Hale (1972d:Prob. IV).

[8] This is one of the few cases where si- modal prefix occurs in the imperfective (YM, 1943b:8).

[9] The rule that deletes h- will be presented in 2.71. Here we are only concerned with the fact that the vowel of the prefix preceding oh- has disappeared.

[10] 'i- has become 'o- by the vowel assimilation rule to be discussed in 2.732.

[11] Significantly, Hoijer (1969) has observed that certain inalienably possessed nouns in Navajo that take a high tone pronominal prefix such as bíla' 'his hand, finger', bíchį́į́h 'his nose', and bíníí' 'his nostril' correspond to Athpaskan cognates with a *ni- prefix (some archaic noun classifying prefix) that is not absorbed by the preceding pronoun. For example, he cites in Kutchin -ni-cį́į́ 'nose', -ni-li' 'hand, finger', and -ni-jik 'nostril', all with a ni- prefix. In Tanaina 'his nose' is benchish, 'my nose' is shenchish (Kari, 1972). Young has recorded 'my nose' in Chipewyan as sIntshį́į and in Carrier as sníintshis (Young, 1940). (Young [personal communication] also notes that at times forms with ni- in Northern Athapaskan do not correspond to a high tone pronoun in Navajo as in Chipewyan singááné, Navajo shigaan 'my arm'.) It appears then that the high tone pronouns in Navajo are derived by ni- absorption. Hence,

/bi+ni+chį́į́h/
ni absorp: [bí+chį́į́h]
ultimately: [bíchį́į́h]

It will be interesting to dertermine the reflexes of the ni- absorption rule in Athapaskan.

[12] It will be demonstrated in 3.6 that seriative h- deletion needs an additional refinement.

[13] It is important to specify that the mode variant is determined by the thematic or derivational prefixes that may appear in the verb base and not by the paradigmatic prefixes such as ji- 4 or yi- direct object. In other words, a verb such as jicha 'he 4 is crying' is of the primary mode variant because no thematic or derivational prefix precedes mode, despite the presence of the conjunct paradigmatic prefix ji-; or 'ajidiz 'he is spinning' is a conjunct mode variant because of the thematized 'i- 3i conjunct prefix and not the paradigmatic ji-.

[14] Two stems that do contain a voiceless stem initial fricative are shééhai 'I spent the winter' and shééshí 'I spent the summer' where no ł- is present in any form to account for the voiceless fricatives. These two stems are clearly nominal in origin and have retained the voicelessness of the initial sound of the source nouns.

[15] The underlying representation for this type of verb will be explained in 3.112.

[16] At this point it may seem simpler to use rule 26, consonant degemination, to reduce ł+ł to ł. However, ordering requirements for the derivation of oh- 2d forms will make it clear why a revised ł- deletion rule is preferable. See below.

[17] The fact that the s- of the si- modal prefix has become sh- in both of these verbs will be discussed in 2.75.

[18] There is some question as to the status of 'y-, preglottalized y-, the rarest Navajo phoneme. Some younger speakers prefer to use in its place an unaspirated dorso-palatal stop, gʸ-, e.g. 'iigʸóół. Also, there is evidence that there are in fact two separate stem initial y-'s, one which, in contrast to the sonorant, appears as dz- when next to d-. Both of these issues will be taken up in 4.112 as part of the discussion of irregular stem initial consonants.

[19] The thematic l- classifier sometimes alternates with ∅ in third person indefinite forms, cf. 'i'niilzhiizh 'he starts to dance' and 'i'niizhiizh 'dancing started'; didoolnish 'he'll start working' and 'adidoonish 'work will start'. This unusual classifier shift supports the analysis that thematic l- classifier is structurally distinct from the d+ł (passive. l-) classifier.

[20] Howren has suggested that the underlying forms of the d- and l- classifiers in Navajo (and in four other Athapaskan languages) are identical to the PA classifiers, /də/ and /łə/ (1971:111). There is no synchronic evidence in Navajo for assuming that the classifiers are syllabic in underlying representation, and this is a needless complication.

[21] The clusters 'd- and zh'd- in 37c and d arise from a vowel elision rule to be discussed in 2.76.

[22] Rule 1d is forced upon Stanley because of the back vowels (rather than i-) he uses in the lexical representation for ni-, si, and ghi- modal prefixes. No reference to the D and E boundaries is needed if i- is posited for these prefixes.

[23] It is worth exploring whether the aa- assimilation correlates with a lower [o] allophone rather than [u] allophone for the high back vowel. This is suggested by Saville-Troike's findings that four of five first grade children in Sanostee-Toadalena (in the east) have the [o] allophone, while the children are evenly divided between [o] and [u] in Greasewood (in the south) and Cottonwood (in the central Reservation) (1973).

[24] It is not certain what underlies the o- imperfectives. For now I assume it is a high tone ó- such as is found in the optative.

[25] Observe that the most exceptional vowel assimilation outputs, 'e'e- (from VCV assimilation) and é- both derive from adjacent i-'s.

[26] I restrict vowel absorption to short vowels because I analyze verbs like nabíigil /na+bí#iid+ghil/ 'we are pushing it around' as having undergone rule 47, vowel degemination, i.e. í#ii → íi, and not vowel absorption.

[27] Similar variants have been cited by Reichard. She also noted that speakers in the Ganado area do not employ vowel fronting, preferring ai- to ei- (1945:164; 1951:372).

[28] The problem that 'away' poses for a statement of vowel assimilation has been raised by Reichard: "In one case a- dominates, in another o- takes precedence" (1951:371).

[29] Further support for the 'i- representation of these prefixes comes from the variants noted by Reichard: 'i'ishnííł and 'i'inííł for 71.1 and 3; 'éshłééh and 'ínílééh for 70.1 and 2 (1951:370, 372). Apparently in these dialects the 'i to 'a rule is dropped. 'éshłééh can be readily explained by an /'í/ representation as having undergone rule 62, vowel absorption. Hoijer notes, "The behavior of 'a- prefixes suggest that they originate from an earlier *'i-, a suggestion that is borne out by comparative evidence" (SH:29). The 3i pronoun appears in all other Apachean languages as 'i- with no 'a- alternation and is a reflex of PA *k^y'ə- (Hoijer, 1971:120).

[30] The 'area' prefix is from PA *xwə- (Hoijer, 1971:120). Golla has proposed a delabialization rule for this prefix in Hupa, xwi → xo / ___{ʔ} (1970:52). In rare cases when hwi- is found next to 'i- 3i there seems to be ambivalence as to the application of rule 78. For example, variants are found for hwé'échééh ∿ hó'échééh 'someone is left out' and hwé'íícháá' ∿ hó'íícháá' 'someone was left out', suggesting that glottal stop is a weak trigger for delabialization. (The high tones on hwí ∿ hó and 'é complicate the analysis of these verbs.) One verb stem shows a velar-labiovelar alternation, -koh, -kóóh, -kwih, -kóóh 'to vomit'. This can be explained by assuming an underlying kw- which becomes k- before o-.

[31] This approach was suggested by Ken Hale (personal communication).

CHAPTER THREE
VERB MODE PHONOLOGY

3.0 Introduction

In this chapter I present an analysis of the phonology of the regular active verb modes. I noted briefly in 2.3 that ten verb mode paradigms can be isolated. (Hoijer figures that there are eleven.) Two of these are parasitic, the usitative, which has the prefix complex of a ∅ imperfective and the stem of the iterative, and the future, which can be shown to be a subset of the progressive. Thus, the mode system consists of eight distinctive constructions.

The eight distinct modes can be derived from the following underlying forms, where X stands for subject pronoun.

    a. ∅ imperfective   ...(X)+⊂

    b. ni imperfective   ...ni+(X)+⊂

    c. iterative   ...ná#...(X)+⊂

    d. optative   ...ó+(X)+∟

    e. progressive   ...ghi+(X)+⊂

    f. ghi perfective   ...ghi+í+(X)I⊂

    g. ni perfective   ...ni+í+(X)+⊂

    h. si perfective   ...si+í+(X)+⊂

In order to present the modes in a complete range of environments, each is discussed in terms of the three mode variants, primary, ##MODE+(X)+⊂; conjunct, +MODE+(X)+⊂; and disjunct, #MODE+(X)+⊂ (with the exception of the iterative which cannot appear in the primary mode variant). In addition, certain modes such as the ni- imperfective and the three perfectives are subdivided further. The mode variants that are discussed represent a set of basic paradigms for the active verb as it has been defined by Sapir and Hoijer.

This chapter is organized, generally, from the phonologically simple to the phonologically complex. I start in 3.1 with the two imperfectives, the ∅ imperfective being the simplest mode. In 3.2, the iterative, which closely parallels the ∅ imperfective, is examined. Third, I discuss the optative (3.3). Fourth, I take up the progressive, including the future (3.4). In 3.5 the three perfectives, which are far more complex than any of the other modes, are discussed. In addition, I discuss the phonology of two highly unusual prefixes, hi- 'seriative' and si- 'destruct' in their various mode forms in 3.6.[1] This chapter is concluded with a discussion of the readjustment rules, the problematic areas in the mode phonology (3.7), and with a summary of the rules presented in this chapter (3.8).

This analysis is largely confined to the regular modes in combination with the more productive derivational prefixes. Some attempt is made to incorporate a few of the more conspicuous aspectual sub-systems such as the mysterious +i+ aspect system (or systems). Numerous idiosyncratic verbs have been overlooked. These include verbs with vowel initial stems such as 'go'; verbs with irregular stem initial consonants; verbs with unusual thematic prefixes such as jii- 'emotion', and sh- 'scold'; and verbs with unusual mode-aspect prefixes such as the o- imperfective and the highly irregular aspectual subsystem formed with yí- 'tentative'. Some of these special topics will be discussed in Chapter Four. Only brief reference is made to neuter verb phonology, a subject that merits additional study.

In this chapter I will focus on the phonological processes that are unique to the modes. Mention will be made of the general rules in Chapter Two only when it is significant to a derivation.

3.1 Imperfective Mode

3.10 Introduction

The obvious place to begin a study of verb mode phonology is with the imperfective, the least marked, semantically and structurally, of the modes. The imperfective signifies, very generally, that "action is incomplete but is in the act of being accomplished, or about to be done" (YM, 1943a:42). Stanley (1969a:Chap 3) and Krauss (1970:224) in their analyses of stem variation as a suffixing process, posit that the imperfective suffix is zero. In addition, I will show that the prefix complex of certain imperfectives is less marked than those for other modes.

As mentioned in 2.3, Hoijer assumes that there are three imperfective mode prefixes, ∅, yi-, and ni-. However, the distribution of the yi-imperfective is curious. Intransitive and transitive verbs with no DPr (derivational prefix) take yi- in modal prefix position unless the transitive verbs contain a direct object in pos. 4 which, Hoijer claims, causes a shift to the ∅ imperfective, i.e. yi- disappears. Also, certain DPr's require a yi- modal prefix but drop it if there is a direct object (SH:27-28). Obviously, a rule that deletes yi- in a morphologically marked environment is very costly.

Krauss has pointed out that if disjunctive and conjunctive prefixes are recognized, yi- and ∅ imperfectives are shown to be in complementary distribution. Yi- occurs when nothing or a disjunctive prefix precedes C_o[, and ∅ occurs when a conjunctive prefix precedes this environment (1970:226). Krauss also suggests that if the yi- imperfective is phonologically derived, then Hoijer's five unpredictable conjugation patterns for the modes (∅ imp.-si perf., yi imp.-si perf., ∅ imp.-yi perf., yi imp.-yi perf., ni imp.-ni perf.) can be reduced to three entirely predictable patterns. All that need be listed for a verb base is its perfective prefix, the imperfective being either ni- if perfective is ni- or ∅/yi- if perfective is si- or yi-. (We return to this suggestion in 3.7.) In formulating phonological rules for imperfectives, I will substantiate Krauss' suggestion that yi- and ∅ are in complementary distribution, and I will provide further proof of the importance of the # disjunct boundary in the Navajo prefix system.

First, in 3.11-3.13 I will examine the ∅ (formerly ∅ and yi-) imperfectives in their conjunct, primary, and disjunct mode variants. I will also include a subcategory of the conjunct imperfectives that takes a vocalic prefix, +i+, in aspect position (3.114). Then I will analyze the ni- imperfective paradigms (3.12).

3.11 ∅ Imperfective

3.111 +(X)+[

In paradigms for (1) 'to plant', (2) 'to sing', and (3) 'to carry an animate object', pos. 6 di- 'inceptive', pos. 5 hwi- 'area' and pos. 4 ni- and shi- direct objects are placed next to ∅ modal prefix. In other words, a range of conjunctive prefixes are directly next to subject pronoun, classifier, or stem initial consonant. These paradigms correspond to what Hoijer calls the regular imperfectives.

(1) 1 k'idishłé[2]   (2) 1 hashtaał   (3) 1 nishteeh
     2 k'idílé   2 hótaał   2 shíłteeh
     3 k'idilé   3 hataał   3 shiłteeh
     1d k'idiilyé   4 hojitaał   1d niilteeh
     2d k'idohłé   1d hwiitaał   2d shołteeh
                              2d hohtaał

All of these forms can be derived by general phonological rules that have been discussed in Chapter Two. The 1sg forms require little explanation. Rule II-18, continuant devoicing, applies to 1.1, rules II-78 and 79, delabialization and ho to ha, apply to 2.1, and rule II-30, classifier deletion, applies to 3.1.

Each of the 2sg forms shows a high tone prefix vowel instead of the underlying ni- pronoun. Recall that ni- absorption, rule II-11, is triggered by the + formative boundary that separates conjunctive prefixes. Thus, 1.2 and 3.2 are derived by rule 11. To obtain the ho- of 2.2 we must first apply delabialization to convert hwi- to ho-; then ho to ha is ordered so that it will be blocked by ni-; finally, ni- absorption applies.

	1.2/k'i#di+ni+lé/	2.2/hwi+ni+taał/	3.2/shi+ni+ł+teeh/
delab:		[ho+ni+taał]	
ho to ha:			
ni absorp:	[k'i+dí+lé]	[hó+taał]	[shí+ł+teeh]
ultimately:	[k'idílé]	[hótaał]	[shíłteeh]

The third person forms, 1.3 and 3.3, require no rules while 2.3 and 4 require only delabialization and, for 2.3 only, the ho to ha rule.

The six first and second dual forms in (1), (2), and (3) contain environments for rule II-12, vowel deletion.

	1.2d/k'i#di+oh+lé/	2.1d/hwi+iid+taał/	3.2d/shi+oh+ł+teeh/
V dele:	[k'i#d+oh+lé]	[hw+iid+taał]	[sh+oh+ł+teeh]
ultimately:	[k'idohłé]	[hwiitaał]	[shołteeh]

As mentioned above, Hoijer would analyze the verbs of (3) with direct object prefixes as shifting from yi- imperfective to ∅ imperfective because related primary forms such as yishteeh 'I bury an animate object' supposedly contain a yi- prefix in mode position (SH:28). Therefore, 3.1 nishteeh, would be derived from /ni+yi+sh+ł+teeh/, and yi- would be deleted by a morphologically marked rule. I am contending in this analysis that all conjunct paradigms for the ∅ imperfective, including direct object forms as in (3), contain no modal prefix. The conjunct ∅ imperfectives are the simplest mode construction in Navajo, and as I have demonstrated, require only general phonological rules.

3.112 ##(X)+C

The intransitive verb 'to cry' (4) and the transitive verb 'to bury' an animate object with preposed łeeh (5) are primary imperfectives; i.e. there are no conjunctive or disjunctive prefixes in front of the mode slot.

(4) 1 yishcha   (5) 1 yishteeh
     2 nicha   2 niłteeh
     3 yicha   3 yiłteeh
     4 jicha   4 jiłteeh
     1d yiicha   1d yiilteeh
     2d wohcha   2d wołteeh

Hoijer and Stanley analyze verbs like (4) and (5) as containing a prefix in pos. 7. (Hoijer posits a yi- prefix and Stanley a hi- prefix.) The second and fourth person forms as well as the third person transitives such as 5.3, must delete the underlying prefix by a readjustment rule (Stanley, 1969a:188-189). If we instead follow Krauss' suggestion that the ∅ and yi- imperfectives are in complementary distribution, the yi- prefix in 4.1, 4.3, and 5.1 (but not 5.3; see below) can be regarded as a meaningless 'peg' element that is attached to these verbs by phonological rule. The 'peg' analysis, as opposed to the yi- modal prefix analysis, is not new. It has been suggested by

Li for the Chipewyan verb 'to cry' hɛstsaɣ, nɛtsaɣ, hɛtsaɣ (1946:413),
by Sapir and Cook for the Sarcee verb 'to cry' ìstsíí, nítsíí, ítsíí
(Cook, 1971b:413), by Golla for Hupa (1970:61), and by Hale (1970:44-47)
and Young and Morgan (1943a:56) for Navajo. The peg element has also
been termed a 'pepet vowel' by Sapir in describing Sarcee (1925:190) and
by Li in describing Mattole (1930:64) and Chipewyan (1933:463).

Hale (ibid.) and Cook (ibid.) have stated the phonological environment
for the insertion of the peg, or pepet vowel, most precisely: a peg
occurs when there is no vocalic constituent in the prefix complex.
Thus, the non-vocalic sh- pronoun requires a peg whereas the vocalic
ni- and ji- pronouns need no peg.

Hale's 1970 formulation of Navajo pegs inserts yi- by a one-step
yi- insertion rule. However, Hale has noted that affinities between
primary and disjunct imperfectives (to be discussed below) suggest that
the peg is best regarded as the result of a three-step process (1972a).[3]

The **pepet vowel insertion** (or vowel insertion) rule, briefly
introduced in 2.73 as part of the vowel assimilation analysis, is the
principal phonological process affecting ∅ imperfectives.

(II-46) $\emptyset \rightarrow i \: / \: \#\_\_\_ \: C_o[$.

Rule II-46 adds i- to an underlying representation with no vowel in the
conjunct portion of the prefix complex. In other words, vowel insertion
states that verbs such as *cha, *shcha, or *łteeh are inadmissable in
Navajo.[4]

Next, a rule is needed to supply an inorganic consonant in front
of the inserted vowel and in front of all other vowel initial prefixes
that appear next to ## word boundary. It is characteristic of word
initial gh- to become y- before i- and w- before o- while word initial

y- is constant before i- and o-. Therefore, we first cover a word initial vowel with gh- by a <u>gamma insertion</u> rule. This gh- then turns to y- before i- and w- before o- by a <u>gliding</u> rule.

(6) ∅ → gh / ##___V

(7) gh → {y/w} / ##___{i/o}

The gliding rule accounts for the phonetic fact noted by Hoijer that word initial yi- and ghi- are indistinguishable. Gamma insertion and gliding have a wider role in the phonology, particularly in the optative, progressive, and ghi- perfective modes.

With rules II-46, 6, and 7, all of the forms in (4) and (5) can be derived. The 1sg forms and 4.3 require all three rules.

	4.3/cha/	5.1/sh+ɨ+teeh/
<u>V insert</u>:	[i+cha]	[i+sh+ɨ+teeh]
<u>gh insert</u>:	[ghi+cha]	[ghi+sh+ɨ+teeh]
<u>gliding</u>:	[yi+cha]	[yi+sh+ɨ+teeh]
<u>ultimately</u>:	[yicha]	[yishteeh]

The 2sg and 4 forms and 5.3 require no rules. Vowel insertion is inapplicable because of the vocalic prefixes, ni-, ji-, and yi-.

5.3/yi+ɨ+teeh/

<u>V insert</u>: _____

<u>ultimately</u>: [yiɨteeh]

The 1st and 2nd dual forms require rules 6 and 7.

	4.1d/iid+cha/	5.2d/oh+ɨ+teeh/
<u>gh insert</u>:	[ghiid+cha]	[ghoh+ɨ+teeh]
<u>gliding</u>:	[yiid+cha]	[woh+ɨ+teeh]
<u>ultimately</u>:	[yiicha]	[woɨteeh]

Of course, rule II-46 does not apply to these verbs because of the vocalic pronouns, iid- and oh-.

The argument in favor of phonologically derived 'peg' yi- prefixes centers on forms like nicha and yiɬteeh which, in the above analysis, need no readjustment or morphologically marked rules to delete an underlying yi- prefix. Instead, they are simply exempt from the vowel insertion rule because of the underlying vowel in their prefix complexes. Further support for the peg analysis is found in the disjunct ∅ imperfectives.

3.113 #(X)+[

Disjunctive prefixes that are low in tone, such as pos. 1 prefixes na- 'about', 'i- 'away', and hada- 'down', appear in ∅ imperfectives in paradigms for (8) 'to swim around', (9) 'to laugh', and (10) 'to drop an animate object'.

(8) 1 naashbé   (9) 1 'iishdlóóh   (10) 1 hadaasht'e'
     2 nanibé   2 'anidlóóh   2 hadaniɬt'e'
     3 naabé   3 'iidlóóh   3 hadeiɬt'e'
     4 njibé   4 'ajidlóóh   4 hadajiɬt'e'
     1d neiibé   1d 'íidlóóh   1d hadeiilt'e'
     2d naohbé ~ naahbé   2d 'oohdlóóh   2d hadaoɬt'e' ~
                                                      hadaaɬt'e'

In comparing the 1sg and 2sg forms in these paradigms, we see an alternation between long and short vowels in the prefix complex. Hoijer regards the derivational prefixes in these verbs as among those that take a yi- modal prefix which in 1sg loses its y- and assimilates its vowel. Thus, 10.1 derives from /ha-da-yi-sh-ɬ-t'e'/. The short vowel in the second and fourth person forms is paralleled with nicha in the primary mode variant, i.e. yi- has been eliminated by a readjustment rule.

If the so-called yi- imperfectives are, in fact, phonologically introduced, can the long vowels in disjunct paradigms be described without recourse to an underlying yi-? Observe that the unanticipated long vowels occur in non-vocalic conjunctive prefix complexes 8.1, 8.3, 9.1, 9.3, and 10.1, i.e. in the same environment that triggers pepet vowel insertion. (The other long vowels are anticipated vowel clusters. For example, in the dual forms the adverbial prefix vowel is adjacent to iid- and oh-.)

Rule II-46, pepet vowel insertion, applies when no vowel appears in #___C_o[. Therefore, the same rule accounts for the peg elements in (4) and (5) and the lengthened vowels in (8), (9), and (10). The pepet vowel in the disjunct verbs is then subject to vowel assimilation.

	8.3/na#bé/	9.1/'i#sh+d+dlóóh/	10.1/ha+da#sh+ɬ+t'e'/
V insert:	[na#i+bé]	['i#i+sh+d+dlóóh]	[ha+da#i+sh+ɬ+t'e']
V assim:	[na#a+bé]	_____	[ha+da#a+sh+ɬ+t'e']
ultimately:	[naabé]	['iishdlóóh]	[hadaasht'e']

In the above derivations vowel assimilation applies when i- is preceded by a-.[5]

As part of his earlier, one-step yi- insertion analysis of ∅ imperfectives, Hale posited that the long vowels in the disjunct forms were derived by a vowel lengthening rule that stated if there is only one vowel in the prefix complex, it is a long vowel (1970:34). However, verbs like hadaasht'e' are counterexamples to such a rule since da- lengthens despite the fact that there are two vowels in the prefix complex. Therefore, Hale's more recent vowel insertion analysis brings out the affinity between the primary and disjunct imperfectives and eliminates the need for a vowel lengthening rule.

As in the primary ∅ imperfectives, vowel insertion does not apply to 2sg and 4 forms in these three paradigms. The 2sg and 4 forms of (9) show an incidence of 'i to 'a, rule II-72, and 8.4 has a syllabic n- as a result of rule II-100.

	8.4/na#ji+be/	9.2/'i#ni+d+dlóóh/
V insert:	_____	_____
'i to 'a:	_____	['a#ni+d+dlóóh]
syllabic n:	[n#ji+bé]	_____
ultimately:	[njibé]	['anidlóóh]

Of course, ni- 2sg prefix in 9.2 is not absorbed because of the preceding # boundary.

Verb (10) is transitive and, therefore, must contain a yi- direct object pronoun in the third person. The y- deletes by rule II-42, y-deletion, and the rule II-67 vowel fronting applies.

	10.3/ha+da#yi+ɨ+t'e'/
y dele:	[ha+da#i+ɨ+t'e']
V front:	[ha+de#i+ɨ+t'e']
ultimately:	[hadeiɫt'e']

According to the vowel deletion rule, none of the dual forms of (8), (9), and (10) should lose adverbial prefix vowels due to the # boundary. 9.1d seems to violate this pattern. However, its underlying vowel cluster, /'i#iid+d+dlóóh/, is shortened by rule II-47, vowel degemination, because it is more than two moras in length, and not by vowel deletion.

The duals are derived by general rules.

	9.1d/'i#iid+d+dlóóh/	9.2d/'i#oh+d+dlóóh/	10.1d/ha+da#iid+ɨ+t'e'/
d dele:	['i#ii+dlóóh]	['i#oh+dlóóh]	[ha+da#ii+l+t'e']
V assim:	_____	['o#oh+dlóóh]	_____

V front: _____   _____   [ha+de#ii+l+t'e']

V degem: ['i#ɨ+dlóóh]   _____   _____

ultimately: ['iidlóóh]   ['oohdlóóh]   [hadeiilt'e']

Disjunctive prefixes with high tone vowels, such as pos. 1 'ákwí- 'that way', bí- 'against', ná- 'encircle', and pos. 2 ná- 'iterative', undergo somewhat different phonological rules than do the low tone disjunctive prefixes. Two transitive verbs containing ná- 'encircle' and bí- 'against' are given in (11) 'to sew it' and (12) 'to push it about'.

(11) 1 náshkad   (12) 1 nabéshhil
      2 nánɨɬkad   2 nabínighil
      3 néíɬkad   3 nayííghil
      4 ñjíɬkad   4 nabíjíghil
      1d néiilkad   1d nabíigil
      2d náɬkad ~ naóɬkad   2d nabóhil

The low tone disjunctive imperfectives have a long vowel in 1sg forms that has been introduced by rule II-46, pepet vowel insertion. But no long vowel appears in 11.1 or 12.1. Nevertheless, I contend that vowel insertion has applied to the underlying non-vocalic prefix complexes. Evidence of vowel insertion is the é- in 12.1 (instead of underlying í-). Recall that rule II-62, vowel absorption, states that a high tone vowel absorbs a short low tone vowel, í#i → é being an exceptional output. This absorption process applies to the phonologically introduced pepet vowel and to the o- of the 2d forms in (11) and (12).

                  11.1/ná#sh+ɨ+kad/   12.1/na+bí#sh+ghil/

V insert: [ná#ish+ɨ+kad]   [na+bí#ish+ghil]

V assim: [ná#ash+ɨ+kad]   _____

V absorp: [ná#sh+ɨ+kad]   [na+bé#sh+ghil]

ultimately: [náshkad]   [nabéshhiɬ]

	11.2d /ná#oh+ɨ+kad/	12.2d /na+bí#oh+ghil/
cont devoic:		[na+bí+oh+hil]
V assim:	([ná#ah+ɨ+kad])	[na+bó+oh+hil]
V absorp:	[ná#h+ɨ+kad] ∿ [náo#h+ɨ+kad]	[na+bó#h+hil]
C degem:		[na+bó#hil]
ultimately:	[náɨkad] ∿ [náoɨkad]	[nabóhil]

The variant forms for 11.2d reflect the two vowel assimilation rules, II-57a and b. Note the application of rule II-26, consonant degemination, to the h+h string in 12.2d.

The difference in vowel length in 11.1d and 12.1d is explained by rule II-47, vowel degemination.

	11.1d /ná#iid+ɨ+kad/	12.1d /na+bí#iid+ghil/
V assim:		
V front:	[né#iid+ɨ+kad]	
V degem:		[na+bí#id+ghil]
ultimately:	[néiilkad]	[nabíigil]

11.2, 3, and 4 and 12.2 and 3 show evidence of rule II-39, tone assimilation.

	11.4 /ná#ji+ɨ+kad/	12.2 /na+bí#ni+ghil/
tone assim:	[ná#jí+ɨ+kad]	[na+bí#ní+ghil]
syllabic n:	[ń#jí+ɨ+kad]	
ultimately:	[ńjíɨkad]	[nabíníghil]

The third person forms are slightly more complex than the second and fourth person forms. Tone assimilation must apply over the y- of the direct object pronoun, which is subsequently deleted by rule II-42, y-deletion.

                    11.3/ná#yi+ɨ+kad/   12.3/na+yí#yi+ghil/

tone assim: [ná#yí+ɨ+kad]   [na+yí#yí+ghil]

y dele: [ná#í+ɨ+kad]   [na+yí#í+ghil]

V front: [né #í+ɨ+kad]   _____

ultimately: [néíɨkad]   [nayííghil]

3.114 +i+ aspect

The preceding analysis of the three mode variants of the ∅ imperfective accounts for the large majority of imperfective verbs. However, a fairly common sub-category of the conjunct imperfectives that takes a vocalic aspect prefix (+i+ or +ii+) of uncertain meaning does not conform to the regular imperfective patterns. It should be pointed out that even assigning +i+ verbs to the ∅ imperfective is tenuous. Perhaps they are some separate type of mode. The phonology of +i+ perfectives lends some support to a separate mode analysis (see 3.514).

As mentioned in 2.3, the seven Navajo modes are crosscut by a vestigial aspect system that is marked by alternations in the stem set and/or prefixes in pos. 6. Most of the research on aspect has centered on stem variations (Hoijer, 1949; SH:101-103; Stanley, 1969a:Chp. 3). Reichard's paradigm chapter remains the most extensive study of the aspect prefixes although her maverick conception of the verb and her insistence on assigning meanings to the most obscure prefixes diminishes the utility of her work. Reichard grouped all verbs with +i+ or +ii+ aspect into a 'cessative system' (recall that Reichard's system is a grouping of related aspects and modes) and glossed them, dubiously, as 'pause while. . .'

The aspectual system could be the subject of an entire study in itself. A thorough explanation would require a study of the syntactic distribution of aspect prefixes and stems, integrated analysis of stem set and aspect prefix phonology, and semantic commentary by Navajo speakers. At present I will attempt to explain the phonological behavior of five aspect subsystems with +i+ or +ii+ in pos. 6, four of which are fairly common.

This vocalic prefix, which I call +i+ aspect, is idiosyncratic phonologically and syntactically. The underlying shape of the prefix, /i/ or /ii/, is unresolved at present. The 1st singular of the ∅ imperfectives and the third and fourth persons of ∅ imperfectives and iteratives are best represented as /ii/. Elsewhere it is best considered as /i/. There is a slightly stronger case for an /i/ rather than /ii/ representation, but either choice requires awkward readjustment rules. I arbitrarily choose to represent the prefix as /i/ and to derive +ii+ by readjustment rules.

The syntactic distribution of +i+ aspect throughout the modes is most eccentric as is illustrated in the following sketches of +i+ paradigms.

a) yii- semelfactive[6]--This aspectual sub-system has +i+ in imperfective and iterative modes only; it always occurs with si- perfective; it does not require the usual negative imperative *t'áadoo yiitałí 'don't kick it'; most noticeably, it always takes an unvaried stem set (Hale, 1972a).

b) yii- attribute--This aspect occurs in the coloring verbs and 'see it' and 'curl it'; +i+ appears is all five modes; it always takes low tone ghi- perfective; it has regular stem variation.

c) nii- inchoative--This aspect takes ni+i+ in all modes except future which takes di+ni; it appears with a low tone ghi- perfective;

it has regular stem variation. (Inchoatives are discussed in YM 1943a:108-111.)

d) dii- abrupt motion[7]--This aspect has di+i+ in all modes except future which has di-; it usually takes low tone ghi- perfective.

e) yaa- 'tilt'--A few verbs contain a ya- disjunct prefix (that is postpositional in origin) and +i+ aspect. These verbs have +i+ in all five modes, low tone ghi- perfective, and regular stem variation.

In addition, +i+ aspect never occurs in the ni- imperfective/perfective and only rarely in the si- perfective. Note that the semelfactives drop +i+ in the perfective and switch to si- perfective.

Phonologically, the imperfectives for the first four of these +i+ aspects are very similar. Below I list paradigms for a semelfactive, (13) 'kick it once'; an attribute verb, (14) 'to redden it, dye it red'; an inchoative, (15) 'to heat it'; and an abrupt motion verb, (16) 'to have a cramp'.

(13) 1 yiishtał   (14) 1 yiishchíík
      2 yiitał   2 yiiłchíín
      3 yiyiitał   3 yiyiiłchíín
      4 jiitał   4 jiiłchíín
      1d yiitał   1d yiilchíín
      2d woohtał   2d woołchíín

(15) 1 niishdóóh   (16) 1 dah diishk'ąąh
      2 niiłdóóh   2 dah diik'ąąh
      3 yiniiłdóóh   3 dah diik'ąąh
      4 jiniiłdóóh   4 jidiik'ąąh dah
      1d niildóóh   1d diik'ąąh dah
      2d noołdóóh   2d doohk'ąąh dah

To keep the +i+ aspect prefix consistent throughout all the modes,
I will assume that /i/ lengthens in front of sh- or in zero environment.
In (17r) (r = readjustment rule) we write an i- lengthening rule. (The
yaa- 'tilt' verbs do not quite conform to this rule, however.)

(17r) +i+ → +ii+ / ___(sh)[

After 17r applies, the 1sg forms in (13) and (14) can be derived like
other vowel initial verbs, by gamma insertion and gliding.

	13.1 /i+sh+tał/	14.1 /i+sh+ł+chííh/
i length:	[ii+sh+tał]	[ii+sh+ł+chííh]
gh insert:	[ghii+sh+tał]	[ghii+sh+ł+chííh]
gliding:	[yii+sh+tał]	[yii+sh+ł+chííh]
ultimately:	[yiishtał]	[yiishchííh]

The 1sg and 3 forms in (15) and (16) and all of the fourth person
forms in the four paradigms also trigger 17r and are derived by vowel
deletion.

	13.4 /ji+i+tał/	15.3 /yi+ni+i+ł+dóóh/	16.1 /di+i+sh+k'ąąh/
i length:	[ji+ii+tał]	[yi+ni+ii+ł+dóóh]	[di+ii+sh+k'ąąh]
V dele:	[j+ii+tał]	[yi+n+ii+ł+dóóh]	[d+ii+sh+k'ąąh]
ultimately:	[jiitał]	[yiniiłdóóh]	[diishk'ąąh]

Unlike other conjunct 2sg forms, +i+ 2sg does not show the usual
high tone on the preceding vowel. I will claim here and in the analysis
of the optatives and the perfectives that rule II-11, ni- absorption, is
not triggered by a prefix of the shape V. In the +i+ verbs, the n- of
the ni- 2sg prefix is deleted by a phonological rule, n- deletion.
(One revision in n- deletion will be made to handle the optative 2sg.)

(18) n → ∅ / +i+___i+[

15.2 /ni+i+ni+ł+dóóh/

n dele:	[ni+i+i+ł+dóóh]
V dele:	[n+i+i+ł+dóóh]
ultimately:	[niiłdóóh]

Third person forms of (13) and (14) deviate from an anticipated *yiitał or *yiiłchiih from /yi+ii+.../. The extra yi- in these forms is inserted by a highly unusual phonological rule, yi- doubling, one of two reduplication rules in Navajo phonology. Yi- doubling applies only if yi- direct object is word initial and if ii- is the only prefix between yi- and [. Notice that 15.3 shows only a single yi- due to the intervening ni- prefix. Later, we will see that a version of yi- doubling also applies to similar environments in the ghi- perfective (see 3.511) and in the imperfective with the hi- seriative prefix (see 3.6).

(19) ∅ → yi / ##___yi+ii+[

14.3 /yi+i+ł+chííh/

i length:	[yi+ii+ł+chííh]
yi doubl:	[yi+yi+ii+ł+chííh]
ultimately:	[yiyiiłchííh]

The dual forms in these four paradigms do not trigger i- lengthening.

13.2d /i+oh+tał/   16.1d /di+i+iid+k'ąąh/

V dele:		[d+i+iid+k'ąąh]
V assim:	[σ+oh+tał]	
V degem:		[d+iid+k'ąąh]
ultimately:	[woohtał]	[diik'ąąh]

The argument that yaa- 'tilt' verbs be grouped with the other four +i+ aspects settles on the long, low tone vowels in 2sg, the ii- that

appears in third person transitive and fourth person forms, and the i-
that appears in future forms like yeideeshtał 'I'll dash off'. However,
there are a number of puzzling phonological questions about yaa- 'tilt'.
Below are listed paradigms for 'dash off' (20) and 'pour it' (21).

(20) 1 yaashtaał   (21) 1 yaassííd
      2 yaaltaał   2 yaazííd
      3 yaaltaał   3 yayiizííd
      4 yajiiltaał   4 yajiizííd
      1d yeiiltaał   1d yeiidzííd
      2d yaołtaał   2d yaohsííd

The chief problem is that in yaa- 'tilt' the i- in 1sg has undergone
vowel assimilation. The i- lengthening readjustment rule, as it is now
defined would apply to 20.1 and 21.1. Since rule II-57, vowel assimilation
is exempt from a#ii sequences by condition a, we assume that the 1sg of
yaa- 'tilt' contains a short i-. Thus we revise rule 17r to lengthen
i- in yaa- 'tilt' only in zero environment and where there is a preceding
conjunct prefix, admittedly an ad hoc device.

(17r) +i+ → +ii+ / $\left\{ \begin{array}{l} ya\#CV+\underline{}+[\\ \underline{}(sh)[\end{array} \right\}$

The 1sg and 2sg forms in (20) and (21) can now be derived.

                20.1/ya#i+sh+l+taał/   21.2/ya#i+ni+zííd/
n dele: _____   [ya#i+i+zííd]
V assim: [ya#a+sh+l+taał]   [ya#a+a+zííd]
V degem: _____   [ya#a+zííd]
ultimately: [yaashtaał]   [yaazííd]

Notice that in 21.3, a transitive, rule 19, yi- doubling, has not
applied. Thus yi- doubling is constrained to apply when no disjunct

prefix is present. (However, see 4.110.)

	20.3 /ya#i+l+taaɬ/	21.3 /ya#yi+i+zííd/
i length:	_____	[ya#yi+i+zííd]
V dele:	_____	[ya#y+ii+zííd]
V assim:	[ya#a+l+taaɬ]	_____
ultimately:	[yaaltaaɬ]	[yayiizííd]

The difficulty in analyzing the +i+ verbs is even further complicated by the puzzling yaa- 'tilt' vowel assimilations.

3.115 ∅ imperfective summary

Krauss' claim that Hoijer's ∅ and yi- imperfectives are in complementary distribution has been substantiated by the pepet vowel insertion rule. In conjunct verbs like nishteeh or yiishtaɬ there is always a vocalic conjunctive prefix, and, thus, no pepet vowel is inserted. In the primary verbs like yishcha and in disjunct verbs like naabé, the peg yi- and the lengthened vowel are both accounted for by the pepet vowel. The advantage over the yi- imperfective analysis is that verbs like nicha and nanibé, which show no trace of a yi- prefix, need not be treated as exceptions.

Following this phonological analysis, only two imperfective mode prefixes need be recognized, ∅ and ni-. As mentioned above, this allows for a simplified statement of the conjugation patterns.[8]

3.12 Ni- Imperfective

3.120 Introduction

Ni- imperfective takes /ni/ in the pos. 7 modal prefix slot and always occurs in conjugation pattern with the ni- perfective. Most ni-imperfectives/ni- perfectives are motion verbs with a terminative meaning, e.g. nish'eeł 'I arrive floating', nishteeh 'I arrive carrying an animate object'. The ni- modal prefix is similar in meaning to pos. 6 ni- 'terminative', niteeh 'he lies down', and to pos. 1 ni- 'end', ninisbąąs 'I park it'. Krauss has suggested that the ni- imperfective/ perfective modal prefix has developed in Athapaskan (i.e., it is not a proto-Athapaskan-Eyak feature) as an extension of the conjunctive pos. 6 ni- prefix, hence its spatial ('arrival at a point') rather than aspectival meaning (1969:81). In other words, ni- modal prefix is the result of a 'slippage' in position, a phenomenon Krauss regards as basic to the Na-Dene hypothesis.

In this section I discuss the mode variants in this order: primary, disjunct, and conjunct. I leave conjunct last because a sub-category, aspect, must be added to the conjunct mode variant to account for the separate course taken by aspect+ni paradigms. In concluding this section, I discuss some pos. 6 ni- 'terminative' ∅ imperfective paradigms to contrast the behavior of the two conjunct ni- prefixes (3.124), and I consider an interesting ni- imperfective neuter verb (3.125).

In analyzing the ni- imperfectives it proves necessary to employ three ad hoc readjustment rules. Affinities between these three rules will be discussed at the end of this section.

3.121 ##ni+(X)+[

The paradigms for (22) 'to arrive flying', an intransitive, and (23) 'to arrive flying it', a transitive, appear to have identical prefix complexes except for the ł- classifier.

(22) 1 nisht'ááh   (23) 1 nisht'ááh
      2 nít'ááh   2 níɫt'ááh
      3 yít'ááh   3 yíɫt'ááh
      4 jít'ááh   4 jíɫt'ááh
      1d niit'ááh   1d niilt'ááh
      2d noht'ááh   2d noɫt'ááh

The ni- mode prefix is actualized in 1sg, 2sg, and the four duals and no further explanation is necessary.

22.1/ni+sh+t'ááh/   23.1d/ni+iid+ɫ+t'ááh/

V dele: _____   [n+iid+ɫ+t'ááh]

ultimately: [nisht'ááh]   [niilt'ááh]

However, high tone and not ni- is present in the third and fourth persons. These high tones can be derived by ni- absorption, rule II-12. Until now the rule has applied only to 2sg prefixes. In the ni- imperfectives we find that the ni- modal prefix goes to a high tone on the vowel of the preceding prefix provided ni- is directly next to [.

22.4/ji+ni+t'ááh/   23.3/yi+ni+ɫ+t'ááh/

ni absorp: [jí+t'ááh]   [yí+ɫ+t'ááh]

ultimately: [jít'ááh]   [yíɫt'ááh]

The anomalous form is 22.3. We would expect *nit'ááh instead of yí- since this is an intransitive paradigm. Hoijer remarks that it is possible that the irregular third person yí- in ni- imperfective intransitives developed by analogy with the transitive yí- (SH:30). I will posit that a readjustment rule, operating before the phonological rules, inserts a yi- 'dummy object' into the surface structure of verbs like 22.3. Below is 24r, <u>dummy object insertion</u>.

(24r) ∅ → yi+/ ##___ni+[

Rule 24r sets up the environment for ni- absorption.

22.3 /ni+t'ááh/

dummy obj:	[yi+ni+t'ááh]
ni absorp:	[yí+t'ááh]
ultimately:	[yít'ááh]

3.122 #ni+(X)+[

Certain pos. 1 adverbial prefixes choose the ni- imperfective/ perfective conjugation pattern. These include ch'í- 'out', bigha- 'through', ni- 'end', and k'í- 'in two pieces'.

First we will examine two intransitives, (25) 'to arrive crawling' and (26) 'to crawl out'.

(25) 1 ninish'nééh   (26) 1 ch'ínísh'nééh
      2 niní'nééh   2 ch'íní'nééh
      3 nii'nééh   3 ch'é'nééh
      4 njí'nééh   4 ch'íjínééh
      1d ninii'nééh   1d ch'ínii'nééh
      2d ninoh'nééh   2d ch'ínóh'nééh

The derivation of the first and seocnd person singular and dual forms in (25) and (26) is essentially the same as in the primary paradigms.

25.2 /ni#ni+ni+d+nééh/   26.1 /ch'í#ni+sh+d+nééh/

ni absorp:	[ni#ní+d+neeh]	
tone assim:		[ch'í#ní+sh+d+nééh]
ultimately:	[niní'nééh]	[ch'ínísh'nééh]

25.1d /ni#ni+iid+d+nééh/   26.2d /ch'í#ni+oh+d+nééh/

V dele:	[ni#n+iid+d+nééh]	[ch'í#n+oh+d+nééh]
tone assim:		[ch'í#n+óh+d+nééh]
ultimately:	[ninii'nééh]	[ch'ínóh'nééh]

Also, the conjunctive prefix ji- absorbs the ni- modal prefix as it does in the primary ni- imperfective.

                26.4 /ch'í#ji+ni+d+nééh/

ni absorp: [ch'í#jí+d+nééh]

ultimately: [ch'íjí'nééh]

The third person forms require closer examination. Note that ni- has disappeared, but, since these are both intransitive verbs, there is no environment for ni- absorption. It is clear from 25.3 that rule 24r, dummy object insertion, does not insert a yi- to set up ni- absorption as is the case in the primaries. The long vowel in 25.3 and the é- in 26.3 are reminiscent of the disjunct ∅ imperfectives that have been affected by pepet vowel insertion. I will posit another readjustment rule that drops ni- when it is bordered by # and [. We list ni- drop as (27r).

   (27r) ni → ∅ / #___[

Ni- drop creates an environment for pepet vowel insertion, i.e. no vowel in #___[.

                25.3 /ni#ni+d+nééh/   26.3 /ch'í#ni+d+nééh/

ni drop: [ni#d+nééh]   [ch'í#d+nééh]

V insert: [ni#i+d+nééh]   [ch'í#i+d+nééh]

V absorp: _____   [ch'é+d+nééh]

ultimately: [nii'nééh]   [ch'é'nééh]

In 26.3 we see that rule II-62, vowel absorption, has converted í#i to é-.

'To break a slender stiff object in two' (28) illustrates a transitive ni- imperfective paradigm.

(28) 1 k'ínishtííh
2 k'ínitííh
3 k'íítííh
4 k'íjítííh
1d k'íniitííh
2d k'ínohtííh

All forms in (28) except 3 can be derived by the same rules that were used for (26). The third person form contains a yi- direct object pronoun which destroys the environment for ni- drop. Thus, yi- absorbs ni-. The y- of the direct object prefix is then deleted by rule II-42, y- deletion.

32.3 /k'í#yi+ni+tííh/

<u>ni absorp</u>: [k'í#yí+tííh]

<u>y dele</u>: [k'í#í+tííh]

<u>ultimately</u>: [k'íítííh]

Therefore, 27r, ni- drop, like 24r, dummy object insertion, applies only to intransitive ni- imperfectives.

3.123 +ni+(X)+[

We have already considered three conjunct ni- imperfectives (22.4, 23.3, and 23.4) where we noted that conjunctive prefixes yi- and ji- absorbed ni- if no prefix is present between ni- and [. Here we will consider more conjunct forms. First I place conjunct prefixes from pos. 4 and 5 next ni-, and second, I examine a different pattern, aspect+ni paradigms. Below is 'arrive carrying an animate object' with a variety of object prefixes (including hwi- 'area' used here as a human object).

(29) a. nishteeh 1
     b. hółteeh   hwi- 3

125

c. hojíłteeh   hwi-4

d. shiníłteeh   1-2

e. boníłteeh   hwi-2

f. ninishteeh   2-1

g. honishteeh   hwi-1

The verbs in (29) lend further support for the inclusion of ɬ in ni-absorption. In 29f and g ni- absorption does not apply to /ni+ni+sh+ɬ+teeh/ because sh- intervenes between ni- and ɬ. In 29b, c, d, and e ni-absorption is triggered next to ɬ.

The one other conjunctive prefix that can occur next to ni- imperfective, pos. 6 aspect, follows a different pattern. This anomalous aspect sub-category appears in other modes such as ni- and si- perfectives.

At least three aspect prefixes can combine with ni- imperfective, di- 'oral noise', as in (30) 'to smile, laugh', ni- 'terminative', as in (31) 'to drive it out', and hi- 'seriative' as in (32) 'to arrive hopping'.

(30) 1 ch'ídinishdlóóh   (31) 1 ch'íninishchééh   (32) 1 hinishchééh

2 ch'ídinídlóóh   2 ch'íniníłchééh   2 hiníchééh

3 ch'ídeeldlóóh   3 ch'íneełchééh   3 heechééh

4 ch'ízhdeeldlóóh   4 ch'ízhneełchééh   4 hijeechééh[9]

1d ch'ídiniildlóóh   1d ch'íniniilchééh   1d hiniichééh

2d ch'ídinołdlóóh   2d ch'íninołchééh   2d hinohchééh

The first and second singular and dual forms correspond to other conjunct ni- imperfectives and need no further explanation.

30.1d/ch'í#di+ni+iid+l+dlóóh/   32.2/hi+ni+ni+chééh/

ni absorp: _____   [hi+ní+chééh]

V dele: [ch'í#di+n+iid+l+dlóóh]   _____

ultimately: [ch'ídiniidlóóh]   [hiníchééh]

However, the third and fourth person forms force us to make a rather ad hoc statement. The ni- is deleted and ee- remains. This ee- vowel will haunt us in our analyses of progressives and the three perfectives, and it will be 'explained' by readjustment rules in each case. Here we will write a highly restricted readjustment rule, <u>ni- replacement</u>.

(33r) ni → ghe / ASP+___+[

Gh- is inserted in order to derive the long vowel, ee-. The gh- blocks vowel deletion which is necessary to preserve the vowel of the aspect prefix. The gh- is then deleted by rule II-41, gamma deletion. Other ee- vowels in this study are derived from a ghe- prefix that is introduced by readjustment rules.

	31.3/ch'í#ni+ni+ɫ+chééh/	32.3/hi+ni+chééh/
<u>ni replac</u>:	[ch'í#ni+ghe+ɫ+chééh]	[hi+ghe+chééh]
V <u>dele</u>:	_____	_____
<u>gh dele</u>:	[ch'í#ni+e+ɫ+chééh]	[hi+e+chééh]
V <u>assim</u>:	[ch'í#ne+e+ɫ+chééh]	[he+e+chééh]
<u>ultimately</u>:	[ch'íneeɫchééh]	[heechééh]

Agentive passives in the ni- imperfective take a compound prefix in pos. 4, /bi+'i+di/, where 'i- is probably a metathesized 3i prefix from pos. 5. If the di- is adjacent to ni- modal prefix, we would expect it to behave like other non-aspect conjunct prefixes as in (29). However, the pos. 4 agentive di- causes ni- replacement.

(34) a. bi'deet'éésh 'they are being led'
    b. bi'deedlóós 'he is being led'
    c. bi'deelt'ááh 'it is being flown'

Evidently, the ni- replacement rule contains the di- 'agentive' morpheme.

(27r)
$$ni \rightarrow ghe \; / \; \begin{Bmatrix} di \\ [agent] \\ ASP \end{Bmatrix} + \underline{\quad} + [$$

34a/bi+'i+di+ni+d+'éésh/

ni replac: [bi+'i+di+ghe+d+'éésh]

gh dele: [bi+'i+di+e+d+'éésh]

V assim: [bi+'i+de+e+d+'éésh]

ultimately: [bi'deet'éésh]

3.124 ∅ imperfective: ni- aspect

In comparing the ni- imperfective with ∅ imperfectives with pos. 6 ni- aspect prefixes, we find that there are some interesting differences in the two paradigms. Certain constraints must be placed on some of the rules we have been using for the ni- imperfective to account for these differences. In (35) I present 'to lie down' and in (36) 'to drive it off of oneself'.

(35) 1 nishteeh   (36) 1 'ak'inishchééh
      2 níteeh   2 'ak'inílchééh
      3 niteeh   3 'ak'iinilchééh
      4 jiniteeh   4 'ak'izhnilchééh
      1d niiteesh   1d 'ak'iniilchééh
      2d nohteesh   2d 'ak'inołchééh
      3p danijah[10]

Note that in 35.2 and 36.2 ni- 2sg is absorbed by ni- 'terminative' but ji- in 35.4 and 36.4 and yi- in 36.3 do not absorb ni- even though it is next to [. Thus we must block the ni- absorption rule from the morphological category, [+ASPECT].

(II-12) CV+ ni [→CV̂
        [-ASP]

Note further that 35.3 and 35.3p should trigger rules 24r, dummy object insertion, and 27r, ni- drop.

This can be avoided by adding the value [MODE] to the readjustment rules: (24r) ∅ → yi /##___ ni [, (27r) ni → ∅ /#___[.
                                                    [MODE]   [MODE]

With these revisions, all forms in (35) and (36) can be derived.

                  35.3/ni+teeh/   35.4/ji+ni+teeh/

dummy obj: _____   _____

ni absorp: _____   _____

ultimately: [niteeh]   [jiniteeh]

Thus, the essential differences in ni- aspect ∅ imperfective and the ni- imperfective are reflected in the morphological restrictions on ni- absorption and the readjustment rules, 24r, 27r, and 33r. These constraints on the ni- imperfective readjustment rules (which are the same readjustments that apply to the ni- perfective) underscore the secondary origin of ni- as a modal prefix. Krauss (personal communication) remarks that ni- is not really a mode prefix but is the ni- aspect prefix "that has gotten partly out of hand."

3.125 Ni- imperfective neuter: ɬi- 'inherent quality'

As an aside, we briefly look at a neuter verb paradigm with the prefix ɬi- 'inherent quality' which appears in adjectival themes as in ɬikan 'it's tasty', ɬikon 'it's flammable', ɬichíí' 'it's red'. When these verbs are conjugated for person, a ni- prefix appears, suggesting that these neuters are based on the ni- imperfective. Note the unusual alternation of the ɬi- prefix when it follows a prefix and is next to STEM in the fourth person and third person plural of 'to be red'.

(37) 1 łinishchíí'

2 łiníchíí'

3 łichíí'

4 jilchíí'

1d łiniichíí'

1p dałiniichíí'

3p daalchíí'

The ni- mode prefix is gone in 3, 4, and 3p. Perhaps a readjustment rule similar to 31r deletes ni-. Since łi- is a conjunctive prefix, we might revise 27r as follows:

(27r) ni → ∅ / {łi+ / #} ___ [.

Then to account for the classifier-like l- in 4 and 3p, we might write a łi to l rule.

(38) łi → l / (#) ___ STEM

42.3/łi+ni+chíí'/   42.4/ji+łi+ni+chíí'/   42.3p/da#łi+ni+chíí'/

ni drop:	[łi+chíí']	[ji+łi+chíí']	[da#łi+chíí']
łi to l:	_____	[ji+l+chíí']	[da#l+chíí']
V insert:	_____	_____	[da#i+l+chíí']
V assim:	_____	_____	[da#a+l+chíí']
ultimately:	[łichíí']	[jilchíí']	[daalchíí']

As mentioned previously, neuter verb phonology is quite tenuous. In (37) ni- modal prefix is not absorbed by łi- as normally is the case when ni- is preceded by a conjunctive prefix in the active ni- imperfectives. Perhaps, as Hale has suggested, there is some neuter prefix in neuter verbs (1972b). A readjustment rule like 27r may be wholly incorrect once more is known about neuter verb phonology and the łi- prefix. But what is most significant is the łi:l alternation. Krauss has suggested that ɬi- 'inherent quality' is a vestige of the proto-Athapaskan *lθ- classifier, the reflex of which is generally l- classifier in present day Athapaskan (1969:57-58).

3.126 Ni- imperfective summary

With a revised version of the ni- absorption rule I have been able to give a fairly straight-forward account of the ni- imperfectives. I have been compelled to make three non-phonological readjustment rules, 24r, 27r, and 33r to account for the third person intransitives of primary and disjunct verbs and the third and fourth person aspect verbs. Interestingly, all three of these readjustment rules apply when ni- modal prefix is next to [. We will see in 3.52 in the analysis of the ni- perfective that these same three readjustment rules have a wider role in the phonology.

3.2 Iterative Mode

3.20 Introduction

The iterative mode expresses repetitive action. It is formed with a ná- prefix in pos. 2 and, variably, a d- classifier, i.e., ∅ classifier becomes d- and ɬ- becomes l.[11] It is obvious that the iterative is derived from the ∅ imperfective. Like the ∅ imperfective, the iterative has no prefix in the modal prefix slot. Furthermore, I will show that the phonology of the iterative is practically identical to that of ∅ imperfectives with high tone disjunctive prefixes such as bí- 'against' or ná- 'encircle'. The ni- imperfective mode prefix is incompatible with ná- iterative, cf. nibínishhííɬ Il and nibínáshgiɬ Rl, 'push it to a point'.

Of course, because of the ná- in pos. 2, there is no primary mode variant for the iterative. I first take up the simplest iterative, the disjunct, including several paradigms in which ná- is preceded by pos. 1 prefixes. Then I will look at conjunct iteratives, including those with +i+ aspect.

3.21 ná#(X)+[

The majority of disjunct iteratives are derived by the same rules that were used for (11) 'sew it', a ∅ imperfective with ná- 'encircle', unless, of course, d- classifier is present and triggers ł- voicing, d- effect, or d- deletion. Below are iteratives for 'tan it' (39), which, according to Young and Morgan, takes no shift in classifier, and 'rip it' (40), which takes a d- classifier (cf. tsiih nighas I2, where the underlying stem initial consonant is shown to be gh-).

(39) 1 nássééh   (40) 1 tsiih násgas
     2 nánísééh   2 tsiih nánígas
     3 nésééh   3 tsiih nśígas
     4 ńjísééh   4 tsiih ńjígas
     1d néiilzééh   1d tsiih néiigas
     2d naóhsééh ~ náhsééh   2d tsiih naóhgas ~ náhgas

Just as in the high tone disjunct ∅ imperfectives, I assume that rule II-46, pepet vowel insertion, has applied and that the inserted vowel has undergone vowel assimilation and has been absorbed by the preceding high tone vowel by rule 60, vowel absorption. This is the case in 39.1 and 40.1.

	39.1/ná#sh+ł+zééh/	40.1/ná#sh+d+ghas/
V insert:	[ná#ish+ł+zééh]	[ná#ish+d+ghas]
V assim:	[ná#ash+ł+zééh]	[ná#ach|d|ghas]
V absorp:	[ná#sh+ł+zééh]	[ná#sh+d+ghas]
d effect:	_____	[ná#sh+gas]
ultimately:	[nássééh]	[násgas]

Vowel absorption also applies to the 2d forms. Of course, vowel assimilation applies optionally to á#o.

        39.2d /ná#oh+ɨ+zééh/

V assim: ([ná#ah+ɨ+zééh])

V absorp: [ná#h+ɨ+zééh] ~ [nao#h+ɨ+zééh]

ultimately: [náhsééh] ~ [naohsééh]

Tone assimilation applies over an intervening consonant in 39.2, 3, and 4 and 40.2, 3, and 4.

        39.3 /ná#yi+ɨ+zééh/   40.4 /ná#ji+d+ghas/

tone assim: [ná#yí+ɨ+zééh]   [ná#jí+d+ghas]

y dele: [ná#í+ɨ+zééh]   _____

V front: [né#í+ɨ+zééh]   _____

ultimately: [néísééh]   [ńjígas]

The ld forms are obtained by vowel fronting and the usual rules that are keyed to d-.

Often when ná- is preceded by an adverbial prefix in pos. 1, no rules beyond those used for (39) and (40) are required. In 'fall down' with hada- 'down' in pos. 1 and in 'push it about' with na- 'about' and bí- 'against' in pos. 1, the underlined prefixes are identical to those in the two previous paradigms with the exception of 41.3, an intransitive that simply lacks the yi- direct object prefix.

(41) 1 hada<u>ná</u>shgoh   (42) 1 nabí<u>ná</u>shgiɨ

      2 hada<u>nání</u>goh   2 nabí<u>nání</u>giɨ

      3 hada<u>ná</u>goh   3 nayí<u>néí</u>giɨ

      4 hada<u>ńjí</u>goh   4 nabí<u>ńjí</u>giɨ

     ld hada<u>néii</u>goh   ld nabí<u>néii</u>giɨ

     2d hada<u>náh</u>goh   2d nabí<u>náh</u>giɨ

One distinctive type of disjunct iterative paradigm occurs when an adverbial prefix of the shape n$\binom{\acute{}}{a}$, such as na- 'about', na- 'down' or ná- 'back' appears in pos. 1. Observe the alternation in the vowel of the adverbial prefix in iterative paradigms for 'sew it' (43) with ná- 'encircle' and 'drop them' (44) with na- 'down'.

(43)   1 nínáshka'   (44) 1 ninásh'niɬ
       2 nínáníɬka'   2 ninání'niɬ
       3 nínéíɬka'   3 ninéí'niɬ
       4 nínájíɬka'   4 ninájí'niɬ
       1d nínéiilka'   1d ninéii'niɬ
       2d nínáɬka'   2d ninóh'niɬ

A <u>na- dissimilation</u> rule is needed to account for the alternation of na- to ni- in these verbs.

(45) na + na → ni + na

Notice that this dissimilation rule is contrary to the vowel assimilation and VCV assimilation rules, in which back vowels dominate over front vowels. One other rule that converts na- to ni- will be formulated in the discussion of the si- perfective (3.53).[12]

Other than na- dissimilation these verbs are derived like other disjunct iteratives.

                  43.2/ná+ná#ni+ɬ+ka'/   44.4/na+ná#ji+d+niɬ/
tone assim: [ná+ná#ní+ɬ+ka']   [na+ná#jí+d+niɬ]
na dissim: [ní+ná#ní+ɬ+ka']   [ni+ná#jí+d+niɬ]
ultimately: [nínáníɬka']   [ninájí'niɬ]

3.22 ná#CV+(X)+[

The conjunct iteratives require little explanation. Below are paradigms for 'say it' (46) and 'herd them back' (47).

(46) 1 ńdísh'niih   (47) 1 nínáníshka'
     2 ńdí'niih   2 nínáníɬka'
     4 názhdí'niih   3 nínéiniɬka'
     1d ńdii'niih   4 nínázhníɬka'
     2d ńdóh'niih   1d nínániilka'
                              2d nínánóɬka'

Tone assimilation applies when just one CV follows ná- (after vowel deletion), as in 47.2d.

47.3/ná+ná#yi+ni+ɬ+ka'/   47.2d/ná+ná#ni+oh+ɬ+ka'/

V dele: [ná+ná#n+oh+ɬ+ka']
tone assim: [ná+ná#n+óh+ɬ+ka']
na dissim: [ní+ná#yi+ni+ɬ+ka']   [ní+ná#n+óh+ɬ+ka']
ultimately: [nínéiniɬka']   [nínánóɬka']

The +i+ aspect verbs that were discussed in 3.114 also take +i+ in the iterative. Below we present iteratives for 'kick it' (48), 'redden it' (49), 'heat it' (50), and 'dash off' (51), a ya- 'tilt' verb.

(48) 1 néishtaɬ   (49) 1 néishchih
     2 néiitaɬ   2 néiɬchih
     3 náyiitaɬ   3 náyiiɬchih
     4 ńjiitaɬ   4 ńjiiɬchih
     1d néiitaɬ   1d néiilchih
     2d náoohtaɬ   2d náooɬchih

(50) 1 ńániishdoh   (51) 1 yanáashtaɬ
     2 ńániiɬdoh   2 yanáaltaɬ
     3 ńániiɬdoh   3 yanáaltaɬ
     4 názhniiɬdoh   4 yańjiiltaɬ
     1d ńániildoh   1d yanéiiltaɬ
     2d ńánooɬdoh   2d yanáaltaɬ

(50) needs no explanation since it patterns just like its imperfective, (15).

An important question is to determine why vowel fronting applies to (48) and (49) while (51) undergoes vowel assimilation. For now I claim that the rather suspect i- lengthening rule, (17r), that applies to most +i+ verbs in ___(sh)[but to ya- 'tilt' in just +___[, operates on (48) and (49) and the long ii- blocks vowel assimilation, while the short i- in (51) is subject to vowel assimilation. Note, however, that this still leaves the differences in the 2sg vowel in (48), (49) and (51) unaccounted for.[13]

	48.1/ná#i+sh+tał/	51.1/ya+ná#i+sh+l+tał/
i length:	[ná#ii+sh+tał]	_____
V assim:	_____	[ya+ná#a+sh+l+tał]
V front:	[né#ii+sh+tał]	_____
ultimately:	[néiishtał]	[yanáashtał]

But notice that this derivation is not quite correct for 48.1. We have derived néiishtał, but the correct form should be néishtał. The 2sg forms, 48.2 and 49.2 are also inconsistent in vowel length. In examining other +i+ iteratives in Young and Morgan we find 1sg forms are néi- but the 2sg forms vary between néii- and néi-, one of the few phonetic inconsistencies in the dictionary. There is a general tendency to hear long vowels before voiceless fricatives as shortened to perhaps 1½ moras (Robert Young, personal communication). This being the case, it is possible that 53.1, 54.1 and 54.2 are affected by a late phonetic vowel degemination rule that operates before a $\begin{bmatrix}+cnt\\-voi\end{bmatrix}$ segment. This is mere speculation at this point. Once again the +i+ verbs resist a principled explanation.

Note that 48.3 and 49.3 do not show the doubled yi- that appears in
the imperfective of these verbs, cf. 13.3 yiyiitał. As we pointed out
for 24.3 yayiizííd, a CV prior to #yi+ii+[destroys the environment for
the reduplication.

One other iterative process deserves mention. Occasionally, when
an iterative is preceded by a pos. 1 adverbial prefix, Young and Morgan
show an iterative prefix that has undergone the n- deletion mentioned
briefly in 2.732. In 'bring it to a boil' (52) compare the imperfective
and perfective forms with the iteratives in 52c-f where the ha+ná
sequence becomes háá-.

(52) a. hanishháásh   Il
     b. hanííłhaazh   Pl
     c. háánishhosh   Rl
     d. háánííłhosh   R2
     e. háázhnííłhosh   R4
     f. háánółhosh   R2d

These iteratives seem to vary freely with hanánishhosh for 52c, etc.
As stated earlier, the conditions on this n- deletion rule are uncertain.
It is usually restricted to pos. 1 ná- prefixes that are preceded by
other disjunct prefixes.

3.23 Iterative Summary

The structural closeness of the iteratives to the imperfectives is
reflected in the duplication of phonological rules for disjunct ∅
imperfectives with high tone prefixes and the iterative. Only the
erratic classifier shifts and the iterative stem variants prevent us
from subsuming the iterative within the imperfective mode as has been
done with the future within the progressive mode.

3.3 Optative Mode

3.30 Introduction

The optative mode expresses desire of potential. Some of the syntactic and semantic properties of the optative have been surveyed by Landar (1962). Optatives generally combine with laanaa or lágo to express positive and negative desire, respectively; e.g. wóshdlį́į́' 'you wish not to drink it, you better not drink it'. Some speakers substitute a future construction for some optatives, diyeeshhééł laanaa instead of sósxééł laanaa 'I wish to kill it'.

To date there has been no straightforward phonological explanation of the tone alternations in the optative mode. Hoijer notes, "The optative paradigm is marked by a prefix having the form gho- in Navaho . . . The tone of the prefix behaves irregularly. No general rule can be given" (1946a:12). Lists of the optative alternations are provided in his 1967 study (SH:40-42). Reichard attempts to explain the low tone optatives by a ghost prefix to the right of the optative prefix. Stanley posits a highly improbable lexical representation, /honhi/, to preserve his a priori assumption that all Navajo prefixes are low in tone in underlying representation.

In this section I will show that the all Navajo optative paradigms can be derived from an underlying /ó/ prefix and two tone lowering rules that are keyed to preceding prefixes. We first take up the primary optatives, then the conjuncts and the disjuncts.

3.31 ##ó+(X)+[

In (53) 'paint it', (54) 'roll it', (55) 'freeze up', and (56) 'eat meat', I give paradigms for primary optatives.

(53) 1 wóshdleesh   (54) 1 wósmáás
     2 wóódleesh   2 wóołmáás
     3 yódleesh   3 yółmáás
     4 jódleesh   4 jółmáás
     1d woodleesh   1d woolmáás
     2d woodleesh   2d woołmáás

(55) 1 wóshtin   (56) 1 wóshghał
     2 wóótin   2 wóólghał
     3 wótin   3 yólghał
     4 jótin   4 jólghał
     1d wootin   1d woolghał
     2d woohtin   2d woołghał

Reichard has suggested that the progressive mode prefix occurs in combination with the optative, ghi+ó, in paradigms such as these (1951:196). On the other hand, I assume that the optative prefix is /ó/ and that if it is word initial as all of the 1sg, 2sg, 1d and 2d forms and 60.3 (an intransitive), then rule 6, gamma insertion, and rule 7, gliding, apply.

                   53.1/ó+sh+dleesh/   55.3/ó+d+tin/

gh insert: [ghó+sh+dleesh]   [ghó+d+tin]

gliding: [wó+sh+dleesh]   [wó+d+tin]

ultimately: [wóshdleesh]   [wótin]

All of the 2sg forms show óó-. Ni- absorption applies only when ni- is preceded by CV+ and therefore will not be triggered by the optative prefix. In the +i+ ∅ imperfectives we found that +i+ triggered an n- deletion rule. Rule 18, n- deletion, can be revised to include ó-.

(18) n → ∅ / {ó̜/i}+___+[

N- deletion is ordered after tone assimilation. After n- deletes, vowel assimilation converts í- to ó-.

56.2 /ó+ni+l+ghaɫ/

tone assim:	[ó+ní+l+ghaɫ]
n dele:	[ó+í+l+ghaɫ]
V assim:	[ó+ó+l+ghaɫ]
gh insert:	[ghó+ó+l+ghaɫ]
gliding:	[wó+ó+l+ghaɫ]
ultimately:	[wóólghaɫ]

Gamma insertion and gliding will not apply to the third and fourth person forms where ó- is preceded by a conjunctive prefix. Instead, vowel deletion applies, leaving ó- high in tone.

54.3 /yi+ó+ɫ+máás/   56.4 /ji+ó+l+ghaɫ/

| V dele: | [y+ó+ɫ+máás] | [j+ó+l+ghaɫ] |
| ultimately: | [yóɫmáás] | [jólghaɫ] |

The dual forms in (53)-(56) show no high tone vowel as is expected by rule II-48, tone lowering, which lowers a high tone vowel when it is followed by a low tone vowel of a conjunct prefix. Vowel assimilation also applies to the 1d forms.

53.1d /ó+iid+dleesh/   55.2d /ó+oh+d+tin/

tone lower:	[o+iid+dleesh]	[o+oh+d+tin]
gh insert:	[gho+iid+dleesh]	[gho+oh+d+tin]
V assim:	[gho+ood+dleesh]	_____
gliding:	[wo+ood+dleesh]	[wo+oh+d+tin]
ultimately:	[woodleesh]	[woohtin]

Also note that just as ni- absorption is not triggered by a V- prefix, vowel deletion does not apply to ó+V in the duals.

3.32 +ó+(X)+[

In (57)-(59) I give paradigms for 'vomit', 'make a mistake', and 'shout'.

(57) 1 dóshkóóh   (58) 1 'ósiih   (59) 1 hadóshgháásh
     2 dóókóóh   2 'óósiih   2 hadóólgháásh
     3 dókóóh   3 'ósiih   3 hadólgháásh
     4 jidókóóh   4 'ajósiih   4 hazhdólgháásh
     1d dookóóh   1d 'oolziih   1d hadoolgháásh
     2d doohkóóh   2d 'oohsiih   2d hadoołgháásh

These conjunct paradigms have the same tone pattern as the primaries. The conjunct prefixes lose their vowels when next to ó-. Otherwise, all of these verbs can be obtained like the primary optatives (excluding gamma insertion and gliding, of course).

                57.3/di+ó+dóóh/   59.2/ha#di+ó+ni+l+gháásh/

V dele: [d+ó+kóóh]   [ha#d+ó+ni+l+gháásh]

tone assim: _____   [ha#d+ó+ní+l+gháásh]

n dele: _____   [ha#d+ó+í+l+gháásh]

V assim: _____   [ha#d+ó+ó+l+gháásh]

ultimately: [dókóóh]   [hadóólgháásh]

The +i+ aspect optatives are distinguished from the other conjuncts by their low tone modal prefixes. In (60) 'lean them side by side' (cf. kíniishoozh I2), (61) 'yellow it', and (62) 'spill', there are no high tone conjunct prefixes except in 2sg.

(60) 1 kínooshóósh   (61) 1 woostsxóóh   (62) 1 yaooshkááł
     2 kínoóshóósh   2 woółtsxóóh   2 yaóókááł
     3 kíinooshóósh   3 yoołtsxóóh   3 yayookááł
     4 kízhnooshóósh   4 joołtsxóóh   4 yajookááł

1d kínoolzhóózh	1d wooltsxóóh	1d yaookáá̶ł
2d kínoohshóósh	2d woo̶ltsxóóh	2d yaoohkáá̶ł

Just as for +i+ imperfectives and iteratives, I assume that there is an underlying +i+ in these verbs. The i- lengthening readjustment rule does not apply.[14]

The +i+ prefix has lowered the tone of the optative prefix in all of these verbs except 62.2 (which defies analysis at this point) and the duals, which lower tone via rule II-48, a separate tone lowering rule. We will see that in the +i+ ghi- perfectives +i+ also lowers tone. Since the tone of the optative prefix remains high until after vowel assimilation, +i+ will have assimilated to +o+ at the time this new tone lowering rule applies. Therefore, we write +V+ tone lowering, +i+ being the only low tone conjunct prefix of the shape +V+.

(63) $\acute{V} \rightarrow V\ /\ +V+\underline{}$

This rule is distinct from the other two tone lowering rules, II-48, tone lowering (the most general of the tone lowering rules), and II-51, optative tone lowering.

	60.1/kí#ni+i+ó+sh+ł+zhóósh/	61.4/ji+i+ó+ł+tsxóóh/
V dele:	[kí#n+i+ó+sh+ł+zhóósh]	[j+i+ó+ł+tsxóóh]
V assim:	[kí#n+o+ó+sh+ł+zhóósh]	[j+o+ó+ł+tsxóóh]
+V+ tone low:	[kí#n+o+o+sh+ł+zhóósh]	[j+o+o+ł+tsxóóh]
ultimately:	[kínooshóóh]	[joo̶ltsxóóh]

Here +i+ has assimilated to o- and has lowered the tone of the optative prefix.

The 2sg forms of the +i+ optatives differ from the usual optative 2sg, óó-. The derivation proceeds as in other 2sg optatives except for +V+ tone lowering, which operates just on the first of the óó- vowels leaving the rightmost unchanged.

61.2 /i+ó+ni+ɫ+tsxóóh/

tone assim:	[i+ó+ní+ɫ+tsxóóh]
n dele:	[i+ó+í+ɫ+tsxóóh]
V assim:	[o+ó+ó+ɫ+tsxóóh]
+V+ tone low:	[o+o+ó+ɫ+tsxóóh]
ultimately:	[woóɫtsxóóh]

Vowel degemination also applies, reducing the three vowel sequence.

As usual, the +i+ verbs leave a question unanswered: why does the ya- 'tilt' verb not follow the +V+ tone lowering rule? In this respect ya- 'tilt' patterns with the disjunct optatives which have óó- in 2sg.

This analysis of the +i+ optatives allows us to reconsider a statement by Krauss on the optatives of 'sg S goes' with ɫ- classifier. Krauss claims that in cases where the irregular stem initial consonant s-, a vestige of the PA y- component, appears in the vowel initial stem of 'sg S goes', the tone of the optative prefix is lowered (1969:70). The only verb with which to illustrate this is 'cure him', nínáábidoossa' Ol, nínéidoosa' O3. However, from looking at other paradigmatic forms of 'cure him', such as nínáábidiishlááh Il, nínáábidiisá Pl, we see that it is a +i+ verb and that the low tone optative prefix is the anticipated form. Thus, there can be no case made here that the low tone optative is a reflex of the y- component.

3.33 #ó+(X)+C

The disjunct optatives received brief mention in the discussion of vowel assimilation. I formulated an optative tone lowering rule, rule II-51, that lowers the tone of the optative prefix when it follows a disjunct prefix. Below are (64) 'make him fall down', (65) 'think about it', (66) 'crawl out', and (67) 'repair it'.

(64) 1 hadaoshgoh[15]
2 hadaóółgoh
3 hadayółgoh
4 hadajółgoh
1d hadaoolgoh
2d hadaoołgoh

(65) 1 ntsóoskees
2 ntsóókees
3 ntsóokees
4 ntsíjókees
1d ntsóokees
2d ntsóohkees

(66) 1 haosh'nééh
2 haóó'nééh
3 hao'nééh
4 hajó'nééh
1d haoo'nééh
2d haooh'nééh

(67) 1 'ánáoshdle'
2 'ánáóódle'
3 'ánáyódle'
4 'ánájódle'
1d 'ánáoolne'
2d 'ánáoohdle'

Wherever ó- is next to the disjunct prefix, it has become o-, as in 64.1, 65.1 and 3, 66.1 and 3, and 67.1. However, the 2sg forms resist optative tone lowering because of the long óó-. The other high tone optatives in these paradigms are next to conjunct prefixes yi- or ji-. I repeat the optative tone lowering rule with the condition that it is not applicable to 2sg forms.

(II-51) ó → o / X#___

condition: ≠ óó

Now all of the forms in (64)-(67) can be derived.

                64.1/ha+da#ó+sh+ł+goh/   67.1/'í+ná#ó+sh+d+le'/

opt tone low: [ha+da#o+sh+ł+goh]   ['í+ná#o+sh+d+le']

ultimately: [hadaoshgoh]   ['ánáoshdle']

Note that rule II-62, vowel absorption, does not apply to 67.1 because ó- is high in tone at the time of its application.

	65.2 /ntsí#ó+ni+kęes/	66.2 /ha#ó+ni+d+nééh/
tone assim:	[ntsí#ó+ní+kees]	[ha#ó+ní+d+nééh]
n dele:	[ntsí#ó+í+kees]	[ha#ó+í+d+nééh]
V assim:	[ntsó#ó+ó+kees]	[ha#ó+ó+d+nééh]
opt tone low:	_____	_____
V degem:	[ntsó#ó+kees]	
ultimately:	[ntsóókees]	[haóó'nééh]

Here optative tone lowering has been blocked by the óó- sequence.

	64.1d /ha+da#ó+iid+i+goh/	67.2d /'í+ná#ó+oh+d+le'/
tone lower:	[ha+da#o+iid+i+goh]	['í+ná#o+oh+d+le']
V assim:	[ha+da#o+ood+i+goh]	
ultimately:	[hadaoolgoh]	['anáoohdle']

In the duals, the general tone lowering rule, II-48, applies prior to vowel assimilation, and thus rule 63 need not apply.

Thus, what is unique to the disjunct optatives is expressed by the optative tone lowering rule.

3.34 Optative Summary

Assuming an underlying /ó/, we have found low tone optatives in two environments, in the +i+ aspect and disjunct paradigms. The question arises, can these two tone lowering rules, II-51 and 63, be collapsed? It seems best to keep them separate. +I+ lowers the tone of the optative prefix in 2sg, whereas a disjunct prefix does not. Furthermore, collapsing +i+ with the disjuncts for tone lowering would deprive us of a generalization: +i+, but not disjunct prefixes, also lowers the tone of the perfective prefix (see 3.514). Thus +i+ is a stronger and broader environment for tone lowering than is the disjunct prefix.

This solution for the optative is considerably more straight-forward than the solutions offered by Stanley and Reichard. Once again, the importance of the # disjunct boundary in Navajo prefix phonology is underscored.

3.4 Progressive Mode

3.40 Introduction

The progressive mode denotes an act performed while going along or an act that is progressively taking place. It is formed with a ghi- prefix in pos. 7. Formally, the future mode can be treated as a conjunct progressive with di- 'inceptive' in pos. 6 plus the progressive modal prefix and stem.

A number of properties of the progressive resist definitive formulation at this time. The progressive is second to the perfective in phonological complexity. There are very interesting semantic problems concerning the distribution of the adverbial prefixes in the progressive. Also, unlike the imperfective, iterative, and optative modes, the addition of da- plural to a progressive is a very complex process which we refer to as "progressive da- shift."

The following topics are discussed in this section: the distribution of adverbial prefixes in the progressive (3.41); the phonology of the three progressive mode variants (3.42); and the progressive da- shift (3.43).

3.41 Distribution of Adverbial Prefixes

The progressive is an important area for research on Navajo word formation. Practically all Navajo verb bases can be conjugated in the future, which is derived from the progressive, but, due to semantic constraints, relatively few verbs take a progressive. Often it is not clear as to the derivational relationship between the progressive paradigm and the active verb base. In Young and Morgan we find unexplained differences in the progressive entries. For example, one primary progressive, náás yisht'ih 'I continue it', is treated as a mode of the base náás ...-t'ih 'to continue it'; but another, yisht'ah 'I am flying it along', is treated as a base separate from -łt'ah 'to fly it'.

While other verb modes, including the future, can take a full range of adverbial prefixes, relatively few can occur in a progressive construction. Of the pos. 1 adverbial prefixes only the more unproductive thematic and postpositional prefixes, ná- 'back', 'í- 'thus', bí- 'against', 'ákwí- 'that way', náá- semeliterative, ká- 'after', and yá- 'speak', can occur next to the ghi- progressive prefix.

A semantic constraint, perhaps keyed to the feature "momentaneous", blocks the appearance of the more productive adverbial prefixes in the progressive. Verbs with pos. 1 ni- 'end' never have a progressive paradigm because of the antithetical semantic properties of the two prefixes. Verb bases with adverbial prefixes in with pos. 1, 'i- 'away', ha- 'up', and na- 'about', may have a progressive paradigm, but the adverbial prefix is no longer present: a) 'i- 'away', 'iishdloh I1, but yishdloh Pg1 'laugh', 'i'ínííł I2, but 'íínił Pg2 'burrow'; b) ha- 'up', tsi'hahodeeshłááł F1, but tsi'hweeshłááł Pg1 'disturb the peace'[16]; c) na- 'about', naalnish I3, but yilnish Pg3 'work', nabéshhil I1 but bééshhił Pg1 'push it'. This semantic constraint is relaxed for na- 'about' if a ná- 'back' prefix occurs in pos. 1. For example, na- can occur in a progressive in naanááshwoł 'I am running back and forth', naanáásbąs 'I am driving back and forth', and naanááshtłish 'I am rushing about in a frenzy'.

These semantic constraints are intriguing but have received little attention to date. Hale noted in his MA thesis, "No class II [adverbial prefix] may occur in a sequence II+Prog+STEM(Prog) without an [intervening] X element. The most common X element for this sequence is di- ['inceptive' in future forms], but certain class II prefixes may occur in the above sequence with other X elements: na- ['about'] may occur in the above sequence with either di- or ná- ['again']" (1956:51).

Perhaps future work in Navajo word formation can isolate the semantic constraints on prefix cooccurrence that would justify the derivation of a progressive such as yishnish 'I am working along' from a deep verb base, na...lnish. Or, in progressives where na- 'about' appears with ná- 'back' perhaps it can be demonstrated that the na- prefix has entered the verb relatively late, overriding the semantic constraint that would eliminate na- 'about' if it were adjacent to the ghi- prefix. These are just suggestions. The deep derivational properties of the progressive are a topic in Navajo grammar that could benefit from the attention of Navajo speaking linguists.

3.42 Progressive Phonology

3.421 ##ghi+(X)+[

The underlying form of the progressive mode, /ghi/, instead of /yi/, as it is sometimes referred to (e.g. YM, 1943a:95), is motivated by the general behavior of gh- in deriving y-w alternations and by the long vowels that occur in the progressive, the ghi- perfective and elsewhere. Also, comparative evidence points to the progressive (and the ghi- perfective) in Navajo being a reflex of PA *ghə- (Hoijer, 1971:141).

Below are primary paradigms for an intransitive, 'trot' (68), and a transitive 'carry it along' (69).

(68) 1 yishtł'éél   (69) 1 yish'ááł
      2 yíltł'éél   2 yí'ááł
      3 yiltł'éél   3 yoo'ááł
      4 jooltł'éél   4 joo'ááł
      1d yiiltł'éél   1d yiit'ááł
      2d wołtł'éél   2d woh'ááł

The first person forms only require gliding to convert gh- to y-. The second person forms also require ni- absorption.

                68.2/ghi+ni+l+tł'éél/   69.1/ghi+sh+'ááł/

ni absorp: [ghí+l+tł'éél]
gliding: [yí+l+tł'éél]   [yi+sh+'ááł]
ultimately: [yíltł'éél]   [yish'ááł]

The vowel initial dual pronouns trigger the deletion of the vowel of the modal prefix.

                68.1d/ghi+iid+l+tł'éél/   69.2d/ghi+oh+'ááł/

V dele: [gh+iid+l+tł'éél]   [gh+oh+'ááł]
gliding: [y+iid+l+tł'éél]   [w+oh+'ááł]
ultimately: [yiiltł'éél]   [woh'ááł]

The intransitive, 68.3, needs no explanation. Gh- has simply glided to y-. However, in 68.4, 69.3 and 4, where the progressive prefix is preceded by yi- and ji-, we find an oo- vowel, a fact that must be handled by a readjustment rule, gho- readjustment, that operates in zero environment when ghi- is preceded by a conjunctive prefix.

(70) ghi → gho / +___[

The gh- prevents the vowel of the conjunct prefix from being deleted and then deletes intervocalically by rule II-41, gamma deletion. After vowel assimilation, oo- is obtained.

	68.4/ji+ghi+l+tł'ééł/	69.3/yi+ghi+'ááł/
gho read:	[ji+gho+l+tł'ééł]	[yi+gho+'ááł]
gh dele:	[ji+o+l+tł'ééł]	[yi+o+'ááł]
V assim:	[jo+o+l+tł'ééł]	[yo+o+'ááł]
ultimately:	[jooltł'ééł]	[yoo'ááł]

3.422 +ghi+(X)+[

Of the conjunctive prefixes pos. 6 hi- 'seriative' and ni- 'terminative' and pos. 5 'i- 3i and hwi- 'area' may occur in progressives. Di- 'inceptive', which can occur thematically, cannot be placed next to ghi-, e.g. dideesdził F1, jidildzííł I4, but yisdził Pgl 'strain'. Also, +i+ never occurs in a progressive.

The future mode can readily be demonstrated to be a conjunct progressive. Compare the prefix complexes of two conjunct progressives, (71) 'resuscitate' and (72) 'set them in a line' with two futures, (73) 'dip it out' and (74) 'string them'.

(71) 1 náheesh'naał   (72) 1 neeshkááł
     2 náhíí'naał   2 nííłkááł
     3 náhoo'naał   3 yinoołkááł
     4 náhijoo'naał   4 jinoołkááł
     1d náhii'naał   1d niilkááł
     2d náhooh'naał   2d noołkááł
(73) 1 hadeeshkááł   (74) 1 deesh'ish
     2 hadííkááł   2 díí'ish

```
        3 haidookááł              3 yidoo'ish
        4 hazhdookááł             4 jidoo'ish
        1d hadiikááł              1d diit'ish
        2d hadoohkááł             2d dooh'ish
```

All four of these verbs can be derived by the same set of rules. The ee- in the 1sg forms, like the oo- in third and fourth person, must be derived by a readjustment rule. However, this cannot be the same readjustment rule, rule 33r, which results in ee- in ni- imperfectives and which is keyed to a preceding aspect prefix since the ee- in the progressive occurs in the first person of <u>all</u> conjunct verbs. Thus, we add <u>ghe- readjustment</u>.

(75r.) ghi → ghe / +___sh

With the addition of this rule, the first person forms in the above verbs can be derived by the same rules used for Coo- in third and fourth person progressives.

```
                    71.1/ná#hi+ghi+sh+d+naał/      74.1/di+ghi+sh+'ish/
    ghe read:       [ná#hi+ghe+sh+d+naał]          [di+ghe+sh+'ish]
    gh dele:        [ná#hi+e+sh+d+naał]            [di+e+sh+'ish]
    V assim:        [ná#he+e+sh+d+naał]            [de+e+sh+'ish]
    ultimately:     [náheesh'naał]                 [deesh'ish]
```

Stanley has written a vowel assimilation rule that is keyed to the lamino-alveolar, sh-, to explain this ee- sequence (1969a:200). However, this still leaves other ee-'s that occur in the ni- imperfective and in the three perfectives unexplained. Although it is not explanatory, I derive all instances of ee- by readjustment rules that have ghe- as an output.

The 2sg forms in (71)-(74) can be derived by ni- absorption, gamma deletion, and tone raising.

	72.2/ni+ghi+ni+ɫ+kááɫ/	74.2/di+ghi+ni+'ish/
ni absorp:	[ni+ghí+ɫ+kááɫ]	[di+ghí+'ish]
gh dele:	[ni+í+ɫ+kááɫ]	[di+í+'ish]
tone rais:	[ní+í+ɫ+kááɫ]	[dí+í+'ish]
ultimately:	[nííɫkááɫ]	[díí'ish]

Due to the conjunct prefixes, the third and fourth person forms trigger rule 70r, gho- readjustment.

	71.3/ná#hi+ghi+d+naaɫ/	74.3/yi+di+ghi+'ish/
gho read:	[ná#hi+gho+d+naaɫ]	[yi+di+gho+'ish]
gh dele:	[ná#hi+o+d+naaɫ]	[yi+di+o+'ish]
V assim:	[ná#ho+o+d+naaɫ]	[yi+do+o+'ish]
ultimately:	[ná#hoo'naaɫ]	[yidoo'ish]

The dual forms are obtained by general rules.

	73.1d/ha#di+ghi+iid+kááɫ/	74.2d/di+ghi+oh+'ish/
V dele:	[ha#di+gh+iid+dááɫ]	[di+gh+oh+'ish]
gh dele:	[ha#di+iid+kááɫ]	[di+oh+'ish]
V assim:	_____	[do+oh+'ish]
V degem:	[ha#di+id+kááɫ]	_____
ultimately:	[hadiikaaɫ]	[dooh'ish]

A few other conjunct progressives are worthy of mention. In (76) I present a paradigm where hwi- 'area' is adjacent to ghi- in 'grope along'.

(76) 1 hweesił

2 hóóził ~ hwííził

3 hooził

4 hojooził

1d hwiidził

2d hoohsił

I have maintained that the /hwi/ rather than /ho/ representation of this prefix preserves the vowel assimilation rule (2.74). In 76.1 I assume that rule II-78, delabialization, has not applied before gamma deletion, and the sequence hwi+e assimilates to hwee-.

76.1 /hwi+ghi+sh+ził/

ghe read:	[hwi+ghe+sh+ził]
gh dele:	[hwi+e+sh+ził]
delab:	_____
V assim:	[hwe+e+sh+ził]
ultimately:	[hweesił]

However, the first variant for 76.2 contradicts this order. Here delabialization has applied before gh- has been deleted.

76.2 /hwi+ghi+ni+ził/

ni absorp:	[ho+ghi+ni+ził]
delab:	[ho+ghí+ził]
gh dele:	[ho+í+ził]
tone rais:	[hó+í+ził]
V assim:	[hó+ó+ził]
ultimately:	[hóóził]

The other variant for 79.2, hwííził, can be derived by the same order used for 76.1, where delabialization follows gamma deletion.

76.2 /hwi+ghi+ni+ziɬ/

ni absorp:	[hwi+ghí+ziɬ]
gh dele:	[hwi+í+ziɬ]
delab:	————
ultimately:	[hwíísiɬ]

The first dual form requires the gamma deletion-delabialization order, and the second dual could be derived correctly by either order. Thus, the delabialization-gamma deletion order of the first variant for 76.2 is paradoxical. The fact that there is variation on this form suggests that there is uncertainty as to the ordering of these two rules.[17] Just why this reordering should be limited to 2sg forms is unclear. Perhaps it is related to the fact that ni- absorption requires a CV prefix in order to operate. Possibly the gh- of the progressive prefix is thereby "reinforced" and the rule reordering proceeds so that gh- triggers delabialization. In any case, the ordering of delabialization before gamma deletion can be assumed to be innovative since it allows a fuller utilization of the rules (Kiparsky, 1968:200).

The future mode can be cross-cut by a number of aspectual subsystems that never appear in other conjunct progressives. The so-called prolongatives (Reichard, 1951:215-216)[18] and inchoatives (YM, 1943a:108-109) appear in the future with /di+í+ní/ (or equally possibly, /dí+ní/) prefixes in pos. 6. Perhaps these two aspects contain the yí- 'tentative' prefix discussed in 2.4. Below is a future prolongative, 'steal it' (77) and a future inchoative 'start to boil it' (78).

(77) 1 dínéesh'į́į́ł   (78) 1 bidí'néeshbish
      2 díníí'į́į́ł   2 bidí'nííłbish
      3 yidínóo'į́į́ł   3 yidí'nóołbish
      4 jidínóo'į́į́ł   4 bizhdí'nóołbish ∿
                                            bidízh'nóołbish
      1d díníit'į́į́ł   1d bidí'níilbish
      2d dínóoh'į́į́ł   2d bidí'nóołbish

These can be derived by almost the same rules I have used for other conjunct progressives. Note, however, that in the 1d and 2d the í- aspectual prefix has not lowered its tone by rule II-48, tone lowering. In addition a metathesis rule that reorders 'i- 3i affects all forms in (78). This metathesis rule is separate from rule II-91 which reorders 'zhC to zh'C. We call the new rule <u>glottal-CV metathesis</u>, and it must follow rule II-86, vowel elision.

(79) '+CV+C → CV+'+C

                77.1/di+í+ní+ghi+sh+'į́į́ł/   78.1/bi+'i+di+í+ní+ghi+sh+ł+bish/

ghe read: [di+í+ní+ghe+sh+'į́į́ł]   [bi+'i+di+í+ní+ghe+sh+ł+bish]
V dele: [d+í+ní+ghe+sh+'į́į́ł]   [bi+'i+d+í+ní+ghe+sh+ł+bish]
gh dele: [d+í+ní+e+sh+'į́į́ł]   [bi+'i+d+í+ní+e+sh+ł+bish]
V assim: [d+í+né+e+sh+'į́į́ł]   [bi+'i+d+í+né+e+sh+ł+bish]
V elision: _____   [bi+'+d+í+né+e+sh+ł+bish]
'CV metath: _____   [bi+d+í+'+né+e+sh+ł+bish]
ultimately: [dínéesh'į́į́ł]   [bidí'néeshbish]

The two variants for 78.4 are an interesting illustration of the two metathesis rules, 79 and II-91. The first variant can be derived by a double application of vowel elision, deaffrication, rule II-91, glottal-zh metathesis, and rule 79, glottal-CV metathesis.

78.4 /bi+'i+ji+di+í+ní+ghi+ł+bish/

gho read:	[bi+'i+ji+di+í+ní+gho+ł+bish]
V assim:	[bi+'i+ji+dí+nó+o+ł+bish]
V elision:	[bi+'+j+dí+nó+o+ł+bish]
deaffric:	[bi+'+zh+dí+nó+o+ł+bish]
'zh metath:	[bi+zh+'+dí+nó+o+ł+bish]
'CV metath:	[bi+zh+dí+'+nó+o+ł+bish]
ultimately:	[bizhdí'nóołbish]

The second variant for 78.4 has the same derivation except that here rule 79, glottal-CV metathesis, has a broader environment that includes zh-. Since these variants appear to be of equal acceptability, I simply add zh- to rule 79.

(79) (zh)+'+CV+C → CV+(zh)+'+C

The second variant includes zh- in the metathesis while the first leaves it out.

78.4 /bi+'i+ji+dí+nó+o+ł+bish/*

V elision:	[bi+'+j+dí+nó+o+ł+bish]
deaffric:	[bi+'+zh+dí+nó+o+ł+bish]
'zh metath:	[bi+zh+'+dí+nó+o+ł+bish]
'CV metath:	[bi+dí+zh+'+nó+o+ł+bish]
ultimately:	[bidízh'nóołbish]

Some of the +i+ aspect verbs take a future form in which +i+ appears to the left of di-. (Just why +i+ should occur to the left of di- in the future but to the right of di- in imperfectives such as diishheeł 'I am quieting down', is another problem concerning +i+.) Below I present paradigms for 'see it' (80), 'dash off' (81), and 'unroll it' (82), an unusual o- imperfective verb.[19]

(80) 1 yideestséél (81) 1 yeideeshtał (82) 1 néideeshtał
    2 yidííłtséél   2 yeidííłtał   2 néidííłtał
    3 yiidoołtséél   3 yeidooltał   3 néidoołtał
    4 yizhdoołtséél   4 yeizhdooltał   4 néizhdoołtał
    1d yidiiltséél   1d yeidiiltał   1d néidiiltał
    2d yidoołtséél   2d yeidooltał   2d néidooltał

When +i+ is in word initial position it is covered by y- via gh-insertion and gliding. This is the case in (80).

      80.2 /i+di+ghi+ni+ł+tséél/ 81.2 /ya#i+di+ghi+ni+l+tał/

gh insert: [ghi+di+ghi+ni+ł+tséél]

ni absorp: [ghi+di+ghí+ł+tséél] [ya#i+di+ghí+l+tał]

gh dele: [ghi+di+í+ł+tséél]   [ya#i+di+í+l+tał]

tone rais: [ghi+dí+í+ł+tséél]   [ya#i+dí+í+l+tał]

gliding: [yi+dí+í+ł+tséél]

ultimately: [yidííłtséél]   [yeidííltał]

The third person of (80) is an interesting exception to the vowel deletion rule. Presumably /yi+i/ would yield y+i after vowel deletion instead of yii-. Many speakers accept yidooltséél as a variant for 80.3.

3.423 #ghi+(X)+[

The disjunct progressives present a number of phonological problems. It is of importance that low tone disjunct prefixes almost never come in contact with ghi-. All but one of the disjunct prefixes that occur in the progressive are of the shape Cá- (on the surface). Below I present progressives for 'speak' (83) and 'carry an animate object back' (84).

(83) 1 yááshtih (84) 1 nááshtééł
2 yááłtih 2 nááłtééł
3 yááłtih 3 náyoołtééł
4 yájoołtih 4 ńjoołtééł
1d yéiiltih 1d néiiltééł
2d yáółtih ~ yááłtih 2d náółtééł ~ nááłteeł

These can be obtained by present rules. In the 1sg and 2d forms and in 83.3 tone assimilation applies before gamma deletion.

        83.3/yá#ghi+ł+tih/   84.2d/ná#ghi+oh+ł+tééł/

V dele: [ná#gh+oh+ł+tééł]

tone assim: [yá#ghí+ł+tih]   [ná#gh+óh+ł+tééł]

gh dele: [yá#í+ł+tih]   [ná#óh+ł+tééł]

V assim: [yá#á+ł+tih]   ([ná#áh+ł+tééł])

ultimately: [yááłtih]   [nááłtééł] ~ [náółtééł]

The vowel assimilation rule applies optionally to 84.2d, depending on dialect.

The 2sg and 1d forms are also derived by general rules.

        83.2/yá#ghi+ni+ł+tih/   84.1d/ná#ghi+iid+ł+tééł/

V dele: [ná#gh+iid+ł+ééł]

ni absorp: [yá#ghí+ł+tih]

gh dele: [yá#í+ł+tih]   [ná#iid+ł+tééł]

V assim: [yá#á+ł+tih]

V front: [né#iid+ł+tééł]

ultimately: [yááłtih]   [néiiltééł]

Vowel assimilation is blocked from 84.1d by condition a on rule II-57 which exempts assimilation from a#ii strings.

The fourth person forms and 84.3 are derived just like other conjunct progressives in zero environment.

84.4 /ná#ji+ghi+ɬ+tééɬ/

gho read: [ná#ji+gho+ɬ+tééɬ]

gh dele: [ná#ji+o+ɬ+tééɬ]

V assim: [ná#jo+o+ɬ+tééɬ]

ultimately: [ńjooɬtééɬ]

Progressives that take the náá- 'semeliterative' prefix undergo an interesting reduplication rule that has some affinity with rule 19, yi- doubling. Below are paradigms for an intransitive, 'crawl along once more' (85) and a transitive, 'carry an animate object once more' (86).

(85) 1 náánááshʼnah   (86) 1 náánááshtééɬ
     2 náánááʼnah   2 náánááɬtééɬ
     3 náánááʼnah   3 nááyooɬtééɬ
     4 náájooʼnah   4 náájooɬtééɬ
     1d náánéiiʼnah   1d náánéiiltééɬ
     2d náánáóhʼnah   2d náánáóɬtééɬ
                              2-1 nááneeshtééɬ

A reduplicated nááná- prefix appears in 1sg, 2sg, 1d, and 2d as well as in 85.3, where there is no direct object prefix. Náá- appears in front of yi-, ji, and ni- second person direct object in 86.2-1, 'I carry you once again'. I will posit that an underlying náá- reduplicates when a vowel is immediately next to # disjunct boundary. If náá-reduplication is ordered after gamma deletion, all forms in (85) and (86) can be predicted.

(87) náá- → nááná / ___#V

Recall that rule 19, yi- doubling, is a reduplication rule triggered by a solitary vowel in conjunct position.

     85.1 /náá#ghi+sh+d+nah/ 86.2 /náá#ghi+ni+ł+téél/

ni absorp:	_____	[náá#ghí+ł+téél]
tone assim:	[náá#ghí+sh+d+nah]	_____
gh dele:	[náá#í+sh+d+nah]	[náá#í+ł+téél]
náá redup:	[nááná#í+sh+d+nah]	[nááná#í+ł+téél]
V assim:	[nááná#á+sh+d+nah]	[nááná#á+ł+téél]
ultimately:	[náánáásh'nah]	[náánáátéél]

On the other hand, the non-reduplicating forms have a CV blocking the environment for rule 87.

     86.2-1 /náá#ni+ghi+sh+ł+téél/

ghe read:	[náá#ni+ghe+sh+ł+téél]
gh dele:	[náá#ni+e+sh+ł+téél]
náá redup:	_____
V assim:	[náá#ne+e+sh+ł+téél]
ultimately:	[nááneeshtéél]

As mentioned above, verbs that take na- 'about' cannot occur in the progressive unless mediated by a ná- 'back' prefix in pos. 1. One such progressive is 'rush back and forth in a **frenzy**'.

(88) 1 naanááshtlish

   2 naanáátlish

   3 naanáátlish

   4 naañjootlish

   1d naanéltlish

   2d naanáóhtlish

What is most conspicuous about this paradigm is the long vowel that appears in the adverbial prefix, naa-. Perhaps a vowel lengthening rule is operating here, but such a rule would be highly idiosyncratic. Alternatively, the long vowel is reminiscent of the postposition naa- 'around' as in hooghan bi<u>naa</u>góó hodiwol 'around the house it is rough' that is the origin of the incorporated na- 'about' adverbial prefix. Perhaps the semantic constraint that prohibits na#ghi is still operative here and it is the synchronically distinct postposition, naa- 'around' and not na- 'about' that is attached to the verb base.

Phonological difficulties are encountered with certain disjunct progressives. Three problematic verbs are 'push it along' (89), 'disappear' (90), and 'progress' (91).

(89) 1 bééshhił   (90) 1 'áashdįįł   (91) 1 náás kwááshnííł
     2 bííghił   2 'áádįįł   2 náás kwáánííł
     3 yíyooghił   3 'áádįįł   3 náás kwáánííł
     4 bíjooghił   4 'ájoodįįł   4 náás kójoonííł
     1d bíigił   1d 'íidįįł   1d náás kwíi'nííł
     2d bóohił   2d 'óohdįįł   2d náás kwááhnííł

All forms in (89) are derived like other progressives except for 89.1 where the éé- is not derivable by present rules. Perhaps, rule 75r, ghe- readjustment, applies here despite the fact that bí- is a disjunct prefix. On the other hand, this vowel is like that found in n- deleting verbs such as déédishjeeh /di+ná#di+sh+ł+jeeh/ 'I am rekindling the fire'. This would imply that in this one member of the paradigm a ná- prefix has been inserted. No solution is obvious at this point.[20]

(90) presents a problem in rule ordering similar to that discussed for the hóó ~ hwíí variants in the conjunct progressive. Here I assume

that pos. 1 'í- 'thus', becomes 'á- before a consonant by rule II-72 which must be ordered before gamma deletion in 90.1-3. But this order is clearly not possible for 90.1d and 2d where 'í- has not become 'á-. Presumably in the duals, gamma deletion applies before the 'i- to 'a- rule. Reichard reports a variant for 90.2, 'íídįįł, where gamma deletion also precedes 'i to 'a (1951:190). Thus, it appears that there is some ambivalence in the ordering relationship of gamma deletion and 'i to 'a.

Finally, (91) presents even greater difficulties. I have been assuming that the pos. 1 'in that way' prefix has the underlying shape /kwí/ with the allomorph [kó] when next to o- or C. Yet the allomorph of this prefix is [kwá] when it is next to V$_{[-lng]}$ in the progressive, a fact that violates the vowel assimilation rule. Perhaps, as suggested for béeshhił, a ná- has been inserted in certain forms. At present, [kwá] can be derived only by an ad hoc readjustment rule.

Could it be that the problematic vowels in these three verbs are related to the fact that bí- 'against', 'í- 'thus', and kwí- 'in that way' are the only disjunct prefixes occurring in progressives that are not of the underlying shape /Cá/? In other words, perhaps there is some analogical patterning influencing the surface forms of these prefixes.

3.43 Progressive Da- Shift

So far we have found no low tone disjunct adverbial prefixes that occur in the progressive. One candidate for such an element would be da- plural. But da- plus ghi- progressive triggers one of the most complex grammatical changes in Navajo. To my knowledge, "progressive da- shift" has been discussed only once in the Navajo literature, a neglect which is probably due to the paucity of paradigmatic material with da-. In their discussion of the progressive mode Young and Morgan state,

> Active transitive [progressive] verbs require a different stem and different prefixes with the addition of the distributive da-. . . . Passive or intransitive verbs can either change in the same fashion as the active verbs with the addition of da- or they can retain the progressive stem and continue regular in this respect. . . The difference is that in the regular form with the progressive stem the action is thought of as being more of a group action, whereas with the change to an imperfective stem and the distinct set of prefixes it is more of an individual action, with each of the individuals in reference taking part in the action (1943a:95).

In other words, the da- shift is obligatory in transitives but optional in intransitives. Also, Haile (1942:58-66) gives some examples of progressive da- shift.

Below are examples of the progressive da- shift in two transitives, (92) 'carry an animate object' and (93) 'push it along', and three intransitives, (94) 'be on a drinking spree', (95) 'go along speaking', and (96) 'rush back and forth in a frenzy'. The abbreviation C. means that the form is a collective plural in denotation (i.e., the non-shifted intransitives), and the abbreviation S. indicates a separate or distributive plural (i.e., the shifted intransitives). In 4.105 we will discuss variation in the use of the da- shifted forms.

(92) 1d yiiltééł

    1p deiníilteeh   S or C

    2p deinółteeh   S or C

    3p deiłteeh   S or C

(93) 1d biigił

    1p bideiníigííł   S or C

    2p bideinóhííł   S or C

    3p yideighííł   S or C

(94) 1d dah 'iidlį́į́ł
    1p dah da'iidlį́į́ł   C
    1p dah da'íníidlįįh   S
    2p dah da'ínóhdlįįh   S
    3p dah da'ídlįįh   S

(95) 1d yéiiltih
    1p yádeiiltih   C
    1p yádeíníiltééh   S
    2p yádeínółtééh   S
    3p yádeíłtééh   S

(96) 1d naanéiitlish
    1p naańdeiitlish   C
    1p naańdeíníitlíísh   S
    2p naańdeínóhtlíísh   S
    3d naańdeítlíísh   S

    In the da- shifted forms the short o- in the 2p and the lack of oo- in the 3p suggest that the ghi- progressive prefix is no longer present. Also, all of the shifted plurals have variants with y-, e.g. 92.1p dayínéiilteeh, indicating that there is an underlying yí-. This yí- may be the 'tentative' prefix mentioned in 2.4. I assume that a /yí+ní/ compound prefix replaces ghi- in the da- shifted forms. The ní- is probably a ni- modal prefix in origin since it disappears in third person forms just as does ni- in the ni- imperfective and perfective.

    All five of the stems in the above da- shifted verbs are momentaneous imperfectives. To demonstrate this, compare the two imperfectives for the stem 'push': nabínígMł 'you push it around' where na- 'about', which always takes a <u>continuous</u> imperfective stem, has chosen -ghił;

and nibíníghííł 'you push it to a point' where ni- 'end', which always chooses the ni- imperfective and a <u>momentaneous</u> imperfective stem, has chosen -ghííł, the same stem as in the da- forms in (93).[21] Even the da- shifted plurals in (96) have switched to the momentaneous imperfective stem despite the presence of na- 'about', which normally requires the continuous imperfective stem. (This could be further evidence that naa- in progressives is separate from the adverbial prefix na- as suggested in 3.423.) Also, that these da- shifted stems parallel those found in the ni- imperfective is strong evidence that the yíní- prefix contains a ni- modal prefix.

Therefore, plural formation in the progressives is a highly marked transformational rule I refer to as <u>progressive da- shift</u>.

(97) ghi + (X) + STEM[progressive] →
     1   2   3

da # yí+ní + (X) + STEM $\begin{bmatrix} \text{imperfective} \\ \text{+momentaneous} \end{bmatrix}$
 4   1   2   3

condition: optional in intransitives

Phonologically, progressive plurals are interesting. The non-shifted intransitives are the only case where a low tone disjunct prefix appears next to ghi- progressive.

               95.1pC /yá+da#ghi+iid+ł+tih/

<u>V dele</u>:   [yá+da#gh+iid+ł+tih]

<u>gh dele</u>:   [yá+da#iid+ł+tih]

<u>V front</u>:   [yá+de#iid+ł+tih]

<u>ultimately</u>:   [yádeiiltih]

The tone on the transformationally introduced ní- prefix is probably inherently high rather than derived by tone assimilation. The lp forms can only be derived from a /yí+ní/ representation since tone assimilation does not apply when V̂ is followed by a long vowel. Also the 1p forms show that -í+iid has resisted rule II-48, tone lowering like the díní- aspect verbs mentioned above in 3.422. Resistance to tone lowering seems to be a trait of the í- prefix (or prefixes) that occurs in pos. 6. Thus, a condition must be added to the tone lowering rule to exempt the í+ní- sequence.

(II-48) V̂ → V / ___+V

        condition: ≠ í+ní+V

Only vowel degemination applies to this sequence.

        92. 1p /da#yí+ní+iid+ɫ+teeh/

y dele: [da#í+ní+iid+ɫ+teeh]

V front: [de#í+ní+iid+ɫ+teeh]

V degem: [de#í+ní+id+ɫ+teeh]

ultimately: [deíníilteeh]

The shifted 2p forms are derived by vowel deletion and tone assimilation.

        94. 2p /da#'i+yí+ní+oh+dlįįh/

V dele: [da#'i+yí+n+oh+dlįįh]

V elision: [da#'+yí+n+oh+dlįįh]

tone assim: [da#'+yí+n+óh+dlįįh]

y dele: [da#'+í+n+óh+dlįįh]

ultimately: [da'ínóhdlįįh]

I assume that the 3p forms also have /yí+ní/ in underlying representation. Ni- absorption applies when ni- is next to [.

93. 3p /yí+da#yí+ní+ghííł/

ni absorp:	[yí+da#yí+ghííł]
y dele:	[yí+da#í+ghííł]
V front:	[yí+de#í+ghííł]
ultimately:	[yídeíghííł]

3.44 Progressive Summary

This analysis of the progressives has raised a number of questions for future research. The phonology of the progressives is confounded by two readjustment rules, 70r and 75r, which obtain the oo- in zero environment and the ee- in 1sg. No more natural solution seems possible at present. In 3.7 I present some evidence that rule 70r, gho-readjustment, is an archaic process present in Alaskan Athapaskan. The most challenging problem in the progressive mode is to explain the derivational processes that underlie the unusual adverbial prefix distribution and the highly marked da- shift. Both of these topics are in urgent need of documentation in other Athapaskan languages.

3.5 The Perfective Mode

3.50 Introduction

The perfectives provide the supreme test for a phonological analysis of the Navajo verb. Three morphemes occur in mode position in the perfective, ghi-, ni-, and si-. These cooccur with a perfective morpheme we represent as /í/. By employing this perfective prefix, a phonological solution can be found for a good proportion of the perfectives. Nevertheless, a total of fifteen readjustment rules are needed in the following analysis. The principal question for future Navajo phonological research is whether these (and other) readjustment rules can in fact

be replaced by legitimate phonological rules. In the summary of this
chapter I present comparative evidence that a number of the perfective
readjustment rules are equally arbitrary processes in other Athapaskan
languages. More than any other mode, the perfective illustrates the
limits of a natural synchronic analysis of Navajo phonology.

The semantics of the three perfective mode prefixes are still vague.
Hopefully, this is a topic that will attract the attention of Navajo
and Athapaskan-speaking linguists in the future. Krauss has noted that
for Athapaskan "insofar as the perfectives contrast, ni- has the marked
meaning 'to a point, completive', ghi- has the marked meaning 'from a
point, inceptive', and si- is unmarked in this respect, 'static'" (1969:82).

Historically, the si- perfective is the oldest Athapaskan perfective.
Eyak has only the si- perfective. The si- perfective in Navajo and
elsewhere in Athapaskan is the only distinctive perfective morpheme.
Ni- perfective (and imperfective) is apparently an extension of the pos. 6
aspect prefix ni- 'terminative', and the ghi- perfective is very likely
an extension of the ghi- progressive prefix (Krauss, 1969:81-82).
There is synchronic evidence in Navajo that si- perfective is older
than the other two perfectives. Ghi- and ni- perfectives have a number
of phonological affinities with one another and, most significantly,
with ghi- progressive and ni- imperfective. Some of these affinities
extend to the si- perfective, but si- also undergoes several highly
unusual morphologically marked rules. Moreover when da- plural is
added to certain ghi- and ni- perfectives, there is a shift to the si-
perfective. These distinctive properties of the si- perfective are
fossil-like signs of its antiquity.22 Krauss regards the si- prefix
as an important link in the Na-Dene hypothesis. In Eyak the si-

perfective _follows_ the subject pronoun and in Tlingit an s- prefix appears in _classifier_ position (1965:24). Thus, at a deep level, the Na-Dene languages appear to have undergone quite radical slippages in the position of the si- morpheme.

Follwing Hale (1972a) I assume that an /í/ perfective prefix is present in all three perfectives.

```
MODE  PERF
si  +  í
ni  +  í
ghi +  í
```

Derivationally, this implies what is assumed to be the historical fact, that ni- and ghi- perfectives are derived from ni- imperfective and ghi- progressive. Reichard has taken a similar approach to the Navajo perfective. "All perfectives are the result of compounded prefixes. The ni-, yi-, and si- perfectives are really compounds of these prefixes with ni- completive" (1951:131). Stanley also assumes that a separate perfective morpheme underlies the perfective. He suggests that it is an /n/ that occurs to the right of the subject pronoun.

There is comparative evidence for assuming a separate perfective prefix, at least for the ni- and ghi- perfectives. Hoijer reconstructs the ghi- perfectives as *gh^W∂n- and ni- perfective as *n∂n-. This final -n is manifest as -n, high tone, or nasal in the third person of ghi- and ni- perfectives in many Athapaskan languages such as Hupa, Mattole, Chipewyan, Sarcee, and Apachean (Hoijer, 1971:138-140). The si- perfective, however, is reconstructed as *s∂-, a fact that accounts for some of the phonological differences between the si- perfective and the other two perfectives in Navajo.

The most problematic phonological question both in Navajo and in Athapaskan in general, is the relationship between the classifiers and the perfective paradigm. The í- perfective prefix is manifest as a high tone in the singular forms if the classifier is ∅ or ɫ- (si-perfective only shows the high tone in 1 and 2). But if the classifier is l- or d- the high tone only appears in the 2sg forms. Furthermore, if the classifier is ∅ or ɫ-, the regular sh- 1sg pronoun does not appear, an anomalous fact that is as old as proto-Athapaskan-Eyak (Krauss, 1969:75). Also, if the classifier is ∅ or ɫ- the usual oh- 2d pronoun is reduced to o-, a process that seems to extend no further than Apachean (Hoijer 1971:129). These classifier dependent phenomena are clearly related to the fact that the Navajo l- and d- classifiers are historically vocalic prefixes, *ɫə- and *də-. At one time there may have been regular phonological rules that deleted the perfective when it cooccurred with a vocalic classifier (or perhaps inserted some perfective prefix when the classifier was non-vocalic), and deleted sh- when it cooccurred with a non-vocalic classifier. However, in Navajo these are historical peculiarities and are not statable as phonological rules. (For some recent comments by Krauss on the perfective classifier subdivision see 3.54.)

The following four sections present an analysis of the phonology of the ghi-, ni-, and si- perfectives and a summary of the readjustment rules and problem areas in this analysis (3.51-3.54). In concluding this section I will examine some of the derivational properties of perfectives, including "perfective choice" and "perfective da- shift" (3.55).

3.51 Ghi- Perfective

3.510 Introduction

If the ghi- perfective is historically related to the progressive, it is divergent in meaning from the progressive now. According to Hoijer's calculations, the ghi- perfective is the most prevalent of the three perfective modes, in contrast to the rather limited distribution of the progressive. Reichard glosses the ghi- perfective as 'progressive completive', a translation that fits nicely with its suggested historical origin. However, many ghi- perfective verbs have no vestige of progressive meaning. For example, ghi- perfectives such as taah yí'ą́ 'put it in the water', taah yishnóód 'I dove into the water' are not progressive in connotation. It seems preferable to gloss ghi- perfective simply as 'completive'.

In this section I take up the two classifier subdivisions in the ghi- perfectives, ∅/ł and d/l, as they appear in their simplest form, the primary mode variant (3.511). Then I look at the ∅/ł perfectives in the conjunct and disjunct (3.512) and the d/l perfectives in the conjunct and disjunct (3.513). Finally, I discuss the +i+ aspect ghi-perfectives which, as usual, raise several problems (3.514).

3.511 ##ghi+í+(X)+⌐

The following four verbs illustrate the classifier subdivision: (98) 'cry', (99) 'ruin it', (100) 'dive in the water' (with preposed taah), and (101) 'drink it'.

(98)   1 yícha   (99)   1 yíłchǫ'
       2 yínícha   2 yíníłchǫ'
       3 yícha   3 yiyííłchǫ'
       4 jíícha   4 jííłchǫ'
       1d yiicha   1d yiilchǫ'
       2d woocha   2d woołchǫ'

(100) 1 yishnóód   (101) 1 yishdláá'
       2 yínílnóód   2 yínídláá'
       3 yilnóód   3 yoodláá'
       4 joolnóód   4 joodláá'
       1d yiilnóód   1d yiidláá'
       2d woołnóód   2d woohdláá'

(98) and (99) are ∅ and ł- perfectives. They show a high tone í-
in all forms but the duals, where, presumably, í- has lowered its tone
by rule II-48, tone lowering. Also, the sh- 1sg pronoun does not
appear, and the oh- 2d pronoun has been reduced to o-. In (100) and
(101), which are d- and l-class perfectives, only 2sg shows a high tone.
The fourth person forms and 101.3 have an oo- just like the conjunct
progressives in zero environment. Sh- and oh appear in their usual
manner.

These ∅/ł and d/l perfectives can be derived from a common underlying
representation, /ghi+í+(X)+[/, with the help of three ordered readjustment
rules. First, in d/l perfectives, the í- perfective prefix deletes in
first person and in zero environment. We call this <u>perfective deletion</u>.

(102) í → ∅ / ___(sh){d̥/l}STEM

In ∅/ł verbs the perfective prefix remains, but two pronoun
readjustments apply, <u>sh- deletion</u> and <u>oh- reduction</u>. These are ordered

after perfective deletion.

(103r) sh → ∅ / í+___

(104r) oh → o / í+___

These three readjustments will be shown to apply in all three perfectives (with an extended version of 102r in the si- perfective).

First, in the ∅/ɨ verbs, the 1sg forms 98.1 and 99.1 lose sh- by rule 103r and then vowel deletion and gliding operate.

99.1 /ghi+í+sh+ɨ+chǫ'/

sh dele:	[ghi+í+ɨ+chǫ']
V dele:	[gh+í+ɨ+chǫ']
gliding:	[y+í+ɨ+chǫ']
ultimately:	[yíɨcho']

The 2sg verbs do not undergo ni- absorption because no CV prefix precedes ni-. The í- perfective prefix, unlike ó- optative and +i+ aspect, does not trigger rule 18, n- deletion. Tone assimilation raises the tone of ni-.

98.2 /ghi+í+ni+cha/

V dele:	[gh+í+ni+cha]
tone assim:	[gh+í+ní+cha]
gliding:	[y+í+ní+cha]
ultimately:	[yínícha]

The fourth person forms in (98) and (99) are derived by vowel deletion, gamma deletion, and tone raising.

99.4 /ji+ghi+í+ɨ+chǫ'/

V dele:	[ji+gh+í+ɨ+chǫ']
gh dele:	[ji+í+ɨ+chǫ']
tone rais:	[jí+í+ɨ+chǫ']
ultimately:	[jííɨchǫ']

101.3 needs no explanation, yí- being derived simply by vowel deletion and gliding. However, the transitive verb, 99.3, is not *yíiłchǫ' as might be expected by analogy with the fourth person forms. Instead an extra yi- prefix is present. This, I claim, is another instance of rule 19, yi- doubling. In +i+ imperfectives we found that yi- direct object reduplicates if no prefix intervenes between it and the +i+ aspect prefix, e.g. 13.3 yiyiitał 'he kicks it'. If we revise rule 19 so that it contains i- (and not ii- as it now states), yi- doubling can apply if either +i+ aspect or the í- perfective prefix is present.

(19) ∅ → yi / ##___yi+i+[

Rule 22 applies to 99.3 after vowel deletion and gamma deletion have eliminated the ghi- prefix.

102.3 /yi+ghi+í+ł+chǫ'/

V dele:	[yi+gh+í+ł+chǫ']
gh dele:	[yi+í+ł+chǫ']
tone rais:	[yí+í+ł+chǫ']
yi doubl:	[yi+yí+í+ł+chǫ']
ultimately:	[yiyíiłchǫ']

Generally, yi- doubling does not apply if yi- is preceded by anything, e.g. dayíiłchǫ' 'they ruined it'. However, in 4.110 we will look at some variation in these forms.

Just like ó- in the optative duals, the í- perfective prefix is lowered in tone when next to the vowel initial dual prefixes. Also, the 2d forms lose h- by the readjustment rule, 104r, oh- reduction.

98.1d /ghi+í+iid+cha/   99.2d /ghi+í+oh+ɬ+chǫ'/

oh reduc:		[ghi+í+o+ɬ+chǫ']
V dele:	[gh+í+iid+cha]	[gh+í+o+ɬ+chǫ']
tone lower:	[gh+i+iid+cha]	[gh+i+o+ɬ+chǫ']
V assim:		[gh+o+o+ɬ+chǫ']
ultimately:	[yiicha]	[wooɬchǫ']

The d/l perfectives (100) and (101) undergo rule 102r, perfective deletion, in the 1, 3, and 4 forms. Perfective deletion and gliding apply to the 1sg forms.

100.1 /ghi+í+sh+l+nóód/

perf dele:	[ghi+sh+l+nóód]
gliding:	[yi+sh+l+nóód]
ultimately:	[yishnóód]

The 2sg forms retain the í- prefix and are derived like analogous ∅/ɬ perfectives.

100.3 has simply lost the perfective prefix.

100.3 /ghi+í+l+nóód/

perf dele:	[ghi+l+nóód]
gliding:	[yi+l+nóód]
ultimately:	[yilnóód]

The oo- vowel in 100.4, 101.3, and 101.4 is reminiscent of the conjunct progressives that require rule 70r, gho readjustment, in zero environment. After í- has been eliminated by perfective deletion, the identical readjustment rule can apply here because the ghi- modal prefix is preceded by a conjunct prefix and is directly next to [.

	100.4/ji+ghi+í+l+nóód/	101.3/yi+ghi+í+d+ląą́'/
perf dele:	[ji+ghi+l+nóód]	[yi+ghi+d+ląą́']
gho read:	[ji+gho+l+nóód]	[yi+gho+d+ląą́']
gh dele:	[ji+o+l+nóód]	[yi+o+d+ląą́']
V assim:	[jo+o+l+nóód]	[yo+o+d+ląą́']
ultimately:	[joolnóód]	[yoodląą́']

Perfective deletion does not apply to the dual forms which are obtained just as the ∅/ł duals except that oh- reduction does not apply.

	101.2d/ghi+í+oh+d+ląą́'/
V dele:	[gh+í+oh+d+ląą́']
tone lower:	[gh+i+oh+d+ląą́']
V assim:	[gh+o+oh+d+ląą́']
ultimately:	[woohdląą́']

3.512 (#)ghi+í+(ł)+STEM

The conjunct and disjunct ghi- perfectives are subdivided by the same readjustment rules that affect the primaries. In (105) 'let go of it' and (106) 'be shelling' I present ∅/ł conjunct paradigms.

(105)	1 bidííchid	(106)	1 'ííłhaal
	2 bidíínichid		2 'íínítłhaal
	3 yiidííchid		3 'ííłhaal
	4 bizhdííchid		4 'ajííłhaal
	1d bidiichid		1d 'iilghaal
	2d bidoochid		2d 'oołhaal

The 1sg verbs lose sh- by the sh- deletion readjustment rule. After ghi- is deleted, tone raising changes the tone of the vowel of the conjunct prefix.

177

106.1 /'i+ghi+í+sh+ł+ghaal/

sh dele:	['i+ghi+í+ł+ghaal]
V dele:	['i+gh+í+ł+ghaal]
gh dele:	['i+í+ł+ghaal]
tone rais:	['í+í+ł+ghaal]
ultimately:	['ííłhaal]

The 2, 3, and 4 forms show Cíí- that is obtained by the same set of rules.

                105.4 /bi#ji+di+ghi+í+chid/   106.3 /'i+ghi+í+ł+ghaal/

V dele:	[bi#ji+di+gh+í+chid]	['i+gh+í+ł+ghaal]
gh dele:	[bi#ji+di+í+chid]	['i+í+ł+ghaal]
tone rais:	[bi#ji+dí+í+chid]	['í+í+ł+ghaal]
ultimately:	[bizhdííchid]	['ííłhaal]

Note that in the third person form, 105.3, rule 19, yi- doubling, has not applied because of the intervening di- prefix.

The dual forms are treated as in the primary ghi- perfectives. Tone lowering applies and oh- reduction affects the 2d verbs.

                105.1d /bi#di+ghi+í+iid+chid/ 106.2d /'i+ghi+í+oh+ł+ghaal/

oh reduc:	_____	['i+ghi+í+o+ł+ghaal]
V dele:	[bi#di+gh+í+iid+chid]	['i+gh+í+o+ł+ghaal]
gh dele:	[bi#di+í+iid+chid]	['i+í+o+ł+ghaal]
tone lower:	[bi#di+i+iid+chid]	['i+i+o+ł+ghaal]
V assim:	_____	['o+o+o+ł+ghaal]
ultimately:	[bidiichid]	['oołhaal]

The disjunct ∅/ł ghi- perfectives are quite similar to the two previous paradigms. They are illustrated by (107) 'drive up' and (108) 'dry it back up'.

(107) 1 hááɫbą́ą́z   (108) 1 nááɫtseii
       2 hainíɫbą́ą́z   2 néíníɫtseii
       3 hayííɫbą́ą́z   3 náyííɫtseii
       4 hajííɫbą́ą́z   4 ńjííɫtseii
       1d haiilbą́ą́z   1d néiiltseii
       2d haooɫbą́ą́z   2d náooɫtseii

Tone raising applies to the 1, 2, 3, and 4 forms of (107).

               107.1/ha#ghi+í+sh+ɫ+bą́ą́z/   107.2/ha#ghi+í+ni+ɫ+bą́ą́z/

sh dele: [ha#ghi+í+ɫ+bą́ą́z]
V dele: [ha#gh+í+ɫ+bą́ą́z]   [ha#gh+í+ni+ɫ+bą́ą́z]
tone assim: [ha#gh+í+ní+ɫ+bą́ą́z]
gh dele: [ha#í+ɫ+bą́ą́z]   [ha#í+ní+ɫ+bą́ą́z]
tone rais: [há#í+ɫ+bą́ą́z]   [há#í+ní+ɫ+bą́ą́z]
V assim: [há#á+ɫ+bą́ą́z]
ultimately: [háá+ɫbą́ą́z]   [haíníɫbą́ą́z]

The verbs in (108) undergo tone raising only in the third and fourth person due to the inherently high tone prefix, ná- 'back'.

The duals lower the tone of the perfective prefix as in other ghi-perfective duals.

3.513 (#)ghi+í+(X)+{l/d}+STEM

The conjunct and disjunct d/l perfectives undergo perfective deletion in 1, 3, and 4 forms like the d/l primaries. Below are conjuncts (109) 'dance' with pos. 5 'i- 3i, (110) 'tell him about it' with pos. 5 hwi- 'area', and (111) 'hex him' with the pos. 6 ni- prefix relating to 'mind'.

(109) 1 'eeshzhiizh   (110) 1 hweeshne'   (111) 1 bineesdzin
      2 'íínílzhiizh   2 hwíínílne'   2 biníínídzin

3 'oolzhiizh	3 hoolne'	3 yinoodzin
4 'ajoolzhiizh	4 hojoolne'	4 bizhnoodzin
1d 'iilzhiizh	1d hwiilne'	1d biniidzin
2d 'oołzhiizh	2d hoołne'	2d binoohdzin

After perfective deletion, the same environments that trigger ghe- readjustment and gho- readjustment in the conjunct progressives-- +ghi+(sh)+[--are present in the conjunct d/l perfectives. Thus in the first singular of the above paradigms rule 75r, ghe- readjustment, applies after í- has been deleted.

	110.1/hwi+ghi+í+sh+l+ne'/	111.1/bi+ni+ghi+í+sh+d+zin/
perf dele:	[hwi+ghi+sh+l+ne']	[bi+ni+ghi+sh+d+zin]
ghe read:	[hwi+ghe+sh+l+ne']	[bi+ni+ghe+sh+d+zin]
gh dele:	[hwi+e+sh+l+ne']	[bi+ni+e+sh+d+zin]
V assim:	[hwe+e+sh+l+ne']	[bi+ne+e+sh+d+zin]
ultimately:	[hweeshne']	[bineesdzin]

The third and fourth person forms of the above verbs are like 101.3 and 4. After perfective deletion, gho- readjustment applies.

	109.3/'i+ghi+í+l+zhiizh/	111.3/yi+ni+ghi+í+d+zin/
perf dele:	['i+ghi+l+zhiizh]	[yi+ni+ghi+d+zin]
gho read:	['i+gho+l+zhiizh]	[yi+ni+gho+d+zin]
ultimately:	['oolzhiizh]	[yinoodzin]

The 2sg forms are obtained like conjunct ∅/ł perfectives by tone assimilation, tone raising, etc. The duals are also as in other conjuncts except, of course, oh- reduction does not apply here because of the d- and l- classifiers.

I should also point out that the agentive passives of ghi- perfectives, which contain a /bi+'i+di/ compound prefix in pos. 4 and a

d- classifier, are derived like other d/l ghi- perfectives; e.g.
bi'doogą́ą́' 'they were killed', yóó' 'abi'doo'nil 'they were lost'.

/bi+'i+di+ghi+í+d+ghą́ą́'/

perf dele: [bi+'i+di+ghi+d+ghą́ą́']

gho read: [bi+'i+di+gho+d+ghą́ą́']

gh dele: [bi+'i+di+o+d+ghą́ą́']

V assim: [bi+'i+do+o+d+ghą́ą́']

ultimately: [bi'doogą́ą́']

Disjunct ghi- perfectives with an l- or d- classifier are relatively rare. These are illustrated by (112) 'exclaim' and (113) 'exhale' (which takes a preposed 'ahiih).

(112) 1 haasdzíí'   (113) 1 hanáásdzíí'
       2 háínídzíí'   2 hanéínídzíí'
       3 haadzíí'   3 hanáádzíí'
       4 hajoodzíí'   4 hańjoodzíí'
      1d haiidzíí'   1d hanéiidzíí'
      2d haoohdzíí'   2d hanáoohdzíí'

These disjuncts differ from the d/l conjuncts in that no ee- or oo- appears in the l or 3 forms, i.e. # blocks the ghe- and gho- readjustment rules from applying. After í- is deleted, the derivation of (113) proceeds just like disjunct progressives such as (84).

112.3/ha#ghi+í+d+zíí'/   113.1/ha+ná#ghi+í+sh+d+zíí'/

perf dele: [ha#ghi+d+zíí']   [ha+ná#ghi+sh+d+zíí']

tone assim: ─────────────   [ha+ná#ghí+sh+d+zíí']

gh dele: [ha#i+d+zíí']   [ha+ná#í+sh+d+zíí']

V assim: [ha#a+d+zíí']   [ha+ná#á+sh+d+zíí']

ultimately: [haadzíí']   [hanáásdzíí']

112.2 and 113.2 illustrate the importance of the C_o[environment for vowel assimilation. Vowel assimilation, rule II-57, is blocked by the ni- prefix and then vowel fronting applies (it is exempt from 112.2 by the condition on the velar+a#i sequence).

     113.2 /ha+na#ghi+í+ni+d+zíí'/

V dele:	[ha+ná#gh+í+ni+d+zíí']
tone assim:	[ha+ná#gh+í+ní+d+zíí']
gh dele:	[ha+ná#í+ní+d+zíí']
V assim:	————————
V front:	[ha+né#í+ní+d+zíí']
ultimately:	[hanéínídzíí']

The fourth person prefix, ji-, triggers gho- readjustment just as in other conjunct d/l ghi- perfectives in zero environment.

The duals are like those for other ghi- perfectives.

    112.1d /ha#ghi+í+iid+d+zíí'/ 113.2d /ha+ná#ghi+í+oh+d+zíí'/

V dele:	[ha#gh+í+iid+d+zíí']	[ha+ná#gh+í+oh+d+zíí']
gh dele:	[ha#í+iid+d+zíí']	[ha+ná#í+oh+d+zíí']
tone lower:	[ha#i+iid+d+zíí']	[ha+ná#i+oh+d+zíí']
ultimately:	[haiidzíí']	[hanáoohdzíí']

3.514 Ghi- perfective aspectual subsystems

A number of aspects crosscut the ghi- perfective. Most conspicuous and most problematic are those which take +i+ aspect and have no high tone perfective prefix throughout the paradigm. Almost all +i+ verbs take this low tone ghi- perfective.[23] I should hasten to point out that it is quite awkward to derive these verbs from /i+ghi+í/ underlying forms as must be the case if these are a subset of the ghi- perfective. It could be that these verbs comprise an entirely separate perfective mode that is formed with a i ∿ ii prefix and no í- perfective prefix.

'See' (114) is an example of a +i+ ghi- perfective with no preceding prefixes. In 'slacken it' (115) and 'leave one's thumb print' (116) +i+ is preceded by a conjunct prefix.

(114) 1 yiiłtsą́ (115) 1 diniiłtłóó' (116) 1 bik'idiishchid
      2 yiniłtsą́   2 dininiłtłóó'   2 bik'idinilchid
      3 yiyiiłtsą́   3 yidiniiłtłóó'   3 yik'idiilchid
      4 jiiłtsą́   4 jidiniiłtłóó'   4 bik'izhdiilchid
      1d yiiltsą́   1d diniiltłóó'   1d bik'idiilchid
      2d woołtsą́   2d dinoołtłóó'   2d bik'idoołchid

The same subdivision between ∅/ł and d/l perfectives is evidenced by the absence of the sh- subject pronoun in 114.1 and 115.1 and its presence in 116.1. With the addition of one readjustment rule, all forms in (114)-(116) can be derived.

114.1 and 115.1 require the sh- deletion rule plus rule 63, +V+ tone lowering, which lowers the tone of í- when preceded by +i+. (This is the same tone lowering rule used to explain +i+ optatives.)

114.1/i+ghi+í+sh+ł+tsá/

sh dele: [i+ghi+í+ł+tsą́]
V dele: [i+gh+i+ł+tsą́]
gh dele: [i+í+ł+tsą́]
+V+ tone low: [i+i+ł+tsą́]
ultimately: [yiiłtsą́]

Sh- deletion and +V+ tone lowering do not apply to 116.1 because of the l- classifier.

116.1 /bikʼi#di+i+ghi+í+sh+l+chid/

perf dele: [bikʼi#di+i+ghi+sh+l+chid]

V dele: [bikʼi#d+i+ghi+sh+l+chid]

gh dele: [bikʼi#d+i+i+sh+l+chid]

ultimately: [bikʼidiishchid]

If a /i+ghi+í+ni/ representation is assumed for the 2sg forms in the above verbs, an ad hoc i- reduction rule must be formulated. We call this rule **i- drop**.

(117) i → ∅ / ___ +i+ni

                114.2 /i+ghi+í+ni+ł+tsą́/   115.2 /dï+ni+ghi+í+ni+ł+tłóóʼ/

V dele: [i+gh+í+ni+ł+tsą́]   [di+n+i+gh+í+ni+ł+tłóóʼ]

gh dele: [i+í+ni+ł+tsą́]   [di+n+i+í+ni+ł+tłóóʼ]

+V+ tone low: [i+i+ni+ł+tsą́]   [di+n+i+i+ni+ł+tłóóʼ]

i drop: [i+ni+ł+tsą́]   [di+n+i+ni+ł+tłóóʼ]

ultimately: [yinił tsą́]   [dininił tłóóʼ]

The arbitrariness of this solution suggests that a generalization is being missed. Perhaps these verbs have only +i+ and no ghi+í in underlying representation.

Rule 19, yi- doubling applies to 114.3 just as it does in primary ∅/ł transitive ghi- perfectives.

                114.3 /yi+i+ghi+í+ł+tsą́/

V dele: [y+i+gh+í+ł+tsą́]

gh dele: [y+i+í+ł+tsą́]

yi doubl: [yi+y+i+í+ł+tsą́]

+V+ tone low: [yi+y+i+i+ł+tsą́]

ultimately: [yiyiił tsą́]

This derivation is somewhat suspect since the direct object prefix has been reduced to y- after vowel deletion and thus y+i- reduplicates. A

+i+ representation would be more direct here.

The other forms in (114)-(116) can be obtained by vowel and gamma deletion and vowel degemination.

By treating the +i+ perfectives as ghi- perfectives we have to resort to an ad hoc i- drop rule to get the 2sg verbs. What is most suspect about this solution is that the posited /ghi+í/ prefixes are never actualized on the surface. Perhaps these can be treated as some +i+ perfective, but the problem with this solution is similar to that raised by the +i+ imperfectives. Certain forms such as 1st and 3rd person would require some sort of +i+ lengthening rule (like rule 17r). For now, tenuously, we leave these low tone perfectives as a subset of the ghi- perfective.

+I+ is not the only aspectual prefix that complicates the analysis of the ghi- perfective. For example, it is not all clear why éé- should appear in the 1, 3, and 4 forms of (118) 'ask him a question', (119) 'fill it with it', and (120) 'look at it'.

(118) 1 nabídééɬkid   (119) 1 hadééɬbįįd   (120) 1 nééɬ'íí'
       2 nabídíínííɬkid   2 hadííníɬbįįd   2 nííníɬ'íí'
       3 nayídééɬkid   3 haidééɬbįįd   3 yinééɬ'íí'
       4 nabízhdééɬkid   4 hazhdééɬbįįd   4 jinééɬ'íí'
       1d nabídííilkid   1d hadiilbįįd   1d níil'íí'
       2d nabídóoɬkid   2d hadooɬbįįd   2d nóoɬ'íí'

The differences in the tones of the dual forms reveal that there is more than one underlying form involved here.

3.515 Ghi- perfective summary

The ghi- perfectives can be derived from a single underlying form /ghi+í/ if a perfective deletion rule and two pronoun readjustment rules

are formulated. Most significantly, we found that conjunct d/l ghi-
perfectives undergo the same two readjustments that affect conjunct
progressives. The low tone perfectives of +i+ verbs are rather awkwardly
derived from the same underlying form as the ghi- perfectives.

3.52 Ni- Perfective

3.520 Introduction

All verbs that take ni- imperfective also take ni- perfective. Ni-
is the most transparent of the three perfectives. Like the ni- imperfective,
it indicates termination of motion or arrival at a point. These verbs
are formed with ni- in mode position and í- in perfective position. I
first examine the ni- perfectives with ∅/ł classifier in primary conjunct
and disjunct (3.521-3.523). Then the d/l ni- perfectives in the three
mode variants are considered (3.524-3.526).

3.521 ##ni+í+(X)+(ł)+STEM

'Arrive' (121) and 'arrive leading it' (122) illustrate transitive
and intransitive ∅/ł ni- perfectives.

	(121)		(122)	
	1	níyá[24]	1	nílóóz
	2	yíníyá	2	yínílóóz
	3	níyá	3	yinílóóz
	4	jiníyá	4	jinílóóz
	1d	niit'aazh	1d	niidlóóz
	2d	noo'aazh	2d	noolóóz

Rule 103r, sh- deletion, and vowel deletion apply to 121.1 and
122.1.

122.1 /ni+í+sh+lóóz/

<u>sh</u> <u>dele</u>:   [ni+í+lóóz]

<u>V</u> <u>dele</u>:   [n+í+lóóz]

<u>ultimately</u>:   [nílóóz]

The 2sg forms are irregular. One would expect that underlying /ni+í+ni/ would yield níní-. However, the n- of the modal prefix has disappeared. Historically, this is probably due to analogical patterning with the yíní- prefix of the 2sg ghi- perfective. (The 2sg form of the si- perfective, síní- does not give way to this analogy.) I write a <u>perfective</u> <u>n-</u> <u>deletion</u> rule that is ordered after rule II-12, vowel deletion.[25]

(123) n → ∅ / ___ +í+ni+[

After n- is removed, the y- is obtained by gamma insertion and gliding.

121.2 /ni+í+ni+yá/

<u>V</u> <u>dele</u>:   [n+í+ni+yá]

<u>pf</u> <u>n</u> <u>dele</u>:   [í+ni+yá]

<u>gh</u> <u>insert</u>:   [ghí+ni+yá]

<u>tone</u> <u>assim</u>:   [ghí+ní+yá]

<u>gliding</u>:   [yí+ní+yá]

<u>ultimately</u>:   [yíníyá]

The third and fourth persons are straightforward. Only vowel deletion applies.

Both 1d and 2d undergo tone lowering. Also oh- reduction applies to 2d, just as in the ∅/ɬ ghi- perfectives.

	121.1d /ni+í+iid+'aazh/	122.2d /ni+í+oh+lóóz/
oh reduc:		[ni+í+o+lóóz]
V dele:	[n+í+iid+'aazh]	[n+í+o+lóóz]
tone lower:	[n+i+iid+'aazh]	[n+i+o+lóóz]
V assim:		[n+o+o+lóóz]
ultimately:	[niit'aazh]	[noolóóz]

3.522 +ni+í+(X)+(ł)+STEM

'Chase it out' (124) and 'stone him to death' (125) are conjunct ∅/ł ni- perfectives.

(124) 1 ch'íninííłcháá'   (125) 1 bił niznííłne'
       2 ch'íníínííłcháá'   2 bił ndzíínííłne'
       3 ch'íínínííłcháá'   3 yił niznííłne'
       4 ch'ízhnínííłcháá'   4 bił niizhnííłne'
       1d ch'íniniilcháá'   1d bił nizniilne'
       2d ch'íninoołcháá'   2d bił niznoołne'

These can be obtained by present rules. The first person forms delete sh- and undergo vowel deletion. In addition, in 125.1 rule II-86, vowel elision and rule II-87, deaffrication, apply.

	124.1 /ch'í#ni+ni+í+sh+ł+cháá'/	125.1 /ni#dzi+ni+í+sh+ł+ne'/
sh dele:	[ch'í#ni+ni+í+ł+cháá']	[ni#dzi+ni+í+ł+ne']
V dele:	[ch'í#ni+n+í+ł+cháá']	[ni#dzi+n+í+ł+ne']
V elision:		[ni#dz+n+í+ł+ne']
deaffric:		[ni#z+n+í+ł+ne']
ultimately:	[ch'ínínííłcháá']	[nizníłne']

The 2sg forms are interesting since the Cíí- sequence provides proof that rule 123, perfective n- deletion, is an ordered phonological rule. If we assume that the ni- modal prefix is deleted by an early readjustment rule, then the ni- and dzi- aspect prefix would lose their vowels by vowel deletion and incorrect forms would be derived. On the other hand, if perfective n- deletion is ordered after vowel deletion, the Cíí-sequence can be obtained by tone raising.

124.2/ch'í#ni+ni+í+ni+ł+chą́ą́'/

V dele:	[ch'í#ni+n+í+ni+ł+chą́ą́']
pf n dele:	[ch'í#ni+í+ni+ł+chą́ą́']
tone rais:	[ch'í#ní+í+ní+ł+chą́ą́']
ultimately:	[ch'ínííníłchą́ą́']

The 3, 4, and dual forms are derived just as in the primary ni- perfectives. 125.4 is interesting because rule II-94, j- deletion, applies.

125.4/ni#ji+dzi+ni+í+ł+ne'/

V dele:	[ni#ji+dzi+n+í+ł+ne']
prog strid assim:	[ni#ji+ji+n+í+ł+ne']
j dele:	[ni#i+ji+n+í+ł+ne']
V elision:	[ni#i+j+n+í+ł+ne']
deaffric:	[ni#i+zh+n+í+ł+ne']
ultimately:	[niizhníłne']

3.523 #ni+í+(X)+(ł)+STEM

'Pull it in two' (126) and 'rape her' (127) are ni- perfectives with ∅/ł classifiers and a preceding disjunct prefix.

(126) 1 k'íníłdlą́ą́d   (127) 1 bił ninídééł
       2 k'ííníłdlą́ą́d   2 bił níínídééł
       3 k'ííníłdlą́ą́d   3 yił niinídééł
       4 k'ízhníłdlą́ą́d   4 bił nizhnídééł
       1d k'íniildlą́ą́d   1d bił niniidééł
       2d k'ínoołdlą́ą́d   2d bił ninoodééł

These verbs need little explanation. The 2sg verbs require perfective
n- deletion and tone raising.

127.2 /ni#ni+í+ni+déél/

V dele:	[ni#n+í+ni+déél]
tone assim:	[ni#n+í+ní+déél]
pf n dele:	[ni#í+ní+déél]
tone rais:	[ní#í+ní+déél]
ultimately:	[níínídéél]

The other forms in (126) and (127) undergo the usual perfective
pronoun readjustments. The derivations are essentially as in primary
and conjunct ni- perfectives.

126.3 /k'í#yi+ni+í+ł+dláád/   127.4 /ni#ji+ni+í+déél/

V dele:	[k'í#yi+n+í+ł+dláád]	[ni#ji+n+í+ł+déél]
V elision:		[ni#j+n+í+ł+déél]
deaffric:		[ni#zh+n+í+ł+déél]
y dele:	[k'í#i+n+í+ł+dláád]	
ultimately:	[k'íiníłdláád]	[nizhníłdéél]

126.1d /k'í#ni+í+iid+ł+dláád/   127.2d /ni#ni+í+oh+déél/

oh reduc:		[ni#ni+í+o+déél]
V dele:	[k'í#n+í+iid+ł+dláád]	[ni#n+í+o+déél]
tone lower:	[k'í#n+i+iid+ł+dláád]	[ni#n+i+o+déél]
ultimately:	[k'íniildláád]	[ninoodéél]

3.524   ##ni+í+(X)+{d/l}+STEM

The d/l ni- perfectives delete the perfective prefix in 1, 3, and
4 forms. Below are two intransitive primaries, 'arrive crawling' (128)
and 'arrive trotting' (129).

(128) 1 nish'na'   (129) 1 nishtł'áh
      2 yíní'na'   2 yíníltł'áh
      3 yí'na'   3 yíltł'áh
      4 jí'na'   4 jíltł'áh
      1d nii'na'   1d niiltł'áh
      2d nooh'na'   2d noołtł'áh

Except for the yí- prefix in 2sg and the long oo- in 2d these are identical to the ni- imperfectives. Perfective deletion sets up an environment in 1, 3, and 4 that is identical to equivalent forms in the ni- imperfective.

                129.1/ni+í+sh+l+tł'áh/

<u>perf dele</u>:   [ni+sh+l+tł'áh]

<u>ultimately</u>:   [nishtł'áh]

The fourth person forms undergo ni- absorption after í- is eliminated.

                128.4/ji+ni+í+d+na'/

<u>perf dele</u>:   [ji+ni+d+na']

<u>ni absorp</u>:   [jí+d+na']

<u>ultimately</u>:   [jí'na']

Since these are intransitive verbs, the yí- in 128.3 and 129.3 cannot be a direct object prefix. These are exactly like third person intransitive ni- imperfectives such as yí'nééh 'he arrives crawling', yíltł'ééh 'he arrives trotting', which are derived by a readjustment rule, 24r, dummy object insertion.

    (24r) ∅ → yi +/ ##___ ni +[
                            [mode]

After the perfective prefix has been deleted, the dummy object is inserted, setting up ni- absorption.

129.3 /ni+í+l+tł'áh/

perf dele:	[ni+l+tł'áh]
dum obj insert:	[yi+ni+l+tł'áh]
ni absorp:	[yí+l+tł'áh]
ultimately:	[yíltł'áh]

The 2sg verbs are derived like ∅/ł ni- perfectives in the primary ni- perfective.

128.2 /ni+í+ni+d+na'/

V dele:	[n+í+ni+d+na']
tone assim:	[n+í+ní+d+na']
pf n dele:	[í+ní+d+na']
gh insert:	[ghí+ní+d+na']
ultimately:	[yíní'na']

The oo- in the 2d forms is due to the underlying í- prefix.

128.2d /ni+í+oh+d+na'/

V dele:	[n+í+oh+d+na']
tone lower:	[n+i+oh+d+na']
V assim:	[n+o+oh+d+na']
ultimately:	[nooh'na']

3.525 +ni+í+(X)+{$\begin{smallmatrix}d\\l\end{smallmatrix}$}+STEM

The conjunct d/l ni- perfectives also parallel the ni- imperfectives. 'Smile' (130) and 'arrive hopping' (131) are conjuncts with a pos. 6 aspect prefix.[26]

(130) 1 ch'ídinishdlo'   (131) 1 hinishcha'
       2 ch'ídíínildlo'   2 híínícha'
       3 ch'ídeeldlo'   3 heecha'
       4 ch'ízhdeeldlo'   4 hijeecha'

  1d ch'ídiniildlo'   1d hiniicha'

  2d ch'ídinooɫdlo'   2d hinoohcha'

It is important to point out that I treat 'arrive hopping' as a d-class verb by inference. No í- appears in 131.1, 3, and 4, and rules 103r and 104r do not apply to 1 and 2d. The d- classifier has been eliminated by rule II-25, d- deletion. Verbs such as this with an absolutely neutralized d- classifier will be called <u>invisible d-class</u> verbs. In 4.101 we discuss some highly significant variation involving invisible d-class verbs.

Again, except for the 2sg and 2d, these verbs are identical to ni- imperfectives with pos. 6 aspect prefixes.

The 1sg forms just delete í- by rule 102r.

The 2sg forms are like 2sg ∅/ɫ conjuncts.

     131.2/hi+ni+í+ni+d+cha'/

<u>V dele</u>:   [hi+n+í+ni+d+cha']

<u>pf n dele</u>: [hi+í+ni+d+cha']

<u>tone rais</u>: [hí+í+ní+d+cha']

<u>ultimately</u>: [híínícha']

What is most interesting about these paradigms is that the ee- is the third and fourth person forms also appears in equivalent ni- imperfectives ch'ídeeldlóóh (30.3) 'he is smiling', hijeechééh (32.3) 'he arrives hopping'. We derived these ni- imperfectives by the readjustment rule, (33r), ni- replacement.

(33r) ni → ghe $\begin{Bmatrix} \text{di} \\ \text{[agent]} \\ \text{ASP} \end{Bmatrix}$+___+[

This same rule applies to these ni- perfectives after the perfective prefix is deleted.

130.4/ch'í#ji+di+ni+í+l+dlo'/ 131.3/hi+ni+í+d+cha'/

perf dele:	[ch'í#ji+di+ni+l+dlo']	[hi+ni+d+cha']
ni replac:	[ch'í#ji+di+ghe+l+dlo']	[hi+ghe+d+cha']
gh dele:	[ch'í#ji+di+e+l+dlo']	[hi+e+d+cha']
V assim:	[ch'í#ji+de+e+l+dlo']	[he+e+d+cha']
ultimately:	[ch'ízhdeeldlo']	[heecha']

The duals are like the other ni- perfective duals.

If a d/l ni- perfective is preceded by a prefix in pos. 4 or 5, one would expect no readjustment rule to apply, as is the case when ni-imperfectives are preceded by direct object prefixes (see the verbs in (33)). I know of no active ni- perfective verbs with d- or l- classifier that have a direct object next to mode. The few transitives with d- or l- classifier have an aspect prefix that intervenes between direct object and mode; e.g. 'ádaa dinisht'á̜ 'I adopted it', 'ádaa shideet'á̜ 'he adopted me'.

However, in agentive passives a pos. 4 di- prefix is next to ni- mode with d- or l- classifier. Here, as is the case in the agentive passives of the ni- imperfectives (see 3.123), ni- replacement applies despite the fact that di- is not an aspect prefix.

(132) a. bi'deedlóóz   'he was led'
      b. bi'deet'eezh   'they were led'
      c. bi'deelmááz   'he was rolled'

132.c/bi+'i+di+ni+í+d+l+mááz/

perf dele:	[bi+'i+di+ni+d+l+mááz]
ni replac:	[bi+'i+di+ghe+d+l+mááz]
ultimately:	[bi'deelmááz]

3.526 #ni+í+(X)+{d/l}+STEM

The disjunct ni- perfectives with d- or l- classifier closely parallel the disjunct ni- imperfectives. Below are 'crawl to a point' (133) and 'run out' (134).

(133) 1 ninish'na'   (134) 1 ch'ínishghod
       2 nííní'na'   2 ch'íínílghod
       3 nii'na'   3 ch'élghod
       4 njí'na'   4 ch'íjílghod
       1d ninii'na'   1d ch'íniijéé'
       2d ninooh'na'   2d ch'ínoojéé'

The 1sg forms delete the perfective prefix and are derived like other d/l ni- perfectives.

      133.1/ni#ni+í+sh+d+na'/

perf dele: [ni#ni+sh+d+na']
ultimately: [ninish'na']

In the 2sg, as in the other ni- perfectives, perfective n- deletion eliminates the n- of the modal prefix.

      134.2/ch'í#ni+í+ni+l+ghod/

V dele: [ch'í#n+í+ni+l+ghod]
pf n dele: [ch'í#í+ni+l+ghod]
tone assim: [ch'í#í+ní+l+ghod]
ultimately: [ch'íínílghod]

The third person forms are exactly like their imperfective counterparts, nii'nééh (25.3) and ch'élgheed (26.3). We recall that these are derived by a ni- drop rule, 27r, that deletes the ni- modal prefix in #___[.

(27r)   ni   → ∅ / #___[
        [mode]

The deletion of í- sets up this same environment in 133.3 and 134.3. After ni- is deleted, pepet vowel insertion applies because there is no longer a vowel in conjunct position. 134.3 is further affected by rule II-62, vowel absorption.

                    133.3/ni#ni+í+d+na'/   134.3/ch'í#ni+í+l+ghod/

perf dele:	[ni#ni+d+na']	[ch'í#ni+l+ghod]
ni drop:	[ni#d+na']	[ch'í#l+ghod]
V insert:	[ni#i+d+na']	[ch'í#i+l+ghod]
V absorp:	————	[ch'é#l+ghod]
ultimately:	[nii'na']	[ch'élghod]

The fourth person forms are like those in primary d/l ni- perfectives.

                    134.4/ch'í#ji+ni+í+l+ghod/

perf dele:	[ch'í#ji+ni+l+ghod]
ni absorp:	[ch'í#jí+l+ghod]
ultimately:	[ch'íjilghod]

The duals are obtained in the usual manner.

3.527 Ni- perfective summary

The ni- perfectives, like the ghi- perfectives, are subdivided into ∅/ɨ and d/l paradigms. The ∅/ɨ ni- perfectives require the same pronoun readjustment rules that affect the ∅/ɨ ghi- perfectives. The d/l ni- perfectives are very similar to the ni- imperfectives. The same three readjustment rules used for the ni- imperfectives are applicable to d/l ni- perfectives.

3.53 Si- Perfective

3.530 Introduction

The si- perfective is a very general mode that denotes action or motion completed and in a durative-static state (YM,1943a:57; Reichard, 1951:280). I choose to derive si- perfectives from an underlying /si+í/ sequence although a distinctive perfective prefix is less certain here than it is in the other two perfectives. Phonologically, the si- perfective is the most obscure mode of the Navajo verb. A series of readjustment rules must be formulated to account for its unusual behavior, and it is obvious that they reflect more about the historical processes that have affected the si- perfective than about the synchronic phonology.

I first take up the primary ∅/ł si- perfective (3.531). Comparison will be made between intransitives and si- perfective neuter verbs. Second, I look at primary d/l forms (3.532). Third, I look at disjunct paradigms in both classifier subdivisions (3.533). Finally, I examine the conjunct si- perfective, reserving for the last the highly unusual aspect+si paradigms (3.534).

3.531 ##si+í+(X)+(ł)+STEM

In (135) and (136) are two transitive primary ∅/ł si- perfectives, 'pile them' and 'freeze it'.

(135) 1 sétł'in   (136) 1 séłtin
       2 sínítł'in   2 síníłtin
       3 yiztł'in   3 yistin
       4 jiztł'in   4 jistin
       1d siitł'in   1d siiltin
       2d sootł'in   2d soołtin

The í- perfective prefix is evidenced by the high tones in 1sg and 2sg and the oo- in 2d. The sh- and oh- pronouns have been altered by rules 103r and 104r just as in the ghi- and ni- ∅/ł perfectives. However, the é- in the 1sg forms is irregular. I derive it simply by a readjustment rule, í- lowering, which lowers í- to é- in front of sh-.

(137r) í → é /si+___+sh

        138.1/si+í+sh+tł'in/   139.1/si+í+sh+ł+tin/

í- lower:	[si+é+sh+tł'in]	[si+é+sh+ł+tin]
sh dele:	[si+é+tł'in]	[si+é+ł+tin]
V dele:	[s+é+tł'in]	[s+é+ł+tin]
ultimately:	[sétłin]	[séłtin]

Perhaps this é- reflects some historical process peculiar to the si- perfective. In eastern Navajo dialects, í- lowering is often suppressed; e.g. sítł'in, síłtin.

The 2sg forms are derived by vowel deletion and tone assimilation.

        136.2/si+í+ni+ł+tin/

V dele:	[s+í+ni+ł+tin]
tone assim:	[s+í+ní+ł+tin]
ultimately:	[síníłtin]

Unlike the ∅/ł ghi- and ni- perfectives, no í- perfective prefix is evidenced in zero environment of the ∅/ł si- perfective. Since other Athapaskan languages such as Hupa show no perfective prefix in this environment there is some question whether there is, in fact, a perfective prefix in the si- perfective. If not, then verbs such as 135.1 and 2 must be explained by other means. Perhaps the 2sg is analogical with the other perfectives, and perhaps the é- in the 1sg reflects something other than the í- perfective prefix (such as the y- component that Krauss has reconstructed for the PA classifier system [1969:75]). In the present analysis I choose to retain the underlying perfective prefix. Therefore I must add a <u>si- perfective deletion</u> rule that deletes í- in any zero environment form regardless of classifier.

(138r) í → ∅ / si+___+[

Si- perfective deletion is not the only readjustment rule that affects the third and fourth person forms in the above paradigms. The si- prefix is non-vocalic in all four forms and in 135.3 and 4, where there is no classifier, s- has been voiced to z-. Both of these processes are widespread in Athapaskan.

A <u>si- syncope</u> rule that reduces si- to s- when it is preceded by something in zero environment must be formulated. In addition, a <u>s- voicing</u> rule that voices s- to z- when it is next to the stem must be added.[27]

(139r) si → s / X___+[

(140r) s → z / ___+STEM

Thus, in 136.3 and 4 s- voicing is blocked by the ł- classifier which is subsequently deleted by rule II-30, classifier deletion.

	135.4/ji+si+í+tł'in/	136.3/yi+si+í+ł+tin/
<u>si pf dele</u>:	[ji+si+tł'in]	[yi+si+ł+tin]
<u>si syncope</u>:	[ji+s+tł'in]	[yi+s+ł+tin]
<u>s voic</u>:	[ji+z+tł'in]	————
<u>cl dele</u>:	————	[yi+s+tin]
<u>ultimately</u>:	[jiztł'in]	[yistin]

The dual forms are obtained like all other perfective duals. Oh- reduction applies to the 2d forms and tone lowering applies to both 1d and 2d.

Intransitive primary si- perfectives differ somewhat from the transitives. Most, if not all, of these si- intransitives are ∅-class verbs that are related to ł-class transitives.

(141) a. sits'il   'it is broken'   síníłts'il   'you broke it'
      b. sit'é   'it is roasted'   soołt'é   'you dpl raosted it'
      c. shibéézh 'it is boiled'   shéłbéézh 'I boiled it'
      d. sigan   'it is dried'   séłgan   'I dried it'

Derivationally, it may be that these intransitives come from deep transitives by a detransitivization rule that deletes the ł- classifier.

The si- perfective intransitives are very close, both structurally and semantically, to the si- perfective neuter verbs. In fact, their only difference is that the active si- perfectives can sometimes be conjugated for mode while the si- neuters appear in only one mode and are conjugated for tense periphrastically; e.g. sik'az 'it is cold', sik'az dooleeł 'it will be cold'.

The similarity in the two forms is illustrated by 'be dried up' (142) a si- perfective intransitive, and 'be standing' (143) a si- perfective neuter.

(142)   1 ségan   (143)   1 sézį́
        2 sínígan   2 sínízį́
        3 sigan   3 sizį́
        4 jizgan   4 jizį́
       1d siigan   1d siidzį́
       2d soogan   2d soozį́

Both of these paradigms are identical with transitives such as (135) except in the third person. Since no yi- object prefix precedes the si- in these third person forms, the si- syncope rule, which is

triggered by some preceding prefix, does not apply. Of course, s-
voicing is then blocked by the intervening vowel.

                142.3/si+í+gan/   143.3/si+í+zį́/

si pf dele: [si+gan]   [si+zį́]

si syncope: ———   ———

ultimately: [sigan]   [sizį́]

The fourth person forms are like the transitives. Ji- triggers si- syncope and then s- voices. Also, in 143.4 consonant degemination applies.

                143.4/ji+si+í+zį́/

si pf dele: [ji+si+zį́]

si syncope: [ji+s+zį́]

s voic: [ji+z+zį́]

C degem: [ji+zį́]

ultimately: [jizį́]

3.532 ##si+í+(X)+{^d_l}+STEM

There are only a few primary si- perfectives with d- or l- classifier that can be conjugated for person. All have a passive-like quality similar to the si- neuters and the si- intransitives. 'Freeze up' (144) is an invisible d-class verb and 'squat' (145) is an l-class verb.

    (144)   1 sistin   (145)   1 shishjį́į́d

               2 sínítin   2 shíníljį́į́d

               3 yistin   3 yishjį́į́d

               4 jistin   4 jishjį́į́d

             1d siitin   1d shiijį́į́d

             2d soohtin   2d shoohjį́į́d

The general characteristics of d/l perfectives are evidenced here. No high tone appears in 1sg and the sh- pronoun has remained. H- has remained in 2d.

Perfective deletion applies to the 1sg forms. 144.1 is affected by progressive strident assimilation which is blocked by condition from 145.1. 145.1 is derived by the regressive strident assimilation rule.

                144.1/si+í+sh+d+tin/   145.1/si+í+sh+l+jíí d/

perf dele:	[si+sh+d+tin]	[si+sh+l+jíí d]
prog strd assim:	[si+s+d+tin]	
strid assim:		[shi+sh+l+jíí d]
ultimately:	[sistin]	[shishjíí d]

The 2sg forms are like those in ∅/ł si- perfectives.

                144.2/si+í+ni+tin/

V dele:	[s+í+ni+tin]
tone assim:	[s+í+ní+tin]
ultimately:	[sinítin]

The fourth person forms are similar to 136.3 and 4. The underlying classifiers block s- voicing and then are deleted.

                144.4/ji+si+í+d+tin/

si pf dele:	[ji+si+d+tin]
si syncope:	[ji+s+d+tin]
s voic:	
d dele:	[ji+s+tin]
ultimately:	[jistin]

The dual forms are the same as in the ∅/ł si- perfectives.

The third person forms require further explanation. These are intransitives, and therefore no yi- direct object is present in underlying form.

It is of importance that passive voice forms of ∅-class si-perfectives contain a yi- like those in 144.3 and 145.3 which cannot be a direct object yi-. Compare the passives in (146) with related active transitives.

(146) a. yisdiz   'it has been spun'   yizdiz   'he spun it'
      b. yishbizh   'it has been braided' yizhbizh 'he braided it'
      c. yishgizh   'it has been cut'   yizhgizh 'he cut it'
      d. yistł'in   'it has been piled'   yiztł'in 'he piled them'

These passives are derivationally related to active transitives in much the same way that the ∅-class verbs are related to transitives with ł- classifier. Here it appears that the passives are derived from deep ∅-class transitives by the insertion of d- classifier. The d- is detected in the passives by the voiceless s ∿ sh (si- modal prefix) whereas the transitives show a z ∿ zh prefix that is the result of s- voicing since s- is next to the stem.

L-class si- perfective passives also contain a yi- prefix in third person like 145.3.

(147) a. yisdił   'it was shaken'   sínildił   'you were shaken'
      b. yisk'is   'it was cracked' doolk'is   'it will be cracked'
      c. yishch'il 'it curled'   yidoolch'ił 'it will be curled'
      d. yist'e   'they became (a certain number)'
                                      doolt'eeł   'they'll become
                                                  (a certain number)'

These l-class verbs (following Stanley's analysis) are probably derivable from deep ł-class transitives with the addition of the d- 'passive' classifier; e.g. yiyiiłch'iił 'he curled it' → yiilch'il 'it is being curled'.

But what of the yi- prefix that precedes the d- and l- intransitives? Krauss has raised this question, stating that this yi- is entirely irregular, perhaps analogical with the peg or direct object prefix (1969: 56-57). Perhaps it is a dummy object such as is inserted in ni- imperfectives and d/l class ni- perfectives.

Alternatively, we recall that ∅/ł si- intransitives and neuters such as sigan (142.3) and siłtsooz do not undergo si- syncope. It could be that when the si- perfective prefix is word initial and is followed by a d- 'passive' classifier, si- syncope is triggered. If that is the case, the yi- prefix can be viewed as a phonologically introduced peg.

I revise si- syncope to operate when preceded by something <u>or</u> when si- appears word initially with d- classifier.

(139r) si → s / $\begin{Bmatrix} \#\#\_\_\_+d \\ X\_\_\_+[\end{Bmatrix}$

After s- is reduced by the first subpart of 139r, a pepet vowel is inserted and gamma insertion and gliding apply.

	143.3 /si+í+d+tin/	147c /si+í+d+ł+ch'il/
perf dele:	[si+d+tin]	[si+d+ł+ch'il]
si syncope:	[s+d+tin]	[s+d+ł+ch'il]
V insert:	[is+d+tin]	[is+d+ł+ch'il]
ł voic:	———	[is+d+l+ch'il]
d dele:	[is+tin]	[is+l+ch'il]
gh insert:	[ghis+tin]	[ghis+l+ch'il]
gliding:	[yis+tin]	[yis+l+ch'il]
ultimately:	[yistin]	[yishch'il]

This approach to an l-class verb such as 150c assumes that it has a passivized ł- classifier, the ł- having been voiced by rule II-24.

3.533 #si+í+(X)+[

Below are four disjunct si- perfectives with ∅ or ł- classifier, two of them transitives (148) 'investigate it' and (149) 'push it about', and two intransitives, (150) 'swim about' and (151) 'think'.

(148)	1 niséłkáá'	(149)	1 nabíséghil
	2 nisíníłkáá'		2 nabísíníghil
	3 neiskáá'		3 nayíízghil
	4 njiskáá'		4 nabíjízghil
	1d nisiilkáá'		1d nabísiigil
	2d nisoołkáá'		2d nabísoogil
(150)	1 nisébį́į́'	(151)	1 ntsísékééz
	2 nisínibį́į́'		2 ntsísíníkééz
	3 naazbį́į́'		3 ntsézkééz
	4 njizbį́į́'		4 ntsíjízkééz
	1d nisiibį́į́'		1d ntsísiikééz
	2d nisoobį́į́'		2d ntsísookééz

The 1sg forms in (148)-(151) are like primary ∅/ł si- perfectives. í- lowering and sh- deletion operate. Note also that in (148) and (150) the na- 'about' prefix appears as ni- in all forms where it is next to a vocalic sV- prefix. I add the following na- alternation rule:

(152) na → ni / ___#sV.

Na- alternation is a late rule that is often suppressed.

 149.1 /na+bí#si+í+sh+ghil/   150.1 /na#si+í+sh+bį́į́'/

í- lower:	[na+bí#si+é+sh+ghil]	[na#si+é+sh+bį́į́']
sh dele:	[na+bí#si+é+ghil]	[na#si+é+bį́į́']
V dele:	[na+bí#s+é+ghil]	[na#s+é+bį́į́']
na alter:	_____	[ni#s+é+bį́į́']
ultimately:	[nabíséghil]	[nisébį́į́']

The 2sg, 1d and 2d forms are derived like analogous forms in the primary si- perfective.

148.2/na#si+í+ni+ɫ+káá'/   151.2/ntsí#si+í+ni+kééz/

V dele:	[na#s+í+ni+ɫ+káá']	[ntsí#s+í+ni+kééz]
tone assim:	[na#s+í+ní+ɫ+káá']	[ntsí#s+í+ní+kééz]
na alter:	[ni#s+í+ní+ɫ+káá']	————————
ultimately:	[nisíníɫkáá']	[ntsísíníkééz]

148.1d/na#si+í+iid+ɫ+káá'/   150.2d/na#si+í+oh+bį́į́'/

oh reduc:	————————	[na#si+í+o+bį́į́']
V dele:	[na#s+í+iid+ɫ+káá']	[na#s+í+o+bį́į́']
tone lower:	[na#s+i+iid+ɫ+káá']	[na#s+i+o+bį́į́']
na alter:	[ni#s+i+iid+ɫ+káá']	[ni#s+i+o+bį́į́']
ultimately:	[nisiilkáá']	[nisoobį́į́']

150.2d is sometimes heard as nasoobį́į́', where na- alternation has not applied.

The fourth person forms in the above paradigms are somewhat similar to 135.4 and 136.4. Si- syncope applies as does s- voicing when s- is next to the stem. The high tone ji- in 149.4 and 151.4 is due to tone assimilation.

151.4/ntsí#ji+si+í+kééz/

si pf dele:	[ntsí#ji+si+kééz]
si syncope:	[ntsí#ji+s+kééz]
s voic:	[ntsí#ji+z+kééz]
tone assim:	[ntsí#jí+z+kééz]
ultimately:	[ntsíjízkééz]

It is the third person forms in these paradigms that are of the most interest. 148.3 is a transitive verb and contains a yi- direct object prefix. The ei- is the result of y- deletion and vowel fronting. In the other transitive, 149.3, the yi- prefix has taken on the tone of the preceding high tone prefix.

148.3 /na#yi+si+í+ɨ+káá'/   149.3 /na+yí#yi+si+í+ghil/

si pf dele:	[na#yi+si+ɨ+káá']	[na+yí#yi+si+ghil]
si syncope:	[na#yi+s+ɨ+káá']	[na+yí#yi+s+ghil]
tone assim:	_____	[na+yí#yí+s+ghil]
y dele:	[na#i+s+ɨ+káá']	[na+yí#í+s+ghil]
V front:	[ne#i+s+ɨ+káá']	_____
ultimately:	[neiskáá']	[nayíízghil]

The intransitives contain aa- in 150.3 and é- in 151.3. These vowels are like those in third person forms of disjunct ∅ imperfectives. After si- has been reduced to s- by si- syncope, rule II-46, pepet vowel insertion applies because these is no vocalic conjunct prefix just as this rule applies to disjunct ∅ imperfectives and to d/l primary si- perfectives (like yistin). In 150.3 vowel assimilation changes i- to a- and in 154.3 í#i becomes é- by vowel absorption.

150.3 /na#si+í+bį́į́'/   151.3 /ntsí#si+í+kééz/

si pf dele:	[na#si+bį́į́']	[ntsí#si+kééz]
si syncope:	[na#s+bį́į́']	[ntsí#s+kééz]
s voic:	[na#z+bį́į́']	[ntsí#z+kééz]
V insert:	[na#iz+bį́į́']	[ntsí#iz+kééz]
V assim:	[na#az+bį́į́']	_____
V absorp:	_____	[ntsé#z+kééz]
ultimately:	[naazbį́į́']	[ntsézkééz]

D- and l-class disjunct si- perfectives parallel the d/l ∅ conjuncts. Below are 'climb up' (153) and 'get sore muscles' (154).

(153) 1 hasis'na'   (154) 1 ńdasisdoh
       2 hasíní'na'   2 ńdasíníldoh
       3 haas'na'   3 ńdaasdoh
       4 hajis'na'   4 ńdajisdoh
       1d hasii'na'   1d ńdasiildoh
       2d hasooh'na'   2d ńdasoołdoh

These paradigms are exactly like the primary d/l si- perfectives, (144) and (145), except for the third person forms, which are derived in the same manner as 150.3.

154.3 /ná+da#si+í+l+doh/

si pf dele:	[ná+da#si+l+doh]
si syncope:	[ná+da#s+l+doh]
V insert:	[ná+da#is+l+doh]
V assim:	[ná+da#as+l+doh]
ultimately:	[ńdaasdoh]

3.534 +si+í+(X)+[

As is the case in the ni- imperfective, two categories of conjunct si- perfective must be distinguished. Si- perfectives that contain poc. 5 prefixes hwi- 'area' or 'i- 3i are entirely straightforward. Below are (155) 'build a hogan', (156) 'paint', and (157) 'commit a crime' (with preposed 'ádąąh dah).

(155) 1 hosééłbį'   (156) 1 'ashédléézh   (157) 1 hosist'ą́
       2 hosíníłbį'   2 'ahínídléézh   2 hosínít'ą́
       3 hasbį'   3 'azhdléézh   3 hast'ą́
       4 hojisbį'   4 'ajizhdléézh   4 hojist'ą́
       1d hosiilbį'   1d 'ashiidléézh   1d hosiit'ą́
       2d hosoołbį'   2d 'ashoodléézh   2d hosooht'ą́

These behave like other ∅/ł and d/l si- perfectives. Note that in these third person forms no long vowel is present. Vowel insertion cannot apply since there is still a vowel in conjunct position after si- syncope.

     156.3/'i+si+í+dlééžh/ 157.3/hwi+si+í+d+'ą́/

si pf dele: ['i+si+dlééžh]   [hwi+si+d+'ą́]

si syncope: ['i+s+dlééžh]   [hwi+s+d+'ą́]

s voic: ['i+z+dlééžh]

delab: [ho+s+d+'ą́]

ultimately: ['ažhdlééžh]   [hast'ą́]

Agentive passive si- perfectives have third person forms just like those in (155)-(157).

(158) a. bi'disdloh 'he was roped'

   b. nabi'dis'nii' 'they were distributed'

   c. bi'dishgąsh 'he was witched'

     161c/bi+'i+di+si+í+d+ł+gąsh/

si pf dele: [bi+'i+di+si+d+ł+gąsh]

si syncope: [bi+'i+di+s+d+ł+gąsh]

ultimately: [bi'dishgąsh]

Thus, si- perfective agentive passives undergo no readjustment rule when di- 'agentive' is next to si-. This is in contrast to ni- imperfective and perfective agentives which inexplicably undergo the ni- replacement readjustment rule (see 3.123 and 3.525).

When si- perfective is preceded by an aspect prefix from pos. 6 such as hi- 'seriative', di- 'inceptive', or ni- 'terminative', the result is the most complex paradigm in the Navajo verb mode system. Verbs of this kind are illustrated below by ∅- and ł-class verbs (159) 'steal it' and (160) 'make a fence' and by d- and l-class verbs (161) 'start to hop' and (162) 'strain, make an effort'.

(159) 1 né'įį'
2 niní'įį'
3 yineez'įį'
4 jineez'įį'
1d neet'įį'
2d noo'įį'

(160) 1 'adéłt'i'
2 'adíníłt'i'
3 'adeest'i'
4 'azhdeest'i'
1d 'adeelt'i'
2d 'adoołt'i'

(161) 1 hidéshcha'
2 hidínícha'
3 hideeshcha'
4 hizhdeeshcha'
1d hideecha'
2d hidoohcha'

(162) 1 désdzil
2 díníldzil
3 deesdzil
4 jideesdzil
1d deeldzil
2d doołdzil

These aspect+si paradigms are unusual because of 1) the disappearance of si- in the first and second singular and dual forms; 2) the ee- vowel in the zero environment and 1d forms; and 3) the é- in the 1sg of the d/l class verbs. None of these facts can be accounted for by particularly natural phonological rules. In 4.103 I will discuss several kinds of variation in the use of aspect+si verbs.

Si- deletes whenever it is preceded by an aspect prefix and is followed by a subject pronoun, i.e. when it is <u>not</u> in zero environment. We call this morphologically marked rule <u>si- deletion</u>.

(163r) si → ∅ / ASP+___+í+X+[

This rule is ordered before the two perfective deletion rules.

The ee- vowels pose a problem once again. Thus far we have seen ee- occurring in +___+sh where ghi- has become ghe- (in the progressive and conjunct d/l ghi- perfective) and in ASP+___+⊏ where ghe- replaces the ni- modal prefix (in the ni- imperfective and conjunct d/l ni- perfective. Here we find ee- in ASP+___+s+ and, more surprisingly, in ASP+___+iid. There is no obvious parallel in these four environments, and I handle these aspect+si alternations simply by adding two readjustment rules. For the ee- in zero environment I write a <u>ghe- insertion</u> rule that adds ghe- and truncates si- to s- in zero environment.

(164r) ASP+si+⊏ → ASP+ghe+s+⊏

For the ld forms I add a <u>ld í- lowering</u> rule that lowers í- to é- after an aspect prefix and before iid, i.e. <u>after</u> si- has been déleted by 163r.

(165r) í → é / ASP+___+iid

The é- in the 1sg of the d/l aspect+si verbs is even more obscure. One would expect that rule 102r, perfective deletion, would have eliminated the underlying í- prefix, e.g. *disdzil or *hidishcha'. The é- that is present is possibly analogical with the é- derived by rule 137r, í- lowering, that occurs in the 1sg of ∅/ł si- perfectives, e.g. ségan. Tentatively, I will account for the unexpected é- by adding a condition to the perfective deletion rule.

(102r) í → ∅ / ___(sh)+$\{^d_1\}$+STEM

condition: ASP+___sh+$\{^d_1\}$+STEM

Then the regular í- lowering readjustment (137r) can apply to the í- that has been spared by condition.

These three readjustment rules plus the condition on perfective deletion join with the general perfective and si- perfective readjustment rules to derive the aspect+si verbs. To summarize this complex situation I list the readjustment rules that affect aspect+si in their order of application.

(137r) í- lowering

(163r) si- deletion

(102r) perfective deletion

(138r) si- perfective deletion

(164r) ghe- insertion

(139r) si- syncope

(140r) s- voicing

(165r) ld í- lowering

(103r) sh- deletion

(104r) oh- reduction

The ∅/ɨ 1sg forms, 159.1 and 160.1, require í- lowering, si- deletion, and sh- deletion while the d/l 1sg forms, 161.1 and 162.1, take í- lowering and si- deletion. (Perfective deletion is blocked by condition.)

	159.1/ni+si+í+sh+'į́į'/	161.1/hi+di+si+í+sh+d+cha'/
í lower:	[ni+si+é+sh+'į́į']	[hi+di+si+é+sh+d+cha']
si dele:	[ni+é+sh+'į́į']	[hi+di+é+sh+d+cha']
sh dele:	[ni+é+'į́į']	
V dele:	[n+é+'į́į']	[hi+d+é+sh+d+cha']
ultimately:	[né'į́į']	[hidéshcha']

The 2sg forms delete the si- modal prefix and then proceed as other si- perfective 2sg verbs.

	160.2/'i+di+si+í+ni+ɨ+t'i'/	161.2/di+si+í+ni+l+dzil/
si dele:	['i+di+í+ni+ɨ+t'i']	[di+í+ni+l+dzil]
V dele:	['i+d+í+ni+ɨ+t'i']	[d+í+ni+l+dzil]
tone assim:	['i+d+í+ní+ɨ+t'i']	[d+í+ní+l+dzil]
ultimately:	['adíníɨt'i']	[díníldzil]

The third and fourth person forms do not delete si- because the pronoun slot is empty. Instead they undergo ghe- insertion.

159.4/ji+ni+si+í+'įį'/   161.3/hi+di+si+í+d+cha'/

si pf dele:	[ji+ni+si+'įį']	[hi+di+si+d+cha']
ghe insert:	[ji+ni+ghe+s+'įį']	[hi+di+ghe+s+d+cha']
s voic:	[ji+ni+ghe+z+'įį']	_____
gh dele:	[ji+ni+e+z+'įį']	[hi+di+e+s+d+cha']
V assim:	[ji+ne+e+z+'įį']	[hi+de+e+s+d+cha']
ultimately:	[jineez'įį']	[hideeshcha']

The first duals are affected by both si- deletion and by ld í-lowering.

159.1d/ni+si+í+iid+'įį'/   162.1d/di+si+í+iid+l+dzil/

si dele:	[ni+í+iid+'įį']	[di+í+iid+l+dzil]
ld í- lower:	[ni+é+iid+'įį']	[di+é+iid+l+dzil]
tone lower:	[ni+e+iid+'įį']	[di+e+iid+l+dzil]
V assim:	[ne+e+eed+'įį']	[de+e+eed+l+dzil]
V degem:	[ne+ed+'įį']	[de+ed+l+dzil]
ultimately:	[neet'įį']	[deeldzil]

The 2d forms delete the si- modal prefix and proceed as other perfective 2d verbs.

160.2d/'i+di+si+í+oh+ł+t'i'/   161.2d/hi+di+si+í+oh+d+cha'/

si dele:	['i+di+í+oh+ł+t'i']	[hi+di+í+oh+d+cha']
oh reduc:	['i+di+í+o+ł+t'i']	_____
V dele:	['i+d+í+o+ł+t'i']	[hi+d+í+oh+d+cha']
tone lower:	['i+d+i+o+ł+t'i']	[hi+d+i+oh+d+cha']
V assim:	['i+d+o+o+ł+t'i']	[hi+d+o+oh+d+cha']
ultimately:	['adoołt'i']	[hidoohcha']

It should be noted that agentive passives in the si- perfective that contain pos. 6 aspect prefixes pattern like other third person aspect+si verbs, e.g. bi'dineest'į́į́' 'he was stolen'.

/bi+'i+di+ni+si+í+d+'į́į́'/

si pf dele: [bi+'i+di+ni+si+d+'į́į́']

ghe insert: [bi+'i+di+ni+ghe+s+d+'į́į́']

ultimately: [bidi'neest'į́į́']

There are certain pos. 6 aspect prefixes such as +i+ aspect, jii- 'emotion', and dzi- 'streak' that are exempt from the si- deletion rule and ghe- insertion rules. In (166) 'start it (a car)' di- 'inceptive' is followed by a +i+ prefix; in (167) 'unroll it' the unusual o- imperfective takes some +i+ prefix in the perfective; in (168) 'treat him with kindness' the unusual jii- 'emotion' prefix is next to si-.

(166) 1 diséłts'ą́ą́'   (167) 1 neiséłtah   (168) 1 jiiséba'
      2 disíníłts'ą́ą́'   2 neisíníłtah   2 jisíníba'
      3 yidiists'ą́ą́'   3 nayoostah   3 joozba'
      4 jidiists'ą́ą́'   4 njoostah   4 jijoozba'
      1d disiilts'ą́ą́'   1d neisiiltah   1d jisiiba'
      2d disoołts'ą́ą́'   2d neisoołtah   2d jisooba'

In (166) the +i+ is detected overtly in zero environment and indirectly by the non-occurrence of si- deletion and ghe- insertion. The i:oo alternation in (167) and (168) is irregular, an interesting parallel between two idiosyncratic prefixes.

Si- perfectives with dzi- 'streak' are rare but extremely interesting phonologically. 'Streak around' (169) is one such verb. (The underlying dzi- 'streak' prefix is clearly visible in the imperfective mode, njisht'ih 1, ndzit'ih 3.)

(169) 1 neisét'i

2 neisínít'i

3 neizt'i

4 neijizt'i ∿ neidzizt'i

1d neisiit'i

2d neisoot'i

Si- has not been deleted and the dzi- prefix has been reduced to i- by a rule very similar to rule II-94, j- deletion. Apparently s- causes the disappearance of dz-. This can be accounted for by revising j-deletion to a <u>strident deletion</u> rule that deletes a non-continuant coronal strident (j- or dz-) when it is followed by a coronal strident that agrees with it in anteriority.

$$(\text{II-94}) \quad \begin{bmatrix} +\text{cor} \\ \alpha\text{ant} \\ -\text{cnt} \\ +\text{str} \end{bmatrix} \rightarrow \emptyset \ / \ \underline{\quad} \ \text{i}+ \begin{bmatrix} +\text{cor} \\ \alpha\text{ant} \\ +\text{str} \end{bmatrix}$$

169.1/na#dzi+si+í+sh+t'i/   169.3/na#dzi+si+í+t'i/

<u>si pf dele</u>:	_____	[na#dzi+si+t'i]
<u>si syncope</u>:	_____	[na#dzi+s+t'i]
<u>s voic</u>:	_____	[na#dzi+z+t'i]
<u>sh dele</u>:	[na#dzi+si+é+t'i]	_____
<u>V dele</u>:	[na#dzi+s+é+t'i]	_____
<u>strid dele</u>:	[na#i+s+é+t'i]	[na#i+z+t'i]
<u>ultimately</u>:	[neisét'i]	[neizt'i]

The fourth person form in this paradigm is significant because it provides proof for my contention that rule II-83, progressive strident assimilation, is a separate and earlier rule than rule II-81, regressive strident assimilation. (See 2.75.) Progressive strident assimilation applies early, converting dz- to j- as in other j- deletion forms. Then

after j- is deleted by strident deletion, some speakers convert j- back
to dz- by the regressive strident assimilation rule.

168.4 /na#ji+dzi+si+í+t'i/

pg strid assim:	[na#ji+ji+z+t'i]
strid dele:	[na#i+ji+z+t'i]
reg strid assim:	([na#i+dz+z+t'i])
ultimately:	[neidzizt'i] ∿ [neijizt'i]

These four non-si deleting, non-ghe inserting pos. 6 prefixes may
be exempted from the two readjustment rules by condition. On the other
hand, it may be that they all contain a +i+ at the time si- deletion
and ghe- insertion apply and are passed over on purely phonological
grounds.

The extreme complexity of this analysis of the aspect+si verbs
suggests that generalizations are being missed. However, it is very
doubtful that such an array of complex changes can be reduced to
entirely well motivated phonological rules. In a sense, aspect+si
is the central problem in the phonology of the Navajo verb modes. At
this point what is most suspect in the analysis of the perfectives is
compounded by the peculiar influence the aspect prefix exerts on si-.
Our only recourse is to tinker with the underlying forms by means of
readjustment rules that have little phonological justification and no
wider role in the grammar. Most dramatically, aspect+si illustrates the
territory in Navajo phonology that resists conventional synchronic analysis.

3.535 Si- perfective summary

The si- perfective stands apart from the other two perfective modes
in several respects. In si- perfective the í- perfective prefix is not
present in zero environment of ∅/ł verbs. The si- modal prefix is

truncated to s- in zero environment when preceded by something or when word initial and followed by a d- classifier. S- becomes z- when next to stem. The perfective morpheme becomes é- in ∅/ɨ 1sg. The higly marked aspect+si paradigms delete si- in non-zero environment, insert ghe- in zero environment, and lower í- to é- in the first dual. At present most of these changes are beyond a motivated synchronic explanation.

3.54 Perfective Summary

In Table 4 I present an ordered summary of the readjustment and restricted phonological rules that have been formulated in this analysis of the three perfectives. In the center column are rules that apply to all forms of each perfective. In the left column are rules that are confined to ∅/ɨ-class verbs and in the right are those that apply to l/d forms.

Three generalizations about the perfectives are apparent from Table 4: 1) the three rules that are common to all three perfectives, perfective deletion and the two pronoun readjustments, reflect the basic classifier subdivision in the perfectives; 2) the ghi- and ni- perfectives, which historically are innovations, are derived exactly like progressives and ni- imperfectives in forms where the perfective prefix has been deleted. This supports the suggestion that the ghi- and ni- perfectives are compounds of the ghi- and ni- modal prefix plus a separate perfective prefix; 3) the si- perfective reflects its maverick and archaic position in the perfective system in the seven unusual readjustment rules that it requires.

Finally, it must be mentioned that Krauss (personal communication) has offered a stimulating alternative analysis to that presented above. He suggests that the í- prefix is not a separate perfective morpheme but is a reflex of his hypothesized proto-Athapaskan-Eyak y-component (Krauss,

TABLE 4
PERFECTIVE RULE SUMMARY

∅/±	All	d/1
	ghi- perfective	
		(102r) perfective deletion
		(70r) gho readjustment
		(75r) ghe readjustment
(103r) sh- deletion		
(104r) oh- reduction		
	ni- perfective	
		(102r) perfective deletion
		(24r) dummy obj insertion
		(27r) ni-drop
		(33r) ni- replacement
(103r) sh- deletion		
(104r) oh- reduction		
	(123) perfective n- deletion	
	si- perfective	
	(137r) í- lowering	
	(163r) si- deletion	
		(102r) perfective deletion
(138r) si- perfective deletion		
	(164r) ghe insertion	
	(139r) si- syncope	
(140) s- voicing		
	(165) ld í- lowering	
(103r) sh- deletion		
(104r) oh- reduction		

1969). In Eyak the y-component accounts for də:di, ɫə:ɬi alternations in the classifiers. Krauss posits that the í- in the ∅/ɫ perfectives in Navajo is the y-component which appears to the left of the ɫ- classifier in <u>subject pronoun position</u> and to the right of d- or l- classifier (which would be the historical equivalent of Eyak də → di, ɫə → ɬi). Of course, a sh- deletion rule is still necessary that states that sh- and í- are incompatible in ∅/ɫ-class verbs. Hence,

$$\begin{Bmatrix} ghi \\ ni \\ si \end{Bmatrix} + \begin{matrix} sh \\ í \end{matrix} + (ɫ)STEM \rightarrow \begin{Bmatrix} ghi \\ ni \\ si \end{Bmatrix} + í + (ɫ)STEM \quad \text{but,}$$

$$\begin{Bmatrix} ghi \\ ni \\ si \end{Bmatrix} + sh + \{^d_l\} + í + STEM \rightarrow \begin{Bmatrix} ghi \\ ni \\ si \end{Bmatrix} + sh + \{^d_l\} + STEM.$$

Krauss also notes that the fact that the si- perfective is low in tone in all zero environment forms is consistent with the y-component analysis in that in PAE it is the case that the y-component is not operative in si- perfective zero environment.

In terms of a synchronic analysis of the Navajo perfective Krauss' y-component analysis would simplify the prefix complex by eliminating the perfective slot. Still, the basic perfective subdivision rules, sh-deletion and some í- metathesis rule, would be no more well motivated phonologically than our sh- deletion and perfective deletion rules. In addition, since the í- in 2sg forms in all the perfectives occurs to the <u>left</u> of the ni- subject pronoun, some other readjustment would be needed. However, because the only high tone í- in the d/l perfectives is in 2sg, and because we have seen that a curious rule, 123, perfective n- deletion operates in the ni- perfective in the 2sg, there could be advantages to explaining perfective 2sg by some special constraint on the í- segment. Also, the y-component analysis leaves the n- of Hupa and Mattole perfectives unaccounted for.

Krauss' y-component analysis is intriguing and deserves further consideration. In particular this illustrates that the perfectives direct the linguist to other Athapaskan languages for clues to what are doubtlessly processes that have been obscured by time.

3.55 Perfective Choice and Perfective Da- Shift

Before concluding this study of the phonology of the perfectives, it is appropriate to mention some of the derivational relationships that hold between the perfective mode and the derivational prefix system. In particular we will look at the ways in which da- plural interacts with adverbial, thematic, and aspectual prefixes and the perfective prefix, a phenomenon that has potential for revealing some of the deeper derivational properties in the Navajo verb.

The degree to which the perfective mode is determined or "chosen" by derivational prefixes in pos. 1, 5, and 6 has received only brief mention in the Navajo literature. Hoijer has devoted some attention to the topic (1948:252-253; SH:97-99).

It should be pointed out that I am side-stepping two important prior questions. It is not clear how perfectives are chosen in primary verbs, i.e. when there are no derivational prefixes and one can only look to the semantics of the stem, the shape of the stem, and the classifier. Also, I offer no explanation why one derivational prefix, ha- 'up and out', which is generally a ghi- perfective chooser, can sometimes take contrastive ghi- and si- perfectives, cf. 'a'aan bii'déé' háálbą́ą́z 'I drove up out of the hole' and dził bąąh hasélbą́ą́z 'I drove up onto the mountain' where the ghi- perfective form indicates an action abruptly completed and the si- perfective an action completed over a period of time resulting in a durative state. It is uncertain why only ha- 'up and out' of the derivational prefixes can appear with an alternant perfective.

The perfective prefix can be predicted with considerable consistency when only one derivational prefix appears with a classifier and stem. In (170) are some of the more conspicuous "perfective choosers". Prefix position is given in parenthesis.

(170) 1. Si- perfective choosers

    a. (6) di- 'inceptive'   deezbaa'   'he went to war'
    b. (1) na- 'about'   nisénii'   'I distributed them'
    c. (1) ha- 'upward'   hashínílzhee'   'you hunted'
    d. (6) ni- 'terminative'   neesk'oł   'he blinked'

2. Ghi- perfective choosers

    a. (1) 'i- 'away'   yóó' ayíídéél   'he threw it away'
    b. (1) na- 'down'   néínine'   'you dropped it'
    c. (1) ha- 'up and out'   háágeed   'I dug it up'
    d. (1) hada- 'down'   hadáágo'   'I fell down'

3. Ni- perfective choosers

    a. (1) ch'í- 'but'   ch'íníłbą́ą́z   'he drove it out'
    b. (1) k'í- 'apart'   k'íiních'iizh   'he sawed it in two'
    c. (1) ni- 'end'   niníłbą́ą́z   'I parked it'
    d. (1) na- 'across'   naní'ą́   'it extended across'
    e. (1) bigha- 'separate'   bighanisht'ą́   'I took it away from him'

Perfective choice is a useful means of deciphering prefixes; e.g., na- 'about', na- 'down', and na- 'across' are phonetically identical, but reveal their distinctiveness by their perfective prefix.

A more complex problem is to determine the basis for perfective selection when a derivational prefix occurs with more than one perfective prefix. Certain derivational prefixes such as bí- 'against' and dzi- 'streak' seem to be neutral to perfective choice. In some verbs bí- 'against' appears with a ghi- perfective, bééłne' 'I pounded it off'. In others it appears with a ni- perfective bíníłkáá' 'I tracked it'. With na- 'about' it takes a si- perfective, nabísínighil 'you pushed it about'. Likewise, when dzi- 'streak' appears with 'i- 'away' as in 'adzíítáál 'I kicked it', it has a ghi- perfective. When it occurs with ni- 'end' as in yił nizníłne' 'he stoned him', it has a ni- perfective; and with na- 'about' it takes a si- perfective, neidzizt'i 'he streaked around'. Prefixes that are neutral to perfective choice either defer perfective selection to another prefix or select the perfective by the semantics of the stem.

A still more complex problem is to determine how perfective gets chosen when two perfective choosers cooccur. It is possible that in these cases there is a hierarchy of perfective choice. For example, ni- 'terminative' normally chooses si- perfective. But in combination with bigha- 'separate' in bighaniníłdee' 'I sifted it' bigha- has dominated in choosing a ni- perfective. This suggests that ni- is a weaker determiner of perfectives than is bigha-. Yet there is more to this problem than listing the combinations of prefixes and finding a hierarchy. For example, is the di- prefix that cooccurs with +i+ and chooses si- perfective in diséłts'aa' 'I started it (the car)' the same as the di- that appears with +i+ and selects ghi- perfective in ntsídiikééz 'I started to think about it'? Or in hadinish'íí' 'I discovered him' is this ha- 'upward' and di- 'inceptive' which have deferred perfective choice to stem semantics in the selection of a ni- perfective?

A thorough study of perfective choice requires 1) a theory of stem semantics and perfective choice; 2) a study of perfectives with combinations of derivational prefixes that takes into account thematic classifiers, prepounded postpositions and adverbials, and stem variation. Perfective choice is also an important topic for comparative research. There is striking correlation between the perfective choice properties of Hupa adverbial prefixes and those in Navajo (Golla, 1970: 121-123).

One process that offers some insight into the process of perfective choice as well as into some of the deeper derivational properties of the verb is the behavior of da- plural in the perfectives. In certain verbs da- plural triggers a shift from ni- or ghi- perfective to si- perfective. This phenomenon, to our knowledge, has received no previous attention in Navajo nor in any other Athapaskan language. Ironically, the only published data on da- shift that I know of is more than 60 years old. The paradigm section of the Franciscan Fathers' dictionary contains several clear examples of the process (1912b:13-19).

The appearance of this da- shift in the perfective is far more nebulous than the progressive da- shift. Numerous syntactic and semantic questions about da- plural and the perfectives remain unexplored. Also, as I will show in 4.104, there is considerable variation in the use of da- shift which complicates a statement of the conditions of the process. Here I try to present what appears to be the more conservative trend in the use of da- and perfective, or as one Navajo puts it, the "plus old" forms.

I first survey verbs that regularly (if not obligatorily) shift to si- perfective when da- is inserted into the verb. Then I look at some non-occurring and ambivalent environments for the shift. Then I attempt to summarize some of the implications of the data on da- shift for the study of word formation in the verb.

The most obligatory environment for da- shift is when a ni- or ghi- perfective contains one of the perfective choosing prefixes from 170.2 or 3. Below I give the perfective choosing prefix in a singular and then a plural verb.[28]

(171) a. ch'íiníłtį́   'he carried out an animate object'
         ch'ídeistį́   'they pl carried out an animate object'
     b. ch'íinílá   'he carried out a rope-like object'
         ch'ídeizlá   'they pl carried out a rope-like object'
     c. ch'íniidlóóz   'we dpl led it out'
         ch'ídasiidlóóz   'we pl led it out'
     d. k'íiních'iizh   'he sawed it apart'
         k'ídeizhch'iizh   'they pl sawed it apart'
     e. k'íiníłdááá   'he pulled it in two'
         k'ídeisdlááá   'they pl pulled it in two'
     f. ninoołbą́ą́z   'you dpl parked it'
         ndasoołbą́ą́z   'you pl parked it'
     g. yóó' 'ayíílóóz   'he led it off'
         yóó' 'adeizlóóz   'they pl led it off'
     h. 'iidzíítáál   'he kicked it'
         'adeidziztáál   'they pl kicked it'
     i. hayííłbą́ą́z   'he drove it up'
         hadeisbą́ą́z   'they pl drove it up'
     j. haiicha   'we dpl cried out'
         hadasiicha   'we pl cried out'

k. hadayíiłgo' 'he made him fall down'

   hadadeisgo' 'they made him fall down'

In Chapter Four I discuss variation in these forms. In many cases a non-shifted plural is allowable, e.g. k'ídeiníłdláád for 171e, but the preference is almost always for the shifted perfective.

Yet da- shift is not restricted to verbs with perfective choosing adverbial prefixes. Verbs with prefixes that are neutral to perfective choice such as bí- 'against' may also undergo the da- shift.

(172) a. yíiníłkáá' 'he tracked it'

   yídeiskáá' 'they pl tracked it'

   b. yíiłne' 'he pounded it off'

   yídeisne' 'they pl pounded it off'

D- and l-class ghi- perfectives that contain no perfective choosing adverbial prefix do not undergo a shift to the si- perfective in the plural. However, if a perfective choosing prefix occurs with a d- or l-class stem, as in 173c-f, da- shift does take place.

(173) a. yoolghal   'he ate meat'
      dayoolghal   'they pl ate meat'
      *deisghal

   b. yooldéél   'he ate pl objects'
      dayooldéél   'they pl ate pl objects'
      *deisdéél

   c. ninii'na'   'we dpl arrived crawling'
      ndasii'na'   'we pl arrived crawling'

   d. ch'ídeeldlo'   'he smiled'
      ch'ídadeesdlo' 'they pl smiled'

   e. hadoolghaazh   'he shouted out'
      hadadeeshghaazh 'they pl cried out'

    f. ch'éldloozh   'he trotted out'

       ch'ídaashdloozh 'they trotted out'

Another environment in which da- shift does not occur is in verbs that contain the +i+ aspect prefix.

(174) a. yayiiką́   'he spilled it'

        yadeiiką́   'they pl spilled it'

       *yadeiiską́

    b. yinii+doi   'he warmed it up'

       deinii+doi   'they pl warmed it up'

      *deiniisdoi

    c. yik'iyiigeed   'he covered it'

       yik'idayiigeed 'they pl covered it'

      *yik'idayiizgeed

Verbs with thematic prefixes such as hasht'e- 'ready', 'í- 'thus', 'i- 3i, 'atí- 'harm' and hwi- 'area' never seem to shift to a si-perfective.

(175) a. 'íit'įįd   'we dpl acted thus'

       'ádeiit'įįd   'we pl acted thus'

      *'ádasiit'įįd

    b. hasht'eiilyaa   'we dpl got it ready'

       hasht'edeiilyaa 'we pl got it ready'

      *hasht'edasiilyaa

    c. 'atíyiilaa   'he injured him'

       'atídayiilaa   'they pl injured him'

      *'atídayiizlaa

    d. hóótáál   'he sang'

       dahóótáál   'they pl sang'

      *dahaztáál

e. 'oolzhiizh   'he danced'
   da'oolzhiizh   'they pl danced'
   *da'eeshzhiizh

It is generally the case that intransitive primary ghi- perfectives with ∅ classifier do not shift to the si- perfective as in 176a and b. However, intransitive primary ni- perfectives such as 176c and d can appear with either ni- or si- perfective. In the latter case, ni- and si- are not variants but in mode contrast, as indicated in the translations given below.

(176) a. yícha   'he cried'
         dáácha   'they pl cried'
         *daazhcha
      b. yíchxǫ'   'it was ruined'
         dááchxǫ'   'they pl were ruined'
         *daazhchxǫ'
      c. yít'a'   'he arrived flying'
         deít'a'   'they pl arrived flying'
         daazt'a'   'they pl flew'
      d. yí'na'   'he arrived crawling'
         deí'na'   'they pl arrived crawling'
         daas'na'   'they pl crawled'

By far the most difficult environment in which to predict da- shift is in primary transitive ghi- perfectives with ∅ or ł- classifier. Here speakers at times report that both shifted and non-shifted forms are possible. Others are preferred as either shifted or non-shifted plurals, but the degree of preference is variable. In (177) I list verbs that are preferred with shifted plurals and in (178) those that are preferred with non-shifted plurals. (Unacceptable forms have * and marginally acceptable have?.)

(177) a. łeeh yiyííłtį 'he buried him'
      łeeh deistį 'they pl buried him'
      *łeeh dayííłtį

   b. yaa yiníłtį 'he gave him an animate object'
      yaa deistį 'they pl gave him an animate object'
      ?yaa deiníłtį

   c. yiníłt'a' 'he arrived flying it'
      deist'a' 'they pl arrived flying it'
      ?deiníłt'a'

   d. yiníłóóz 'he led it'
      deizłóóz 'they pl led it'
      ?deiníłóóz

(178) a. yiyíínizh 'he plucked it'
      dayíínizh 'they pl plucked it'
      ?deizhnizh

   b. yiyííghą́ą́' 'he killed them'
      dayííghą́ą́' 'they pl killed them'
      *deizghą́ą́'

   c. yiyííłchxǫ' 'he ruined it'
      dayííłchxǫ' 'they pl ruined it'
      ?deishchxǫ'

   d. yiyííłchozh 'he ate greens'
      dayííłchozh 'they pl ate greens'
      *deishchozh

This is only a preliminary investigation of the distribution of perfective da- shifts. Further research should focus on the ways in which da- shift interacts with syntactic constraints on plural marking. Brief investigation has yielded no evidence of interaction between perfective da- shift and noun ranking.[29]

Even though our knowledge of perfective da- shift is incomplete, several interesting patterns can be observed. Most conspicuously, the adverbial prefixes that regularly choose the ni- and ghi- perfective also regularly undergo the da- shift. D- and l-class verbs that shift to si- perfective must have a perfective choosing adverbial prefix (as in 173c-f). On the other hand thematic prefixes such as hwi- 'area' and 'i- 3i as illustrated in (175) retain their perfective with da-. This suggests that there is a looser, more secondary derivational relationship between the productive adverbial prefixes and the perfective mode than with the derivational prefixes that are thematized to stems. In a theory of Navajo word formation, the phenomena of perfective choice and da- shift might be explainable by assuming that deep si- perfectives underlie stems such as 'carry an animate object': /si+ɫ+tį́/. If a ha- 'up and out' prefix cooccurs with this base, ghi- perfective is chosen in place of si-: /ha#ghi+ɫ+tį́/. If a ch'í- 'out' prefix coocurs with it, ni- perfective is chosen: /ch'í#ni+ɫ+tį́/. If da- plural is inserted into either of these two derived bases, the perfective simply remains si-. From this point of view then, non-occurring da- shifts as in (175) can be explained by the presence of an underlying ghi- perfective. Such information then as perfective choice and perfective da- shift might be stated as general rules of word formation.

Several important questions must be resolved before such an approach to the organization of the verb might be taken. It is not certain how da- shift interacts with transitivity. The trend seems to be that intransitive ∅ and l-class verbs do not shift to si- perfective unless they are preceded by a perfective chooser. Also, it is not clear how da- shift might be handled in verbs such as in (172) that are neutral to perfective choice. Can it be said that a si- perfective underlies these verbs as well? Also, a clearer notion of the influence of the stem semantics on perfective might clarify the different patterns in da- shift in (172) and (178). Perhaps a verb like 177b is an underlying si- perfective that selects ni- perfective in the context of 'terminated motion' and retains si- with da-.

Because the proto-Athapaskan perfective is si-, there is considerable comparative appeal to the suggestion that perfective choosing, da- shifting verbs are underlying si- perfectives. This is an urgent issue for comparative research. In Western Apache, where da- is a non-singular, i.e. it is inserted in duals as well as in plurals, there is some evidence for perfective da- shift; cf. 'áyíílaa 'he made it', 'ách'ílaa 'he (4) made it' and 'ádai̱zlaa 'they dpl/pl made it', 'ádaats'i̱zlaa 'they (4) dpl/pl made it' (Perry, 1972:95). Interestingly 'make' does not shift with da- in Navajo.

Phonologically, da- shifted verbs are straightforward. They are obtained like other si- perfectives.

3.6 The Phonology of Hi- 'Seriative' and Si- 'Destruct'

In this chapter I have purposely made little reference to verbs with the pos. 6 prefix hi- 'seriative' because of the highly restricted phonological rules this prefix undergoes.[30] Before concluding this chapter I examine the unusual set of rules that apply to hi-. In addition, I demonstrate a surprising fact: two of the restricted rules that apply to hi- also apply to a separate prefix, si- 'destruct', which appears in just one verb base, 'kill it'. In this section I present the 'regular' hi- and si- rules. In 4.108 and 4.109 variation in the application of these rules will be examined.

I know of no systematic account of hi- 'seriative' and its allomorphs in the Navajo literature. Reichard attempted to isolate some of its properties, but her analysis introduces much confusion to the problem. She notes,

> In some instances the position of hi- is clear and generally
> agreed upon, but speakers do not agree about the forms which
> combine with yi-, si-, and the like, and they give varying
> forms. In fact, the differentiation of the repetitive aspects
> is secured from old men rather than from today's speakers.
> The latter may realize and use some of the forms, but do not
> distinguish meanings and often even confuse the repetitives
> with the cessatives [i.e. +i+ verbs]. These remarks are
> illustrated by many of Morgan's mixed paradigms (1951:263).

The chief problem with Reichard's analysis of hi- is her assumption that there is a _separate_ repetitive prefix, yi-, which she glossed as 'repetitive action' (while hi- was glossed as 'move repeatedly'). She comments that "both repetitive prefixes are composed of unstable sounds, and they have many overlapping forms, both with each other and with other combinations of yi- prefixes. They are therefore considered separately to differentiate the changes occurring with them, and to indicate the effects of their respective positions" (1951:250).

Reichard's two repetitive prefixes, hi- and yi-, are explainable as allomorphs of a single hi- prefix. Although there is quite a bit of variation in the use of hi- and its allomorphs because the phonological rules involved are highly marked, it is clear that Reichard's remarks about "overlapping forms" and "Morgan's mixed paradigms" are motivated by her failure to link the hi- and yi- prefixes.

In the discussion of the # disjunct boundary in 2.6 we formulated a rule, II-13, that deletes the h- of the hi- prefix when it is preceded by a conjunct prefix. Seriative h- deletion is operative in third and fourth person forms of verbs where hi- is the lone derivational prefix or where hi- is preceded by a disjunct prefix as in imperfectives for (179) 'break them off one after the other', (180) 'break it up' and in the iterative for (181) 'break it up'.

(179)	1 heshtííh[31]	(180)	1 nihishtííh	(181)	1 nináháshtih
	2 hítííh		2 nihítííh		2 nináhítih
	3 yiyiitííh		3 niyiitííh		3 nináyiitih
	4 jiitííh		4 njiitííh		4 ninájiitih
	1d hiitííh		1d nihiitííh		1d nináhiitih
	2d hohtííh		2d nihohtííh		2d nináhóhtih

These verbs are just like other conjunct ∅ imperfectives and conjunct iteratives in all forms but the third and fourth persons. Here the yi- and ji- prefixes trigger rule II-13, seriative h- deletion.

180.3/ni#yi+hi+tííh/   181.4/ni+ná#ji+hi+tih/

ser h dele:	[ni#yi+i+tííh]	[ni+ná#ji+i+tih]
ultimately:	[niyiitííh]	[ninájiitih]

The yiyii- prefix in 182.3 is due to the operation of rule 19, yi- doubling, after h- has been deleted.

179.3/yi+hi+tííh/

ser h dele:	[yi+i+tííh]
yi doubl:	[yi+yi+i+tííh]
ultimately:	[yiyiitííh]

If we look more closely at the hi- 'seriative' verbs, we find paradigms such as the optative of disjunct verbs where hi- alternates

with y-. Below are the optatives for 'break it up' (182) and 'tie it
to it' (183).

(182) 1 nihóshtih   (183) 1 bíhóshtɬ'óóɬ
      2 nihóótih   2 bíhóóɬtɬ'óóɬ
      3 niiyótih   3 yíiyóɬtɬ'óóɬ
      4 njiyótih   4 bíjiyóɬtɬ'óóɬ
      1d nihootih   1d bíhooltɬ'óóɬ
      2d nihoohtih   2d bíhooɬtɬ'óóɬ

In Reichard's view these would be considered mixed paradigms showing
the two repetitive prefixes. But the appearance of y- is entirely
predictable here and elsewhere. When hi- is followed by a vowel in an
environment where we would expect the seriative h- deletion rule to apply,
i.e. when there is a conjunct prefix preceding hi-, h- becomes y-. Thus,
it appears that rule II-13 applies only when hi- is next to C_o[. If we
make this revision in seriative h- deletion, we can then add an h- glide
rule that converts h- to y- before a vowel and after a conjunct prefix.

(II-13) h → ∅ / +___i+C_o[

(184) h → y / +___V

Rule 184 is ordered after vowel deletion and seriative h- deletion.
In 182.3 and 4 and 183.3 and 4 seriative h- deletion does not apply
because hi- is not adjacent to C_o[. After vowel deletion, h- becomes y-.

182.4/ni#ji+hi+ó+tih/   183.3/yí#yi+hi+ó+ɬ+tɬ'óóɬ/

V dele: [ni#ji+h+ó+tih]   [yí#yi+h+ó+ɬ+tɬ'óóɬ]
h glide: [ni#ji+y+ó+tih]   [yí#yi+y+ó+ɬ+tɬ'óóɬ]
ultimately: [njiyótih]   [yíiyóɬtɬ'óóɬ]

Hi- 'seriative' undergoes still more exotic changes. In the future
mode and in other verbs in which hi- occurs with a di- prefix in pos. 6,

we find hi- alternating with y- in the third and fourth person, but hi- precedes di- while y- follows di-. Below is the future of (185) 'break it up' and various forms from (186) 'hang an animate object up' (with preposed dah).

(185) 1 nihideeshtih   (186) a. hidiishteeh
      2 nihidíítih   b. hidiiłteeh
      3 niidiyootih   c. yidiyiiłteeh
      4 nizhdiyootih   d. hidiiłtį́
     1d nihidiitih   e. yidiyiiłtį́
     2d nihidoohtih   f. ndiyiiłtį́
                                      g. shidiyiiłtį́

I assume that in underlying representation hi- is to the left of di-. If hi+di is preceded by a conjunct prefix such as ji- or a direct object, a +hi+di metathesis rule applies. In the above verbs this metathesis places hi- next to some vowel (oo- in the futures, +i+ in 'hang it up') so that h- glide then applies.

(187) +hi+di → +di+hi

                         185.4/ni#ji+hi+di+ghi+tih/   186c/yi+hi+di+i+ł+teeh/

gho read: [ni#ji+hi+di+gho+tih]   _____

+hi+di metath: [ni#ji+di+hi+gho+tih]   [yi+di+hi+i+ł+teeh]

gh dele: [ni#ji+di+hi+o+tih]   _____

V assim: [ni#ji+di+ho+o+tih]   _____

h glide: [ni#ji+di+yo+o+tih]   [yi+di+yi+i+ł+teeh]

ultimately: [nizhdiyootih]   [yidiyiiłteeh]

This metathesis is most unusual. It is clearly related to the fact that hi- 'seriative' is highly unstable when preceded by a conjunct prefix. Functionally, this metathesis avoids an environment where hi-would be preceded by a conjunct prefix and not be either next to C_0[or a vowel.

Having determined these three rules that affect hi- 'seriative' when it is preceded by a conjunct prefix, it is possible to explain certain verbs that have highly irregular alternations as containing an underlying thematic conjunct prefix plus hi- 'seriative'. Two such verbs are 'beat one's wife' with 'i- 3i (188) and 'plow' with hwi- 'area' given here in its imperfective (189), future (190), and perfective (191) modes.

(188) 1 'iisą́   (189) 1 nahwiishdlaad
       2 'ayízą́   2 nahwiyíɫdlaad
       3 'iizą́   3 nahwiiɫdlaad
       4 'ajizą́   4 nahojiiɫdlaad
       1d 'iidzą́[32]   1d nahwiyiildlaad
       2d 'ayohsą́   2d nahwiyoɫdlaad

(190) 1 nahodiyeeshdlaɫ (191) 1 nahwiyéɫdláád
       2 nahodiyííɫdlaɫ   2 nahwiyíníɫdláád
       3 nahodiyooɫdlaɫ   3 nahwiisdláád
       4 nahozhdiyooɫdlaɫ   4 nahojiisdláád
       1d nahodiyiildlaɫ   1d nahwiyeeldláád
       2d nahodiyooɫdlaɫ   2d nahwiyooɫdláád

These verbs are treated by Reichard as containing a yi- repetitive prefix. Alternatively, I claim that there is an absolutely neutralized hi- prefix here which never appears as such because of the conjunct prefix that is present in all forms. The presence of hi- can be inferred because the set of processes that affects these verbs is identical to those we know are characteristic of hi-.

(188) is explainable if /'i+hi/ is assumed, and the 'plow' paradigms can be derived from a /hwi+hi/ representation. In 188.1, 3, and 4 and 189.1, 3, and 4 seriative h- deletion applies because hi- is next to C_0[.

                188.3/'i+hi+zą́/   189.1/na#hwi+hi+sh+ł+dlaad/

ser h dele: ['i+i+zą́]   [na#hwi+i+sh+ł+dlaad]

ultimately: ['iizą́]   [nahwiishdlaad]

The y- in 188.2 and 2d, 189.2, 1d, and 2d is due to the vowel that occurs to the right of hi-.

                188.2d/'i+hi+oh+zą́/   189.2/na#hwi+hi+ni+ł+dlaad/

V dele: ['i+h+oh+zą́]

ni absorp: [na#hwi+hí+ł+dlaad]

h glide: ['i+y+oh+zą́]   [na#hwi+yí+ł+dlaad]

ultimately: ['ayohsą́]   [nahwiyíłdlaad]

All of the future forms in (190) undergo +hi+di metathesis because of the hwi- conjunct prefix.

                190.4/na#hwi+ji+hi+di+ghi+ł+dlał/

+hi+di metath: [na#hwi+ji+di+hi+gho+ł+dlał]

V assim: [na#hwi+ji+di+ho+o+ł+dlał]

h glide: [na#hwi+ji+di+yo+o+ł+dlał]

ultimately: [nahozhdiyoołdlał]

                190.1d/na#hwi+hi+di+ghi+iid+ł+dlał/

+hi+di metath: [na#hwi+di+hi+ghi+iid+ł+dlał]

V assim:

h glide: [na#hwi+di+yi+i+iid+ł+dlał]

ultimately: [nahodiyiildlał]

The aspect+si perfective of 'plow' deserves an award for being the most complex Navajo verb paradigm. Here hi- triggers the usual aspect+si readjustment rules and then h- turns to y- next to a vowel in 191.1, 2, 1d, and 2d and deletes next to s- in 3 and 4.

    191.1/na#hwi+hi+si+í+sh+ɫ+dláád/ 191.1d/na#hwi+hi+si+í+iid+ɫ+dláád/

í lower:	[na#hwi+hi+si+é+sh+ɫ+dláád]	
si dele:	[na#hwi+hi+é+sh+ɫ+dláád]	[na#hwi+hi+í+iid+ɫ+dláád]
1d í lower:		[na#hwi+hi+é+iid+ɫ+dláád]
sh dele:	[na#hwi+hi+é+ɫ+dláád]	
h glide:	[na#hwi+y+é+ɫ+dláád]	[na#hwi+y+e+iid+ɫ+dláád]
ultimately:	[nahwiyéɫdláád]	[nahwiyeeldláád]

    191.3/na#hwi+hi+si+í+ɫ+dláád/

si pf dele:	[na#hwi+hi+si+ɫ+dláád]
si syncope:	[na#hwi+hi+s+ɫ+dláád]
ser h dele:	[na#hwi+i+s+ɫ+dláád]
ultimately:	[nahwiisdláád]

The third and fourth person forms of (191) are particularly interesting because no ee- vowel appears as it usually does in aspect+si verbs in zero environment. Apparently ghe- insertion is exempted from these hi- forms, and seriative h- deletion applies.

Thus verbs such as 'plow' and 'beat one's wife' contain an absolutely neutralized hi- that can be posited with some confidence since it is in Kiparsky's terms "strongly embedded" in the grammar by its participation in more than one rule (Kiparsky, 1971:590). Further support for this analysis is offered by the fact that the large percentage of Reichard's yi- repetitives contain a thematic conjunct prefix (Reichard, 1951:250-253).

Still more happens to hi- 'seriative' In verbs where a sequence ji+hi has not been altered by either seriative h- deletion or +hi+di metathesis, an additional metathesis can apply, e.g. hizhdiłnaah 'he is moving it', where pos. 6 hi- precedes pos. 5 ji-. Here a ji+hi metathesis rule applies.

(192) ji+hi → hi+ji / ___X+C_o [

/ji+hi+di+ł+naah/

<u>ji hi metath</u>: [hi+ji+di+ł+naah]

<u>V elision</u>: [hi+j+di+ł+naah]

<u>deaffric</u>: [hi+zh+di+ł+naah]

<u>ultimately</u>: [hizhdiłnaah]

In other instances the ji+hi metathesis rule seems to vary with non-metathesized y- forms; e.g. hijeeghał ∿ jiyeeghał 'he arrives wriggling'. This variation will be discussed in 4.108, and at that time rule 192 will be refined.

Another problem with the hi- prefix is that certain verbs appear to have a <u>double</u> occurrence of hi; e.g. hizhdiyootih 'he will break them off'. This seems to be a <u>hi- copying</u> rule. These forms are used variably and will also be discussed in Chapter Four.

I have accounted for the three allomorphs of hi- 'seriative' [hi], [y], and [i] and two metatheses by formulating four rules that operate when hi- is preceded by a conjunct prefix. It would be useful to examine the behavior of hi- 'seriative' in other Athapaskan languages.

There is yet another surprising gact about the unusual behavior of hi-. It is quite apparent that one other aspect prefix which appears thematically with only one stem, si- 'destruct', undergoes an s- deletion rule in the same environment as seriative h- deletion and turns to y- when h- does.[33]

Below are imperfective (193), future (194), perfective (195), and optative (196) paradigms for 'kill it' and the imperfective paradigm for 'kill self' (199).

(194) 1 sisxé   (195) 1 diyeeshxééł   (196) 1 séłxį́
      2 síłxé   2 diyiiłxééł   2 sínííłxį́
      3 yiyiiłxé   3 yidiyoołxééł   3 yiyiisxį́
      4 jiiłxé   4 jidiyoołxééł   4 jiisxį́
      1d siilghé   1d diyiilghééł   1d siilghį́
      2d sołxé   2d diyoołxééł   2d soołxį́

(197) 1 sósxééł   (198) 1 'ádiishghé
      2 sóółxééł   2 'ádiyílghé
      3 yiyółxééł   3 'ádiilghé
      4 jiyółxééł   4 'ázhdiilghé
      1d soolghééł
      2d soołxééł

When si- is next to C₀[and is preceded by a conjunct prefix as in
193.3 and 4, 195.3 and 4 and 197.1, 3, and 4, s- is deleted. This can
be handled by revising the seriative h- deletion rule to delete s- as
well as h-. The revised rule will be called h/s deletion.

(II-13) $\left\{ \begin{matrix} [\text{ASP}]^s \\ h \end{matrix} \right\} \rightarrow \emptyset\ /\ +\underline{\quad}i+C_0[$

The morphological marking on s- in this rule and in the following rule
is necessary to distinguish this s- from that of si- modal prefix.

In addition, yi- doubling applies to 193.3 and 195.3.

                193.3/yi+si+ł+ghé/   197.1/'á#di+si+sh+d+ł+ghé/
h/s dele: [yi+i+ł+ghé]   ['á#di+i+sh+d+ł+ghé]
yi doubl: [yi+yi+i+ł+ghé]   _____
ultimately: [yiyiiłxé]   ['ádiishghé]

If si- is next to a vowel and is preceded by a conjunct prefix as
in all forms of 194, 196.3 and 4 and 197.2, s- becomes y-. This, of

238

course, can be explained by expanding the h- glide rule to include s-.
Below is h/s glide.

(184) $\left\{ \begin{matrix} s \\ [ASP] \\ h \end{matrix} \right\} \rightarrow y\ /\ +\_\_V$

One difference between si- 'destruct' and hi- 'seriative' is that in the future paradigm (194), si- always appears to the right of di- (cf. (185) and (186) above). Thus I assume that si- is to the right of di- in underlying representation and no metathesis has applied. (195) is a regular aspect+si paradigm except that, like the perfective of 'plow', (191), ghe- insertion does not apply to the third and fourth person.

194.1/di+si+ghi+sh+ł+ghééł/ 196.3/yi+si+ó+ł+ghééł/

ghe read:	[di+si+ghe+sh+ł+ghééł]	
V dele:		[yi+s+ó+ł+ghééł]
gh dele:	[di+si+e+sh+ł+ghééł]	
V assim:	[di+se+e+sh+ł+ghééł]	
h/s glide:	[di+ye+e+sh+ł+ghééł]	[yi+y+ó+ł+ghééł]
ultimately:	[diyeeshxééł]	[yiyółxééł]

195.2/si+si+í+ni+ł+ghį́/ 196.2/'á#di+si+ni+d+ł+ghé/

si dele:	[si+í+ni+ł+ghį́]	
ni absorp:		['á#di+sí+d+ł+ghé]
h/s glide:		['á#di+yí+d+ł+ghé]
ultimately:	[síníłxį́]	['ádiyílghé]

I have demonstrated a highly improbable fact: the si- 'destruct' prefix undergoes two of the same rules that apply to hi- 'seriative', a duplication of two highly restricted phonological rules. Comparative evidence on the verb 'kill it' shows that the this instability in si- is unique to Navajo.[34] Thus, the treatment of si- in Navajo seems to be due to a peculiar analogy with hi- 'seriative' and its phonological rules.

3.7 Mode Phonology Summary

In this chapter I have tried to present a complete analysis of the phonology of the eight regular active verb modes. The majority of verbs can be derived from relatively secure underlying representations by legitimate phonological rules (some of which are quite restricted). However, certain forms in the ni- imperfective, the conjunct progressive, the three perfectives, and most paradigms in which +i+ aspect occurs require readjustment rules. To what extent these readjustment rules can be redefined as legitimate phonological rules is the principal task of future Navajo phonology research.

One important affinity is noted between six of the readjustment rules that have been formulated in this chapter. Compare the following:

(70r) gho readjustment -- ghi → gho / +___+[

(24r) dummy object insertion -- ∅ → yi+/ ##___ni+[

(27r) ni- drop -- ni → ∅ / #___+[

(33r) ni- replacement -- ni → ghe / ASP+___+[

(164r) ghe- insertion -- ASP+si+[→ ASP+ghe+s+[

(139r) si- syncope -- si → s / X___+[

These rules all apply when aspect, mode, +, #, or X are in the environment _____+[, the zero environment. This is the very environment in which pepet vowels are inserted in certain forms of the ∅ imperfective, the ni- imperfective/perfective, and the si- perfective. Also, the unusual yi- doubling rule applies when yi+i is in zero environment. Perhaps additional phonological rules are operative here, but no natural solutions are evident at present.

Krauss remarks in his review of Sapir-Hoijer,

> For the future, in the analysis of structures that are
> presently unanalyzable or only marginally analyzable, this
> writer speculates that there will be a highly beneficial
> further breakdown of the barriers between synchronic and
> historical-comparative linguistics. Every synchronic
> language state is the result of historical process, and shows
> it, especially in the problematic areas . . . in which the
> concept of synchronic morpheme becomes highly arbitrary.
> In Navaho these areas which resist analysis in conventional
> synchronic terms . . . are quite large. It becomes increasingly
> evident then that description of a synchronic state of a
> language (especially one like Navaho), to be truly satisfying,
> will require understanding of the historical processes that
> have led to that state (1970:227-228).

The Navajo readjustment rules, the rough edges in this study of the verb modes, are the very place to initiate a comparative study of Athapaskan phonology as Krauss' y-component analysis of the perfectives admirably illustrates. Based on the Athapaskan languages for which there is adequate documentation, it is clear that many of the Navajo readjustment rules are operative elsewhere. For example rule 70r, gho- readjustment that operates in the progressive and the d/l ghi- perfective has reflexes throughout Athapaskan. Krauss (personal communication) notes an analogous vowel alternation in the Minto future, təgə → tɔ in zero environment; təghəs'ɔł 'I'll handle a round object', təghi'ɔł 2sg, yətɔ'ɔł 3 where ɔ- equals PA a- (Navajo oo equals PA u-). Despite the lack of vowel correspondences, there is some relationship in these vowel changes in zero environment.

As we have seen, the maximally marked aspect+si paradigm requires extreme readjustment rules. Below I present the aspect+si paradigm in Chipewyan (Li, 1946:89) and in the Apachean languages (Hoijer, 1946a:8-9). We find that it is equally idiosyncratic in other languages.

(198) Chipewyan--'be drowned'

    1 tunesdą

    2 tunįdą

    3 tunéedą

    1d tunééíídą

    2d tunuhą

    3d tuhenéedą

(199) San Carlos--'run across'

    1 naadééshghod

    2 naadénlghod

    3 naadeesghod

    4 naach'ideesghod

    1d naadęęlghod

    2d naadeesołghod

(200) Mescalero--'crawl'

    1 dédǫ́ǫ́dz

    2 déndǫ́ǫ́dz

    3 deesdǫ́ǫ́dz

    4 ch'ideesdǫ́ǫ́dz

    1d dęędǫ́ǫ́dz

    2d dádǫ́ǫ́dz

(201) Chiricahua--'start to carry a round obj'

    1 dé'ą́

    2 dén'ą́

    3 yidees'ą́

    4 jidees'ą́

    1d deet'ą́

    2d da'ą́

(202) Jicarilla--'hide oneself'

    1 naanésht'į́'

    2 naanént'į́'

    3 naaneest'į́'

    4 naach'ineest'į́'

    1d naanęęt'į́'

    2d naanát'į́'

(203) Lipan--'spread it over something'

    1 bik'iidí^{n}dił

    2 bik'iidíni^{n}dił

    3 yik'iidiis^{n}dił

    4 bik'iishdis^{n}dił

    1d bik'iidįįh^{n}dił

    2d bik'iidá^{n}dił

(204) Kiowa Apache--'choose'

    1 bikadééshgeesh

    2 bikadáá^{n}digeesh

    3 yikadeesgeesh

    4 bikashdeesgeesh

    1d bikadąągeesh

    2d bikadaahgeesh

There are striking similarities with the Navajo aspect+si. 1) Just as in Navajo, the si- perfective prefix (Chipewyan=ee) has disappeared in all seven paradigms. 2) In 198.1d and in 199.2d si- has remained. In 4.103 I discuss parallel cases in Navajo where si- has not been deleted in the duals of aspect+si. 3) As in Navajo, in third and fourth person si- has been reduced to s- and there is some alteration in the preceding syllable. In Chipewyan 198.3 and 3d an é- appears in front of s-. In all the Apachean languages the vowel becomes ee- (as in Navajo) except in Lipan where ii- appears. Krauss has noted this tendency for vowels to lengthen compensatorily with si- syncope (1969:56). Golla finds a CV̆ → CV vowel lengthening process in Hupa before all instances of the si- perfective, a fact which he regards as an extension of the usual environment of this rule (1970:64). Futhermore, Hoijer notes that in Chiricahua, Mescalero, Jicarilla, and Lipan any prefix (not just aspect) preceding zero environment in the si- perfective has a lengthened vowel; e.g. Chir. naagojiis'á, Nav. nahojiz'á 'he made plans' (1946a:8). An interesting question is to determine the original environment for this vowel lengthening (vowel insertion?) rule. 4) The aberrant ee- in the 1d forms in Navajo has reflexes in the éeíí- sequence in the Chipewyan first dual and in the nasalized vowels, ęę- in all the Apachean first duals (except Chiricahua which has ee-). 5) The inexplicable é- in the 1sg of Navajo d/l aspect+si verbs is present as e- in Chipewyan 198.1, as éé- in San Carlos 199.1 and Kiowa Apache 204.1, and as é- in Jicarilla 202.1. Thus, all the rules that are highly arbitrary in Navajo aspect+si seem to be operative and equally arbitrary in all the other Apachean languages and in Chipewyan. A better understanding of the synchronic phonological rules operating in some of the other Athapaskan languages might allow us to enter some of the Navajo readjustment rules, such as 164r ghe- insertion, as phonological rules.

In concluding this chapter we observe that based upon this analysis of the mode system (particularly upon the elimination of the yi- imperfective as a separate mode) all Navajo verbs can be placed into one of three conjugation patterns.

	Imperfective	Perfective	Prog-Future	Iterative	Optative
A.	∅	ghi+í	(di)+ghi	ná	ó
B.	∅	si+í	(di)+ghi	ná	ó
C.	ni	ni+í	(di)+ghi	ná	ó

The conjugation pattern for a given verb base can be marked simply by a listing of the perfective prefix, all other forms being predictable. And, as we have seen in the discussion of perfective choice, the perfective prefix is to a certain extent predictable from the derivational prefix complex.

According to Hoijer's calculations based on about 5,000 verb bases, conjugation pattern A occurs in 44% of the verbs, B in 39%, and C in 17% (SH:95).

The conjugation patterns arrived at in this chapter are the consequence of the Sapir-Hoijer conception of the Navajo mode-aspect system. However, as Krauss has noted (personal communication), in Navajo and in Athapaskan we have yet to arrive at substantial definitions for mode or aspect, and there are lacunae in the present system. Why do an aspect (di-) and a mode (ghi-) combine to make a mode (future)? Are the ni- imperfective and ni- perfective in fact an aspectual system? Why should iterative and usitative be treated as separate modes when they can be subsumed in the ∅ imperfective? A more radical analysis might posit that the paradigmatic mode system is simpler, perhaps just ∅ imperfective, ghi-perfective, si- perfective, progressive, and optative. The iterative, usitative, future, and ni- imperfective/perfective might then be treated as derivational variants of these basic paradigms. It is obvious that there is need for further research on the structure of the Navajo mode-aspect system.

3.8 Rule Summary

(6) gamma insertion   ∅ → gh / ##___V

(7) gliding   gh → {y/w} / ##___{i/o}

(17r) i- lengthening   +i+ → +ii+ / $\begin{Bmatrix} ya\#CV+\underline{\quad}[\\ \underline{(sh)[} \end{Bmatrix}$

(18) n- deletion   n → ∅ / {ó/i} +___+[

(19) yi- doubling   ∅ → yi / ##___yi+i+[

(24r) dummy object insertion   ∅ → yi + / ##___ ni +[
                                              [MODE]

(27r) ni- drop   ni   → ∅ / $\begin{Bmatrix} \pm i+ \\ \# \end{Bmatrix}$ ___[
                 [MODE]

(33r) ni replacement $\begin{Bmatrix} di \\ [agent] \\ ASP \end{Bmatrix}$+ ni + [→ $\begin{Bmatrix} di \\ [agent] \\ ASP \end{Bmatrix}$ + ghe + [

(II-12) ni- absorption   CV+ ni [→ CV̂[
                              [-ASP]

(38) ɨi to l   ɨi → l / (#)___STEM

(45) na- dissimilation   na + na → ni + na

(63) +V+ tone lowering   V̂ → V / +V+___

(II-51) optative tone lowering   ó → o / X#___
        condition: ≠ óó

(70r) gho- readjustment   ghi → gho / +___[

(75r) ghe- readjustment   ghi → ghe / +___sh

(79) glottal-CV metathesis   (zh)+'+CV+C → CV+(zh)+'+C

(87) náá- reduplication   náá → nááná / ___#V

(97) progressive da- shift   ghi+(X)+STEM [progressive] →
　　　　　　　　　　　　　　　1　　2　　3

　　　　　　　　　　　　　　da.#yí+ní+(X)+STEM [imperfective
　　　　　　　　　　　　　　 4　　1　　2　　3　 +momentaneous]

　　　　　　　　　　　　condition: optional in intransitives

(II-48) tone lowering   v́ → V / ___+V

　　　condition: ≠ í+ní+V

(102r) perfective deletion   í → ∅ / ___(sh)+{d/i}+STEM

　　　condition: ≠ ASP+___sh+{d/i}+STEM

(103r) sh- deletion   sh → ∅ / í+___

(104r) oh- reduction   oh → o / í+___

(117) i- drop   i → ∅ / +___+i+ni

(123) perfective n- deletion   n → ∅ / ___+í+ni+[

(137r) í- lowering   í → é / si+___+sh

(138r) si- perfective deletion   í → ∅ / si+___+[

(139r) si- syncope   si → s / { ##___+d / X___+[}

(140r) s- voicing   s → z / ___+STEM

(152) na- alternation   na → ni / ___#sV

(163r) si- deletion   si → ∅ / ASP+___+í+X+[

(164r) ghe- insertion   ASP+si+[→ ASP+ghe+s+[

(165r) ld í- lowering   í → é / ASP+___+iid

(II-94) strident deletion $\begin{bmatrix}+cor\\ \alpha ant\\ -cnt\\ +str\end{bmatrix}$ → ∅ / ___i+ $\begin{bmatrix}+cor\\ \alpha ant\\ +str\end{bmatrix}$

(II-13) h/s deletion $\left\{\begin{array}{c}[A\tilde{S}P]\\ h\end{array}\right\}$ → ∅ / +___i+C₀[

(184) h/s glide $\left\{\begin{array}{c}[A\tilde{S}P]\\ h\end{array}\right\}$ → y / +___V

(187) +hi+di metathesis   +hi+di → +di+hi

(192) ji+hi metathesis   ji+hi → hi+ji / ___X+C₀[

Notes to Chapter III

[1] Organizationally, the treatment of hi- and si- perhaps belongs in 2.7 with other non-mode dependent processes. However, the highly unusual phonology of hi- and si- is more easily understood within the context of the analysis of the modes. As it is, this section functions as a review of the mode analysis.

[2] This paradigm shows that the mode variant 'conjunct' is defined by the derivational prefix that comes immediately before the mode slot, in this case pos. 6 di-. The disjunct prefix k'i- does not make this a disjunct verb.

[3] Once again Li (1933) proves very insightful. In discussing the implications of the primary-secondary (conjunctive-disjunctive) prefix division, he notes, "We may add here the existence of an inorganic 'h-' which appears where there is originally a vowel without any consonant. Mattole has a glottal stop instead of h-, Navajo y-, Chip. hès'áɬ, Nav. yish'aɬ 'I am chewing it' . . . This syllable hè-, which is developed from a supporting pepet vowel ĕ is dropped in the second person and in all forms in other tenses where there is a syllabic prefix and where this supporting vowel is not necessary, thus nè'áɬ 'you are chewing it', ghwàs'áɬ 'I shall chew it'" (p.463). Thus Li associated the peg element with the non-syllabic prefix complexes, and he saw the initial h- or y- as an inorganic or derived element acting as a cover for the pepet vowel.

[4] Only rarely will an Athapaskan language allow a lone stem without a peg element, e.g. Navajo ní 'he says', Tanaina chegh 'he cries'.

[5] Certain basic noun stems are pluralized with the addition of da-. In these instances the same pepet vowel insertion-vowel assimilation processes that occur in the disjunct ∅ imperfective apply. We find daa- if there is no conjunct prefix between #___[; daató 'waters', daakǫ 'fires', daaɬid 'smokes', kédaayah 'lands'; but cf. dabito 'his waters' where bi- prevents the vowel insertion rule from applying. Note also the problem we would have in explaining these noun plurals with an underlying yi- prefix.

[6] This use of semelfactive is narrower than that of Hoijer who used the term for any verb that connotes "a single act as abstracted from an unanalyzable series" (1949:14).

[7] There appear to be several aspectual systems comprised of di+i-. 'Abrupt motion' is formed with the di- 'inceptive' prefix. Di- 'oral' may occur with +i+, diishch'ééh 'I am opening my mouth'; di- 'elongated object' may also take +i+, nábidiish'nééh 'I am standing it on end'.

[8] In recent publications Hoijer continues to recognize three imperfective paradigms. In his 1971 article he writes, "The conjunct imperfective is employed when the verb contains some other prefix, either one of several adverbial prefixes of positions 1 and 6, or an

inflectional prefix of positions 4 or 5. The [yi] disjunct imperfective occurs when the verb has no prefix in positions 1, 4, 5, or 6, or when the verb base includes an adverbial prefix that requires the disjunct imperfective" (p.137). Hoijer is using the terms conjunct-disjunct as he did in 1945 without reference to the fundamental phonological nature of the two prefix classes. Thus he is forced to assign yi- lexically to certain prefixes.

[9]This metathesis of ji- (pos. 5) and hi- (pos. 6) is one of the unusual processes affecting the hi- 'seriative' prefix and will be discussed in 3.6.

[10]This is a usitative plural form, 'they customarily sleep'.

[11]The variability of the ná- classifier shift will be discussed in 4.107.

[12]According to rule II-100, syllabic n, one would expect the iterative prefix to reduce to n- in 43.4 and 44.4. However, nínjíłka' is not too acceptable. This suggests that the syllabic n- rule should be constrained by condition from nV- prefixes that are preceded by another nV-.

[13]Note that in 51.1 we would expect that vowel absorption would apply to á#a, but it does not. Obviously this analysis is defective.

[14]In 4.106 I will discuss the optatives for the +i+ semelfactives. I will present evidence that some speakers have generalized the +i+ prefix to the semelfactive optative paradigm.

[15]The 1sg and 3sg of disjunct optatives are reported inconsistently in Young and Morgan. Low tone disjuncts are given as CVoo- or as CVo-. If the disjunct prefix is high in tone it is given as CV̂o-. There is no phonological motivation for the oo- in disjuncts, and Young (personal communication) regards it as an inconsistency. There is a perceptible, though slight, length difference between the vowel of 1sg and 3sg and those of the duals.

[16]Ha- 'up and out' does not appear in the progressive with nááʼ 'semeliterative' as does na- 'about', but it does occur in at least one progressive, ha'oo'ááł 'it is rising up' as in jóhanaaʼéí t'óó ha'oo'áłígo 'just as the sun is rising'.

[17]In hwi- progressives speakers may be lexicalizing one of the two forms. For example, one speaker gave hóóził 'you grope along' hóółááł 'you are carrying on a ceremony', but hwííłtééł 'you are carrying him along'.

[18]'Prolongative' may be a misnomer (Reichard, 1951:215). Reichard's gloss for 77.3 would be 'he will prolongatively steal it', a translation that is not acceptable to Navajos. There may be more than one díní- prefix. The inchoatives denote the start of an action as in 78.1 'I will start to boil it'.

[19] One of the peculiarities of the o- imperfective is that it takes a +i+ in three modes. Just why +i+ should occur to the left of di- in future constructions but to the right of di- in imperfectives such as (16) is uncertain. Perhaps these are two different +i+ prefixes.

[20] Hale (personal communication) has suggested that 89.3 be derived by yi- doubling. In other words, only the yi- that is incorporated with the postposition í- would be in underlying representation and the internal yi- would be derived by yi- doubling which would call for a revision of the yi- doubling rule. Since we find oo- in this verb, it seems preferable to assume that the yi- direct object is in underlying form providing the environment for gho- readjustment. Therefore, the underlying form would be /yi+í#yi+ghi+ghi+/ and no revision in yi- doubling is needed.

[21] See Hale 1956:54-58 for a discussion of some of the stem set choosing properties of adverbial prefixes, an important topic for future Navajo research.

[22] Another illustration of the primacy of the si- perfective is in the Hupa wesi- perfective which is a compound of the wi- progressive and the si- perfective (Golla, 1970:66).

[23] +I+ is rarely found in a si- perfective, e.g. yidiists'ą́ą́' 'he started it (the car)'.

[24] This is the irregular verb 'to go'. In singular forms the underlying stem is vowel initial, -á, cf. deesháá+ Fl. The y- is introduced by a restricted rule.

[25] At present an equally good case could be made that the ni- modal prefix simply deletes by a readjustment rule. However, I present evidence below from the conjuncts that perfective n- deletion is a legitimate though highly restricted phonological rule.

[26] In 4.102 I present evidence of variation in the third and fourth persons of these paradigms.

[27] Krauss has suggested that a voicing rule first operates, $V-s\partial-C \rightarrow V-z\partial-C$, and then a syncope rule, $V-z\partial-C \rightarrow V-z-C$ (1969:55,774). This order is untenable synchronically for Navajo since forms such as 136.3, which do not show z- because of the +- classifier, would then have to be devoiced. The opposite order, si- syncope, s- voicing, will work. An exception to s- voicing (or to perfective deletion) is 'ásédįįd 'I disappeared', 'ásdįįd 'it disappeared' where 1sg appears to be ∅- classifier but s- voicing has not operated in 3.

[28] These plurals were elicited in sentences such as 'ashkii 'awéé' ch'íníłtį́ 'the boy carried out the baby', ashiiké dóó hastóí 'awéé' ch'ídeistį́ 'the boys and men carried out the baby'.

[29] In other words, sentences of the following type show no change in preference for the da- shifted forms: 'ashiiké náshdóí yídeiskáá' 'the boys tracked the lion', 'ashiiké dlǫ́ǫ́' bídeiskáá' 'the boys were tracked by the prairie dog'. See Hale 1973a for an explanation of noun-ranking.

[30]Reichard suggested that there are two hi- prefixes. One is the 'seriative' (or 'repetitive') prefix, and the other Reichard glossed as 'change position' as in hiinaah 'he is alive', hinishcha' 'he hopped'. It does appear that hi- does not always have a 'one after another' connotation. This is another question that requires the attention of Navajo speakers. Phonologically, all hi-'s behave alike.

[31]The e- in 179.1 is exceptional and varies with i-.

[32]This form is evidently an exception. We would expect 'ayiidzą́. See 4.108.

[33]Besides si- 'destruct' two other si- prefixes occur in pos. 6. Young and Morgan give 'ahosidiyoolts'ííł 'several sounds will be heard fading off' (1951:199) and łeeh sidínóotsis 'it will sink into the soil' (1951:289). These are very rare and do not behave like si- 'destruct'.

[34]In the following Lipan future paradigm for 'kill it' from Hoijer (1946a:11), the si- (zi-) prefix is not altered at all:
1 dizooshxáíł
2 dizǫ́ǫ́łxáíł
3 yidizałxáíł
4 ch'idizałxáíł
1d dizǫǫłgáíł
2d dizaałxáíł.

CHAPTER FOUR

MORPHOPHONEMIC VARIATION

4.00 Introduction

Although students of Navajo have often remarked on the considerable amount of linguistic diversity that can be detected across the Navajo Reservation, the field of Navajo dialectology and linguistic variation is still very much in its infancy. To date there have been only three short studies that deal directly with dialect and variation issues (Reichard, 1945; 1951:396-382; Saville-Troike, 1973). Clearly this is a field that will advance as more Navajos become interested in linguistic research. Future work on Navajo linguistic variation promises to be of real practicality now that Navajo bilingual education has become a reality. Also, the study of linguistic variation can deepen our insight into all levels of Navajo grammar, particularly into the intricate morphophonology. Furthermore, because of Navajo's synchronic complexity, research on Navajo linguistic variation can contribute greatly to our understanding of the substantive conditions on language change.

This chapter attempts in a preliminary way to document and to analyze a dozen categories of variation in the Navajo verb. All of the examples discussed can be loosely labeled 'deep morphophonemic' variations. They arise from differences in the underlying representations of certain verbs or in differences in the phonological rules that affect the underlying forms. The analysis is focused on this one category of variation because of its relevance to the preceding analysis of the verb modes and because it has yet received no significant attention in Navajo linguistics.

I am purposely ignoring other types of variation that have been reported by Reichard and Saville-Troike. These include variation in lexical items (vocabulary replacement and independent innovations) and an array of late phonetic differences such as variation in nasalization, length, and quality of vowels or differences in the degree of aspiration. Variation in very late phonological rules such as rule II-81 strident assimilation, rule II-44 VCV assimilation, and rule II-100 syllabic n- are also ignored.[1]

In particular I take issue with the recent statement by Saville-Troike that the morphophonemic rules comprise "the most stable component in the grammar" (1973). This component of Navajo grammar is by no means stable. Rather, there has been little empirical data on morphophonemic variation to date. Reichard's two studies contain some examples of this type of variation, but this study is the first attempt to sample the variants and to provide some analysis.

We must distinguish morphophonemic variation from the more familiar regional dialect markers. It is well known that there is a distinctive eastern Navajo dialect that is characterized by the assimilation of o- to a- (see 2.732), by the dipthongizing of ee- to ei-, by the replacement of é- by í-, by certain lexical items such as zas instead of yas 'snow'. In contrast to these markers, it is hypothesized, following Kiparsky 1968, that many of the deeper morphophonemic variants discussed in this chapter are not being diffused regionally but are happening in random clusters as people independently simplify rules or reanalyze segments.

It appears that many of the variations discussed in this chapter are being used differentially through an individual's lexicon. Although data were not gathered with this objective in mind, some variations may illustrate Wang's hypothesis that linguistic changes are "phonetically abrupt and lexically gradual".

> According to this view, during the early phase of the change only a small sector of the relevant morphemes is affected. Some of the affected morphemes change to the Y-pronunciation directly. Other morphemes, however, will at first have both the X-pronunciation and the Y-pronunciation, fluctuating either randomly or according to some such factor as tempo or style. (For the most part, morphemes do not have more than two pronunciations. In the phonetic literature these dual forms have sometimes been referred to as 'doublets'.) But the X-pronunciation will gradually be suppressed in favor of the Y-pronunciation (Wang, 1969:15).

Throughout the early stages of gathering language data for this study certain variations in forms were noted. As a sense for the regular patterns in the verb modes became refined, it became increasingly evident that the instances of variation were patterned phenomena. The variants that received further investigation were selected for their relevance to the study of the prefix phonology.[2] The items discussed range in productivity from those that occur in every instance of a given mode to those that are lexically confined to certain verb bases.

The documentation on these dozen types of variation is uneven. From eight to twenty-nine Navajo speakers were surveyed on each type. Most of this material was elicited from paradigms; e.g. "You know sisxé 'I kill it'? What's the second person singular form?" Admittedly, the data may be of diminished significance because we are dealing with the most stigmatized, self-conscious level of speech usage. However, paradigms are a convenient way to organize and present large amounts of material in short sessions. A further danger in paradigm elicitation, as is pointed out by Harris and Voegelin, is that "constant asking for parallel forms invites analogizing" (1953:68). To augment the data on a given form a speaker was generally asked to give his opinion of a variant form. Often sentences were constructed to measure the variants. Responses on two variants were recorded on a three-fold scale: strong preference for one form, equal preference for both forms, and preference for one form but acceptance of the other. In this latter category "acceptance" ranged from comments like "I use it sometimes" to "Some people say it that way". Despite the shortcomings of the data-gathering techniques and the unevenness of the sample, most categories that were investigated reveal a trend as to degree of acceptance. (An exception to this is the data on the 'scold' prefix, which follows no clear pattern.)

In analyzing the motivation behind each type of variation extensive reference is made to Kiparsky 1971, which contains a number of hypotheses on the substantive conditions upon linguistic change. At the conclusion of this chapter several implications of the findings will be discussed.

The data presented here do not presume to be the final word on these variants. Rather, they serve to indicate that there are in fact doublets or "another way to say it". The methodology for placing these forms in natural speech and for including a broader sample of Navajo speakers remains a topic for further research. Inevitably, this research will be carried out by Navajo speaking linguists.

4.10 Types of Variation

4.101 Oh- reduction

In the analysis of the perfectives, two pronoun readjustment rules, III-103r and III-104r were formulated to account for the absence of sh- 1sg and the reduction of oh- 2d to o- in $\emptyset/\ddagger$ paradigms. In checking other Athapaskan languages, it is apparent that sh- deletion is a very old rule, present throughout Athpaskan and in Eyak, while oh- reduction is a newer rule that is confined to Apachean (Hoijer, 1971:127, 129). In Navajo the sh- deletion rule operates without exception or variation, but the oh- reduction rule is being used with considerable variability. What makes the variation in the use of oh- reduction of particular interest is that for many speakers, perhaps even the majority of speakers, the rule is both suppressed and extended.

According to oh- reduction, we would expect the following 2d perfectives in ∅-class verbs.

(1) a. sootał   'kick it'
    b. shoodlééžh   'paint it'
    c. haoogeed   'mine it'
    d. soolįh   'taste it'
    e. sooloh   'rope it'
    f. noolóóz   'lead it'
    g. nabísooghil   'push it around'.

Rule III-104r applies to all of these verbs.

(III-104r) oh → o / PERF+___(ł)+STEM

                le/si+í+oh+loh/

oh reduc: [si+í+o+loh]

V dele: [s+í+o+loh]

tone lower: [s+i+o+loh]

V assim: [s+o+o+loh]

ultimately: [sooloh]

However, the oh- reduction rule is frequently dropped as in these variants for the verbs in (1).

(2) a. soohtał

b. shoohdlééezh

c. haoohgeed

d. soołįh

e. soołoh

f. noołóóz

In 2d-f the unaltered oh- pronoun has caused continuant devoicing and then has been deleted by rule II-32, h- deletion.

2e /si+í+oh+loh/

V dele:	[s+í+oh+loh]
tone lower:	[s+i+oh+loh]
V assim:	[s+o+oh+loh]
cont devoic:	[s+o+oh+łoh]
h dele:	[s+o+o+łoh]
ultimately:	[soołoh]

Based on a sampling of twenty-five speakers on these forms, two speakers indicated a preference for oh- in certain verbs. Almost all tolerate an h- in 2a-c (next to a non-continuant stem initial consonant). Fewer speakers queried accept an h- (i.e. ł-) in 2d-f, and none accept a devoiced alternant for 1g, *nabísoohil. Thus it appears that the oh- reduction rule is dropped next to non-continuant stem initials by many speakers some of the time. Fewer speakers, perhaps less than 5%, drop the rule next to l-, i.e. when h-'s presence is particularly conspicuous. Many speakers perceive the inclusion of h- in these verbs as a regularization.

Technically speaking, there is no direct proof that oh- reduction applies to ł-class perfectives, e.g. noołt'a' 'you dpl flew it', since rule II-32, h- deletion applies to any hɫC- sequence. Based on the fact that sh- deletion is clearly operable in both ∅ and ɫ- perfectives and not in l- and d- perfectives, it is reasonable to infer that oh- reduction has the same distribution. Obviously, there is no variation in the 2d ɫ-class perfectives, since a non-deleted h- (by the suppression of rule III-104r) would be eliminated by h- deletion.

Thus, it appears that the morphologically marked oh- reduction rule, which is actually detectable only in ∅-class perfectives, is becoming optional. It might be that Kiparsky's substantive condition on language change, "allomorphy tends to be regularized in a paradigm" (1971:598-9) is operating here. Speakers find the oh- reduction rule hard to learn and are tending to regularize the ∅-class perfective paradigm by dropping the rule.

Yet this is not the whole story. In 3.524 there was brief reference to perfectives with an "invisible" d- classifier, an absolutely neutralized d- that is inferred by the appearance of sh- in the lsg, oh- in the 2d and, in si- perfectives, by s- instead of z- in zero environment. We would expect the following 2d forms in invisible d- perfectives:

(3) a. hasoohtih   'get old'
    b. soohtin   'freeze'
    c. yisoohdlaad   'believe it'
    d. néisoohkan   'beg'
    e. nooht'a'   'arrive flying'
    f. nisoohkai   'go pl'.

However, these are often heard without h-.

(4) a. hasootih
    b. sootin
    c. yisoodląąd
    d. néisookan
    e. noot'a'
    f. nisookai

In fact, it is quite certain that the variants in (4) are more frequent than those in (2). This is demonstrated in the Young and Morgan dictionaries, where there are no cases of h- in 2d ∅-class perfectives but, occasionally, deleted h-'s in the invisible d- verbs are found. Further indication of the uncertainty about h- in invisible d-'s is that speakers tend to be much hazier about determining the conservative variant than they are with the ∅-class verbs. Also, it is important to note that relatively few speakers accept 4f because 'go' is a high frequency word.

The variants in (4) reflect an irregularization, the extension of a highly arbitrary rule, and, thus, they contradict the substantive condition that allomorphy tends to regularized. What is happening in (4) illustrates confusion about the absolutely neutralized d- classifier. Speakers are treating these verbs as having a ∅ classifier and then applying oh- reduction. These invisible d- classifiers are in a fairly small subset of the vocabulary. They reflect another of Kiparsky's substantive conditions, that "underlying distinctions which do not directly correspond to surface distinctions are hard to learn" (1971:596). In fact, what makes this oh- problem of importance is that it appears that in Navajo the absolutely neutralized d- classifier is harder to learn than the morphologically marked oh- reduction rule, so much so that the trend toward the regularization of allomorphy is overridden.

4.102 Ni- replacement

A highly interesting variation has been detected in zero environment forms of the aspect+ni perfective with d- or l- classifier. Recall that these verbs as well as the aspect+ni imperfective require a readjustment rule, III-33r, ni- replacement. This rule is illustrated below in derivations for 'smile' and 'arrive hopping'.

III-33r ni → ghe / $\left\{\begin{matrix}\text{di}\\\text{[agent]}\\\text{ASP}\end{matrix}\right\}$+___+[

/ch'í#di+ni+í+l+dlo'/   /hi+ni+í+d+cha'/

perf dele: [ch'í#di+ni+l+dlo']   [hi+ni+d+cha']
ni replac: [ch'í#di+ghe+l+dlo']   [hi+ghe+d+cha']
gh dele: [ch'í#di+e+l+dlo']   [hi+e+d+cha']
V assim: [ch'í#de+e+l+dlo']   [he+e+d+cha']
ultimately: [ch'ídeeldlo']   [heecha']

The first hint of variation in these forms came incidentally as one speaker reported for the two above verbs, ch'ídooldlo', hoocha'. Upon further examination, this speaker consistently had an oo- vowel instead of ee- in the third and fourth person of aspect+ni perfectives with d- or l- classifier. In ni- imperfectives this speaker often had a high tone CV̂ instead of ee- in the zero environment forms, e.g. ch'ídíldlóóh instead of ch'ídeeldlóóh 'he is smiling'. Thus this speaker lacks or has suppressed the ni- replacement rule. It is clear that this person is using in its place in the perfectives rule III-70r, gho- readjustment, that is usually for conjunct ghi- perfectives with d- or l- classifier.

(III-70r) ghi → gho / +___+[

Upon further examination with nine other speakers, no one was found who advocated oo- in this environment as strongly as did the first speaker. No other speaker accepted oo- in the active verbs 'smile' or 'hop'. Two other speakers accepted oo- in hoolghal, 'he arrived wriggling' instead of heelghal. However, in agentive passives such as ch'íbi'deedlóóz 'he was led out', bi'deelmááz 'he was rolled', ch'íbidi'neelchą́ą́' 'he was chased out' there was considerably greater tolerance of oo- in place of ee-, e.g. ch'íbidi'noolchą́ą́'. One speaker felt that oo- is an optional variant in passive forms but is inadmissable in actives, while others were less precise about when oo- might occur.

Based upon this very limited sample it is possible to make a hypothesis as to the cause of this variation. Ni- replacement is a highly marked readjustment rule that applies only to a handful of active verbs in the ni- perfective, those with an aspect prefix and a d- or l- classifier. The agentive passive ni- perfectives are a more productive environment for ni- replacement, but, as was pointed out in 3.525, it is surprising to find that rule II-33r, ni- replacement, applies here since the di- prefix is in pos. 4, not in pos. 6, and should not trigger the readjustment rule. (The agentive passive si- perfectives do not trigger a readjustment rule.) We can handle this only by adding a condition to the readjustment rule.

The agentive passives are the strongest environment for the oo- variant, suggesting that the innovation is starting here. In all likelihood this began because of the doubly marked nature of the ni- replacement rule in agentive passives. The gho- readjustment rule that has been extended to this environment is of much higher frequency than is ni- replacement, and it is triggered by *any* preceding conjunct prefix making it a less restricted rule. Thus the oo- variant in agentive passives represents a regularization in the grammar, the loss of a highly marked readjustment rule from an exceptional environment and the extension of the more productive readjustment rule that is used in the progressives and ghi- perfectives. A very few speakers have further generalized this use of the gho- readjustment rule to the other environment for ni- replacement, the active ni- perfectives with aspect and d- or l- classifier. It remains to be documented to what extent the gho- readjustment rule is being so generalized. It appears to be a very weak innovation at this time.

In passing, it is worth pointing out that a similar extension of gho- readjustment has been detected in imperfectives of náhi- 'turn over' verbs which in Young and Morgan contain an inexplicable ee- in third and fourth person, e.g. náhideejish 'he is rolling over', náhideeghał 'he is rolling over'. These are frequently treated like futures with gho- readjustment replacing the more restricted rule that produces ee-, e.g. náhidoojish, náhidooghał. (The future for these verbs is still distinctive, náhididooghał.)

4.103 Aspect+si

In the analysis of the si- perfectives the aspect+si verbs were demonstrated to be the most highly marked verbs in the mode system requiring a total of seven readjustment rules beyond the three general perfective readjustments. It is not surprising that we find considerable variation in the use of certain aspect+si forms.

Statements in the literature on aspect+si reveal that there has been variation in the duals of aspect+si for a long time. Hoijer notes the following variants for aspect+si duals: 1d can be Cee(d) or Cisii(d);

2d can be Coo(h) or, less often, Cisoo(h) or rarely siCoo(h) (SH:37). The si- perfective paradigm section in Young and Morgan 1943a lists alternants for the duals (pp. 92-94), and aspect+si verbs in their dictionaries are listed with varying patterns in the duals. Reichard also gives occasional variants for aspect+si duals (1951:181).

Investigation of several aspect+si verbs with nine Navajo speakers yielded three types of variation, the well documented non-application of the si- deletion rule in the duals, the less cited metathesis of si- and the aspect prefix, and the loss of the ld í- lowering rule, III-165r.

In the analysis of aspect+si perfectives we accounted for the ee- in the ld forms by the highly restricted ld í- lowering rule.

(III-165r) í → é / ASP+___+iid

We also saw that this rule is analogous to the apparently idiosyncratic nasal vowel in aspect+si paradigms in several other Athapaskan languages. Based on initial responses, the speakers queried were about evenly divided between the ee- form and an unchanged ii-, e.g. deeldzil or diildzil 'we strained', deebaa' or diibaa' 'we went to war'. Most of the nine speakers sampled regard both forms as being equally acceptable. A minority of speakers, including William Morgan (personal communication) show a consistent preference for the ee- form. This trend toward the loss of the idiosyncratic ld í- lowering rule represents a regularization of allomorphy in the aspect+si paradigm.

The variation in the application of rule III-163r, si- deletion, in the duals is harder to explain. For the majority of aspect+si verbs it appears that the most common variant is the "regular" one where si- has been deleted; e.g. deebaa' ∿ diibaa' 'we went to war'

heetí' ∿ hiiti' 'we broke them off', doobaa' 'you went to war', hooti'
'you broke them off'. All nine speakers accepted these verbs with a
non-deleted si- prefix, disiibaa', hisiiti', disoobaa', hisooti'. One
speaker who consistently employs the 1d í- lowering rule renders
these first duals as diseebaa', hiseeti', but this seems to be unusual.
Less frequent, and for many speakers an unacceptable variant for these
verbs, is a form with metathesized aspect and mode prefixes, sidiibaa',
sidoobaa'.[3] However, one speaker consistently preferred the metathesized
version, sidi- to the non-metathesized disi-, with deleted si- still the
best alternant. Thus, if si- is not deleted, there seems to be an
optional metathesis rule:

(5) di + si → si + di

Interestingly, aspect+si verbs that contain the ni- 'terminative'
prefix do not vary in quite the same way as di+si or hi+si. Again,
deleted si- is the preferred form, neet'į́į' ∿ niit'į́į', noo'į́į 'steal
it'; neeltł'ah ∿ niiltł'ah, nooltł'ah 'prevent it'. The only acceptable
alternant to these forms is the metathesized siniit'į́į', sinoo'į́į';
siniiltł'ah, sinooltł'ah. Non-metathesized *nisiit'į́į' or *nisooltł'ah
are incorrect for all speakers queried. For some obscure reason if si-
perfective does not delete by rule III-163r, then a metathesis rule
must apply to a ni+si sequence. Rule 5 can be collapsed into an
aspect+si metathesis rule that operates on ni- and optionally on di-.

(5) $\begin{Bmatrix} di \\ ni \end{Bmatrix}$ + si → si + $\begin{Bmatrix} di \\ ni \end{Bmatrix}$

condition: optional or dialect dependent for di-

Below I give derivations for two aspect+si duals where si- deletion
has not applied.

/di+si+í+iid+baa'/   /ni+si+í+iid+ł+tł'ah/

si dele: _____ _____
asp si metath: ([si+di+iid+baa'])   [si+ni+iid+ł+tł'ah]
ultimately: [sidiibaa'] ∼   [siniiltł'ah]
               [disiibaa']

There are three separate stages to the variation in the aspect+si duals. First, the ld í- lowering rule has become optional in first duals. Second, the si- deletion rule has become optional for almost all aspect+si duals. Third, an aspect+si metathesis rule applies to all instances of ni+si, optionally to di+si, and never to hi+si (due to the fact that this would alter the unstable hi- 'seriative' prefix by placing a conjunct prefix, si-, to the left of hi-).

As we stated, the optionality of the ld í- lowering rule is readily explained as a regularization of allomorphy by the suppression of a morphologically marked rule. The optionality of si- deletion is more difficult to account for. Si- deletion is certainly an unnatural phonological rule. Its suppression might stem from an effort to keep si- as a surface marker for the perfective. Yet why do the 1sg and 2sg forms never show the si- prefix? Perhaps the vowel initial dual pronouns constitute a weaker environment for si- deletion as is indicated in this revised version of the rule.

(III-163r) si → ∅ / ASP+___+X+[

condition: optional if X = VC

The aspect+si metathesis rule is particularly intriguing. The metathesis seems in no way to be a simplification in the grammar. Since the "slippage" of the si- prefix is a crucial link in the Na-Dene hypothesis, the fact that ni+si requires a metathesis reflects some deep historical property of these two prefixes. The optional di+si metathesis may be based upon analogy with the ni+si process.

Thus, the variation in the highly marked aspect+si perfectives reflects both simplification and a curious historical irregularization. Further research may also reveal that variation in this paradigm is to a certain extent regional, i.e. that particular dialects may be more prone to optional si- deletion or di+si metathesis (Robert Young, personal communication).

4.104 Perfective da- shift

The perfective da- shifts, as indicated in 3.55, are being used with considerable variation. Although our understanding of this process is very vague at this point, a few generalizations can be made about this variation.

The most visible da- shifting verbs, those that have a ghi- or ni- perfective choosing adverbial prefix such as ch'í-, ha-, ni-, or 'i- generally can take a non-shifted variant in the plural. Of thirteen speakers questioned on a list of plurals, all tended to give the da- shifted form as their initial response for most of the verbs, including III-173c-g, which contain a d- or l- classifier. But most speakers also accept non-shifted forms as variants as in the right hand forms of (6).

(6) a. ch'ídeizlá ∿ ch'ídeinílá
 b. k'ídeizhch'iizh ∿ k'ídeiních'iizh
 c. yóó' 'adeizlóóz ∿ yóó' 'adayíílóóz
 d. ndeisbą́ą́z ∿ ndeinííbą́ą́z
 e. ch'ídadeesdlo' ∿ ch'ídadeeldlo'
 f. hadadeeskeez ∿ hadadoolkeez

Some speakers claimed that both variants were equally acceptable, but most regard the si- perfective forms as preferable. One speaker said that the non-shifted variants are "young Navajo". William Morgan (personal communication), however, is strict about the da- shift and regards the non-shifted variants as incorrect.

On the other hand, certain verbs are less acceptable in non-shifted form. For example, hadeisbą́ą́z 'they pl drove it up' is strongly preferable to hadayííłbą́ą́z since the non-shifted form is homophonous with a hada- 'down' verb, hadayííłbą́ą́z 'he drove it down'. In this case the competing homonym makes the da- shifted form relatively obligatory. It remains to be determined to what extent homophony and other factors affect the acceptability of perfective da- shift variants.

No variation in plurals was found for the non-shifting verbs with +i+, with thematic prefixes, or with d/l class verbs having no adverbial prefixes that were discussed in Chapter Three (174) and (175), i.e. deiniiłdoi not *deiniisdoi 'they pl warmed it up', dahóótáál not *dahaztáál 'they sang'.

As was noted in III-(176)-(178), it is still not possible to predict the plural for ∅ or ł-class ghi- perfectives with no derivational prefixes. Some ghi- perfectives such as dayííghą́ą́' 'they killed them' and dayíínizh 'they plucked them' are almost never given with si- perfectives, *deizghą́ą́', *deizhnizh, while others seem to be equally acceptable with both plurals, dayííts'ǫ́ǫ́z or deizts'ǫ́ǫ́z. Ni- perfectives with ∅/ł classifier and no adverbial prefixes seem to be equally acceptable with non-shifted and shifted plurals, deiní'eezh or deizh'eezh 'they pl led them', deiníłóóz or deizłóóz 'they pl led it'. William Morgan only accepts the shifted si- perfectives for these ni- perfective plurals (personal communication). In checking these forms what is most significant is the consistency with which the plurals are reported, either as definitely non-shifting or as shifting or non-shifting, suggesting that there is some active mechanism for distinguishing between them.

Generally speaking, the greatest amount of variation in perfective da- shift is in verbs with the productive perfective choosing adverbial prefixes. In these verbs the si- perfective is still predominant, but Robert Young (personal communication) feels that there is far greater tolerance of non-shifted plurals in these forms than there was thirty years ago. At that time non-shifted plurals were weakly tolerable in first and second person plurals, e.g. ch'ídaniilyá, ch'ídanoołá. But, he recalls, in third person plurals variants were generally never heard. The only published source on perfective da- shift, the Franciscan Fathers' verb paradigms gathered over 60 years ago, corroborate Young's intuition in that da- shifted plurals are presented with no hint of variation (while variation is noted for other forms) (1912a:13-19).

Perfective da- shift must be a difficult structure to learn. This trend toward greater tolerance of non-shifted plurals represents a simplification in the grammar. The mechanism that triggers the shift to a si- perfective in these verbs, whether it is an underlying si- perfective that is overridden by the perfective choosing properties of the adverbial prefix or whether it is some more obscure semantic constraint on the perfective morphemes, is wholly abstract from the surface forms. The non-shifted forms are a reanalysis based on the surface form of the perfective, i.e. ghi- and ni- perfectives construct their plurals just by adding da-.

Numerous questions about variation in the perfective da- shift remain unexplored. It would be of interest to determine the age at which this structure is being acquired and the extent to which young people do not have the shift or have it only weakly. Of the twelve speakers questioned in this study, only one person tended to prefer non-shifted plurals in the perfective choosing verbs (but this was not the case with this person for all such verbs). It is also possible that some younger speakers at times over-generalize the da- shift, as seems to be the case in the two instances of deizhnizh 'they pl plucked them' that were recorded (instead of the generally preferred dayíínizh).

4.105 Progressive da- shift

The plural formation rule in the progressive, III-97 progressive da- shift, is one of the most complex grammatical rules in Navajo.

(III-97) $\#ghi + (X) + STEM \rightarrow$
$\quad\quad\quad 1 \quad\quad 2 \quad\quad 3 \;\;$ [progressive]

$da \# yi\text{+}ni + (X) + STEM$
$\;\;4 \quad\quad 1 \quad\quad 2 \quad\quad 3 \;\;$ [${}^{\text{imperfective}}_{\text{momentaneous}}$]

Undoubtedly, progressive da- shift is acquired quite late, and it is not surprising that some younger speakers are simplyfying this rule or, in some cases, are simply not learning it.

In checking the plurals of seven progressive verbs with nine speakers, some variation was found in each verb. For example, three speakers rendered dah da'íníidlįįh 'we pl are on a drinking spree' as dah da'íníidlį́į́ł. One speaker gave yídeíghííł 'they pl are pushing it along' as yídeíghił. Two speakers said yádeíníiltééh 'we pl are speaking' as yádeíníiltih. One speaker, in place of deínółteeh 'you pl are carrying an animate object' had deínółtééł. All of these variants reflect a simplification of rule III-97 where the stem remains progressive instead of shifting to the momentaneous imperfective. Only one speaker seemed to do this consistently with all the progressive plurals. William Morgan (personal communication) is strict about shifting to the momentaneous imperfective stem and regards the progressive stems as incorrect in plurals. One speaker tolerated the progressive stem but said it sounded like young, simplified Navajo.

Other variation in progressive da- shift was noted. One speaker in some third person forms observed the stem shift but did not replace the progressive with yíní-, e.g. deiyoołteeh 'they pl carry an animate object along' (which this person strongly preferred to deíłteeh), or yídeiyooghííł, 'they pl are pushing it along' instead of yídeíghííł.

Another speaker did not have the progressive da- shift at all. In intransitives this person only had the non-shifted variants, dah da'iidlį́į́ł 'we pl are on a drinking spree', yádeiiltih 'we pl are speaking'. In transitives this speaker retained the progressive prefix and stem, dayoołtééł 'they pl are carrying an animate object along', bídaoohił 'you pl are pushing it along', yídeiyooghił 'they pl are pushing it along'. It is obvious that this person constructs plurals simply by adding da- to the progressive.

It is not certain to what extent the progressive da- shift is optional in intransitives with a distinct collective plural meaning in non-shifted plurals and a separate plural meaning in the shifted forms as has been suggested by Young and Morgan. Many speakers recognize such a distinction upon suggestion, but it remains for a Navajo speaking linguist to determine how clearly it is maintained.

Although the progressive da- shift still predominates, they are signs that this complex rule is becoming simplified. Many speakers use or accept the progressive stem in place of the momentaneous imperfective stem and a few speakers do not have the rule at all. Further documentation on Navajo speech usage will probably reveal that progressive da- shift is a marker of generational differences.

4.106 Semelfactive optative 1sg

The highly visible aspectual system, the semelfactive, that was discussed in 3.114 and 3.22 as part of the analysis of ∅ imperfectives and iteratives, is considered to take a +i+ prefix in aspect position in the imperfective and iterative modes only. In the other three modes the semelfactives show no evidence of the +i+ prefix. However, in the first person singular of the semelfactive optative paradigm there is considerable variation between the anticipated ó- and a form that contains +i+, oo-.

One sign of this variation is that out of twenty semelfactive optatives listed in Young and Morgan, nine are with ó- in 1sg (e.g. wósiih 'I wish to miss it', wóshtał 'I wish to kick it'); eight are with oo- (wooshgoh 'I wish to butt it', wooshgąsh 'I wish to witch it'); and three contain o- (woshhash 'I wish to bite it', woshkah 'I wish to shoot it with an arrow'). The length variation in the low tone o- forms is merely a phonetic inconsistency (Robert Young, personal communication).

Upon examination of these semelfactives with a dozen speakers, the ó- form was found to be the favored variant with almost everyone tolerating oo- as correct. Three persons stated that both forms were equally correct, and one person preferred the oo- variant. One speaker had an unexplainable óó- variant for these verbs, e.g. wóóshtał, wóóshłoh. A few persons reported that ó- is preferred in positive optatives with laanaa and that oo- best occurs in negative optatives with lágo (wóshtał laanaa 'I wish to kick it', wooshtał lágo 'I wish not to kick it'). Most speakers, however, do not adhere to such a distinction.

Thus, the +i+ aspect prefix is being generalized to just one member of the optative paradigm, the first person singular, where its presence is detected by the oo-. This extension of +i+ is probably due to the unusual distribution of +i+ in the semelfactives, the oo- variant being like the other +i+ aspectual systems that always contain +i+ in the optative. Just why this extension of +i+ does not proceed to other members of the semelfactive optative paradigm such as 2sg, 3 and 4 is not certain.

4.107 Iterative classifier shift

The variable nature of the classifier shift in the iterative paradigm has long been detected by students of Navajo. Haile notes that iteratives "often employ the d- form of the stem" (1947:87). Reichard states, "Often, but not always, the d- classifier is used with the customary [iterative] prefixes" (1951:133).

Hale (personal communication) remarks that the iterative classifier shift is conditioned by transitivity. ∅-class intransitives almost always shift, ∅-class transitives vary, and ł-class transitives are generally not shifted.

In checking the use of iteratives with more than a dozen speakers, it is clear that the classifier shift is still the predominant iterative pattern. Based on initial responses, the shifted forms (nabínáshgił 'I repeatedly push it around', néinil'įįh 'he repeatedly sees it', násdlóós 'I repeatedly lead it') are heard most frequently. The majority of speakers accept the non-shifted forms (nabínáshhił, néinił'įįh, násłóós) as variants. With certain verbs of high frequency the shifted form is more strongly preferred: néisdzįįh 'I repeatedly stand up' rather than néisįįh, ńdísh'niih 'I repeatedly say it' rather than ńdishniih. On the other hand certain ł-class verbs that are apparently strongly transitive in connotation tend to remain unshifted: náníłchosh 'you repeatedly eat greens' is preferred to nánílchosh, náníłchį́į́h 'you repeatedly smell it' is preferred to nánílchį́į́h. It is uncertain why some ł-class transitives such as néinil'įįh are preferred with a shifted classifier while others are not.

Of the several "voice" functioning prefixes that require a classifier shift ('ádi- 'reflexive', 'ahi- 'reciprocal', bi'di- 'agentive passive', and ná- 'iterative') the iterative is the only one in which the classifier shift is variable. The iterative classifier shift has become variable because this process is "opaque" with respect to the phonetically identical ná- 'encircle' prefix, which never takes a classifier shift (nánił'ah 'you are skinning it', nánííkad 'you are sewing it'). According to Kiparsky "a rule is opaque if a representation of the sort it eliminates exists on the surface" (1971:627). In other words, the iterative classifier shift is hard to learn because another ná- prefix contradicts this process by never requiring a classifier shift.

There is yet another ná- prefix, ná- 'back', which adds to the opacity of the iterative classifier shift. Ná- back appears in both shifted and non-shifted forms; ńdeeshdáál 'I will go back', nísísdlį́į́' 'I will become again' are high frequency verbs that always require a d- classifier with ná- 'back'. On the other hand, nání'ą́ 'I gave it back' is almost interchangeable with a shifted form, nánísht'ą́, with some speakers characterizing the former as being more archaic. Another verb, nánííłtį́ 'I gave an animate object back' is usually preferred to its shifted form náníshtį́. Thus it is not clear as to the classifier shifting properties of ná- 'back'. Robert Young (personal communication) feels that in old Navajo ná- 'back' more frequently caused a classifier shift than it does now. On the other hand, intuitions of speakers on a number of these forms suggest that the non-shifted verbs are more archaic.[4]

This uncertainty about ná- 'back' coupled with the non-shifting ná- 'encircle' prefix, plus the possibility that certain ł-class verbs are more overtly transitivized and less prone to classifier shifts, conspire to make the iterative classifier shift rule opaque. Though it appears that there has been variation on the iterative classifier shift for some time, it is still the preferred variant.

4.108 Hi- 'seriative'

We saw in 3.6 that the hi- 'seriative' prefix is highly unstable phonologically. Reichard has noted several types of variants for hi- (1951:375-376). Also, an examination of hi- verbs in Young and Morgan reveals certain inconsistencies. In addition, in a sampling of hi- 'seriatives' with nine Navajos, three categories of variation appeared.

There is a tendency for some speakers to streamline hi- verbs that require rule III-187, +hi+di metathesis, and rule III-184, h/s glide. For example, five of nine speakers gave some or all of the right hand variants in (7) for 'hang an animate object up' and three of nine persons gave some or all variants in the right hand column of (8) for 'plow'.

(7) a. dah yidiyiiłteeh ~ dah yidiiłteeh
    b. dah yidiyiiltį́ ~ dah yidiiłtį́
    c. dah ndiyiiłtį́ ~ dah ndiiłtį́
    d. dah shidiyiiłtį́ ~ dah shidiiłtį́

(8) a. nahodiyeeshdlał ~ nahodeeshdlał
    b. nahodiyį́į́łdlał ~ nahodį́į́łdlał
    c. nahodiyoołdlał ~ nahodoołdlał

These right-hand variants show a loss of the hi- where metathesis and h/s glide should have applied.

There are signs that some hi- verbs with y- have been reanalyzed without hi- for some time. For example, according to the h/s glide rule, we would expect h- to become y- in nahwiyiildlaad 'we dpl are plowing', nahwiyołdlaad 'you dpl are plowing'. In Young and Morgan these are given as nahwiildlaad, nahoołdlaad. In checking these forms the ones without y- were found to be more prevalent, with speakers indicating some awareness that the forms with y- are more archaic. Despite the dictionary entry, William Morgan (personal communication) prefers the y- forms.

In the analysis of hi- 'seriative' in 3.6 I made brief reference to a ji+hi metathesis rule, rule III-192, that must be added to the grammar to derive verbs such as hizhdiłnaah. However, there is variation in the use of this rule when the element to the right of hi- is a vowel and competition is created between ji+hi metathesis and h/s glide. The following verbs illustrate this variation:

(9) a. hijeechééh ~ jiyeechééh 'he arrives hopping'
    b. hijeeghał ~ jiyeeghał 'he arrives wriggling'
    c. hijooghał ~ jiyooghał 'he is wriggling along'

   d. hijótííh   ∿   jiyótííh   'he wishes to break them off'
   e. bíhijóɬtɬ'óóɬ ∿   bíjiyóɬtɬ'óóɬ 'he wishes to tie it to it'
   f. hijiiɬnaah   ∿   jiyiiɬnaah   'he gives it life'.

 In investigating these forms no clear trend was determined. Most persons accept both forms as being interchangeable with only a slight perception on the part of a few persons that the y- form is more archaic.

 As was stated in Chapter Three the ji+hi metathesis rule applies when ji+hi appears before a subsequence, X, that is in turn before C_o[, i.e. when h/s deletion is blocked. However, as I have just demonstrated, if the subsequence is a vowel, the rule is optional.

 (III-192) ji + hi → hi + ji / ___+X+C_o[

    condition: optional if X = V

 If rule III-192 does not apply by condition, then h- turns to y- before the vowel. The two variants for 9d would be derived as follows:

    9d/ji+hi+ó+tííh/

ji+hi metath: ([hi+ji+ó+tííh])

V dele: [hi+j+ó+tiih]   ∿   [ji+h+ó+tííh]

h/s glide: _____   ∿   [ji+y+ó+tííh]

ultimately: [hijótííh]   ∿   [jiyótííh]

We have already detected that there is a tendency for the y- allomorph of the hi- 'seriative' prefix to be reanalyzed. Certainly the presence of the ji+hi metathesis rule which bleeds the rule that produces y- contributes to the instability of the y- forms.

 One other type of hi- variation has been detected. Occasionally, certain verbs have a variant form with hi- in word initial position as in the right-hand column below.

(10) a. yiyiitííh ∿ hiyiitííh
　　 b. jiitííh ∿ hijiitííh
　　 c. łeeh yiyiinííł ∿ łeeh hiyiinííł
　　 d. yidiyootih ∿ hidiyootih
　　 e. dah yidiyiiłtį́ ∿ dah hidiyiiłtį́

Note that d and e actually show a <u>double</u> occurrence of hi- (since the y- is an underlying hi-).

Frequently, fourth person forms of hi- 'seriative' appear in triplets: a form that has ji- initially with h- gliding to y-, a ji+hi metathesized form (where h/s glide has been bled), and a form with both hi- and y-. Examples of such variants are given below.

(11) a. jidi<u>y</u>ootih ∿ hi<u>z</u>hdootih ∿ hi<u>z</u>hdi<u>y</u>ootih
　　 b. łeeh jidi<u>y</u>oonił ∿ łeeh hi<u>z</u>hdoonił ∿ łeeh hi<u>z</u>hdi<u>y</u>oonił
　　 c. dah jidi<u>y</u>iiłteeh ∿ hi<u>z</u>hdiiłteeh ∿ dah hi<u>z</u>hdi<u>y</u>iiłteeh
　　 d. dah <u>jidiy</u>iiłtį́ ∿ hi<u>z</u>hdiiłtį́ ∿ dah hi<u>z</u>hdi<u>y</u>iiłtį́

Variants similar to those in (10) and (11) have been reported by Reichard (1951:375-376).

Looking closely at the forms in (11), we see that these are verbs where <u>both</u> III-187, hi+di metathesis, and rule III-192, ji+hi metathesis can apply. In the left-hand variant hi+di metathesis has applied and in the center variant ji+hi metathesis is operative. Since either rule bleeds the other, this is a case of what Kiparsky refers to as "mutual bleeding", i.e. only one of two rules can apply to an environment and that is the one which occurs first. In such a case Kiparsky suggests that the innovating order is the one that minimizes allomorphy (1971:600).

I presume that the left-hand variants in (11) are the original forms. The center variants are innovative and reflect a reduction in allomorphy since, after ji+hi metathesis applies, the troublesome y- is eliminated from the paradigm and hi- is preserved. The right-hand variants seem to have a doubled hi- which yields a surface form that looks as if <u>both</u> metatheses have been employed. This is apparently the same hi- that appears in (10). There must be an optional <u>hi- copying</u> rule operating here (Ken Hale, personal communication). This rule precedes ji+hi metathesis.

(12) hi+(di)+X → hi+(di)+hi+X
     1   2   3   1   2   1   3

The doubled hi- variants in (10) and (11) can now be derived.

	10b/ji+hi+tííh/	11a/ji+hi+di+ghi+tih/
<u>gho read</u>:		[ji+hi+di+gho+tih]
<u>hi copy</u>:	[ji+hi+hi+tííh]	[ji+hi+di+hi+gho+tih]
<u>ji+hi metath</u>:	[hi+ji+hi+tííh]	[hi+ji+di+hi+gho+tih]
<u>h/s dele</u>:	[hi+ji+i+tííh]	
<u>h/s glide</u>:		[hi+ji+di+yi+o+tih]
<u>V elision</u>:		[hi+j+di+yi+o+tih]
<u>deaffric</u>:		[hi+zh+di+yi+o+tih]
<u>ultimately</u>:	[hijiitííh]	[hizhdiyootih]

In sampling the verbs in (11) I found that the center and right-hand variants are about equally acceptable and that both are slightly preferred to the left-hand, ji- initial forms. William Morgan (personal communication) states that he would not use the ji- initial variants.

The three types of variation in the use of the hi- 'seriative' prefix are a consequence of the fact that the "regular" alternations that hi- undergoes are so unusual. The loss of y-, the variation in ji+hi metathesis, and the doubling of hi- are all motivated by an effort to give a more concrete analysis to the hi- prefix.

4.109 Si- 'destruct'

Since we know that the si- 'destruct' prefix follows two of the same exotic phonological rules as does hi- 'seriative', it is relevant to inquire whether it too is being used variably. It turns out that the verb 'kill it' is being reanalyzed in a different and much more radical way than are any of the hi- 'seriative' verbs.

In examining older textual material, particularly that of Haile, one finds that 1sg of the future paradigm of the verb 'kill it' is often recorded as diyeesxééł instead of diyeeshxééł (Haile, 1948:159; 1951:168).[5] In checking these variants with about fifteen Navajos I heard diyeesxééł as an initial response from no one. However, two persons (including William Morgan) said that they would be more likely to use the s- form than the sh- form. All but three of the persons questioned claimed to have heard the s- form, and almost everyone identified it as an archaism.

The derivation of diyeesxééł is of particular interest. The sh- pronoun has been converted to s- by rule II-83, progressive strident assimilation, by the s- of the si- 'destruct' prefix before that s- is turned to y- by rule III-184, h/s glide.[6]

/di+si+ghi+sh+ł+ghééł/

ghe read:	[di+si+ghe+sh+ł+ghééł]
prog strid assim:	[di+si+ghe+s+ł+ghééł]
h/s glide:	[di+yi+ghe+s+ł+ghééł]
ultimately:	[diyeesxééł]

The more prevalent form, diyeeshxééł, has reordered progressive strident assimilation after h/s glide. The reordering is understandable since the s- that triggers progressive strident assimilation does not appear on the surface in any form in the future paradigm. The reordering suggests that speakers are treating the future of 'kill it' more concretely.

This trend toward a more concrete analysis of 'kill it' is more apparent in the variation recorded for other modes of 'kill it'. In fact, from the extent of the reanalysis it appears that si- 'destruct' and its rules are posing more of a learning problem than hi- 'seriative' and its rules. There is a strong trend to reanalyze 'kill it' as though it contains a ɬiɬ aspect prefix instead of si-. Of twelve speakers questioned, eight showed restructuring in at least one member of the imperfective paradigm. Below I give the usual imperfective of 'kill it' in the first column and then I list four of the ways in which it was recorded.

(13) 1 sisxé   yiishxé   yiishxé   yiishxé   sisxé
      2 síɬxé   yiiɬxé   yiiɬxé   síɬxe   síɬxé
      3 yiyiiɬxé   _____   _____   _____   _____
      4 jiiɬxé   _____   _____   _____   _____
      1d siilghé   yiilghé   yiilghé   yiilghé   siyiilghé
      2d soɬxé   wooɬxé   soɬxé   soɬxé   siyoɬxé

In addition, six of eight persons questioned gave the negative command (the optative 2sg) as wóóɬxééɬ lágo instead of the anticipated sóóɬxééɬ lágo. One gave it as siyóóɬxééɬ lágo.

The perfective forms were found to be generally more intact. However, the following variants were recorded; the expected forms are given at the left.

(14) 1 séɬxį́   yiséɬxį́
      2 síníɬxį́   yisíníɬxį́   siyíníɬxį́
      4 jiisxį́   jiyiisxį́
      1d siilghį́ siyiilghį́   yeelghį́

Thus, what we viewed to be a trend toward a more concrete analysis of si- in the futures has now given way to wholesale reanalysis of the paradigm for many speakers. Si- 'destruct' is being replaced by a +i+ aspect prefix, hence yiiɫxé instead of síɫxe in the imperfective 2sg. The reanalysis is as yet incomplete and most persons vary on some forms. There is a clear perception that the s- forms are "the old way to say it". The perfective has received less reanalysis since the original perfective shows no evidence of a separate si- prefix (after modal prefix si- has been deleted by rule III-163r, si- deletion); i.e. it looks like a regular si- perfective. This reanalysis is clearly based on the semelfactive aspect: +i+ in the imperfective and si- perfective.

This radical reanalysis of 'kill it' is motivated by the unnatural status of the phonological rules that apply to si- 'destruct', h/s glide and h/s deletion. Since si- 'destruct' appears in just one verb base, these rules are less likely to be learned than the analogous rules that apply to the fairly productive hi- 'seriative' prefix. Because the hi- 'seriative' rules are being used variably, the unusual analogy between the two prefixes is breaking down. The zero environment forms, yiyiiɫxé and jiiɫxé, are providing the model for the reanalysis; after s- has deleted, these verbs appear to be like ordinary semelfactive +i+ verbs such as yiyiitaɫ, jiitaɫ.

4.110 Yi- doubling

We have seen that rule III-19, yi- doubling, applies to three distinct environments, in the imperfective and perfective of +i+ aspect verbs, in ghi- perfectives, and in hi- 'seriatives' and si- 'destruct'.

(15) a. yiyiiɫgąsh   /yi+i+ɫ+gąsh/
      b. yiyíínizh   /yi+ghi+í+nizh/
      c. yiyiitííh   /yi+hi+tííh/

In each case the element to the right of yi- is a vowel at the time the reduplication rule applies. The rule is blocked by any conjunct prefix that appears in the string ##yi+i+[, e.g. yinii₁dóóh 'he heats it'.

However, there is variation in the application of the yi- doubling rule when there is a disjunct prefix preceding yi- direct object. For example, when da- plural is inserted into a verb that can undergo yi- doubling, two forms are heard.

(16) a. dayii₁gǝsh ∿ deiyii₁gǝsh 'they witch him'
     b. dayíínizh ∿ deiyíínizh 'they plucked them'
     c. dayiitííh ∿ deiyiitííh 'they broke them off'
     d. dayíí₁chxǫ' ∿ deiyíí₁chxǫ' 'they ruined it'

Thus yi- doubling has applied despite the presence of a preceding disjunct prefix. The dei- variant is very common for these verbs. It is used at least occasionally by the majority of Navajo speakers, although it is still the weaker variant.

The same variation seems somewhat less common in iteratives, but speakers, upon questioning, almost always accepted both of the following variants.

(17) a. náyii₁tsééh ∿ néiyii₁tsééh 'he repeatedly sees it'
     b. náyii₁gah ∿ néiyii₁gah 'he repeatedly whitens it'
     c. náyii₁ch'i₁ ∿ néiyii₁ch'i₁ 'he repeatedly curls it'

It could be, then, that the yi- doubling rule has been generalized to operate after a disjunct prefix instead of only after ##. Rule III-19 might be so revised.

(III-19) ∅ → yi / #___yi+i+[

On the other hand, it is also possible that this variation may not be a change in the yi- doubling rule, but, rather, at the time of plural formation, the phonologically introduced yi- may have been reanalyzed as an underlying prefix.

The ya- 'tilt' verbs contain a ɬiɬ aspect prefix and, conceivably, could provide an environment for variation in the third person.

(18) a. yayiizííd ∿ yeiyiizííd 'he pours it'
    b. yayiiziid ∿ yeiyiiziid 'he poured it'
    c. yayiikaah ∿ yeiyiikaah 'he spills it'
    d. yayiiką́ ∿ yeiyiiką́ 'he spilled it'

In checking these ya- 'tilt' forms with ten speakers only one person gave the yei- (yi- doubled) form initially. Most, but not all persons tolerate the yei- form as correct.

Thus, the acceptance of the doubled yi- is considerably greater in da- plural than it is in ya- 'tilt'. This is understandable since in the ya- 'tilt' verbs, unlike the plurals and iteratives given above, the original environment for yi- doubling is never present in some form of the paradigm because of the thematic ya- prefix. Since there is no surface yiyii- form, reanalysis or the generalized yi- doubling rule is not as likely.

4.111 Sh/shi- 'scold'

The verb 'scold him' contains an unusual prefix that occurs in no other verb. It is uncertain whether this prefix is /sh/ or /shi/ in underlying representation, and it floats in position between pos. 6 and 10. In (19) are listed several forms from 'scold him' as they are given in Young and Morgan (with preposed bich'a) (YM, 1951:276).

(19) a. hoshishkééh I1

b. hoshíkééh I2

c. hashkééh I3

d. hodeeshkeeł F1

e. hodííshkeeł F2

f. hodooshkeeł F3

g. hodiikeeł F1d

h. hodoohkeeł F2d

i. hoshííshkeed P1

j. hóóshkeed P3

In a and b this prefix seems to be shi- in pos. 6 but in c sh- appears next to the stem. In d, g, and h this prefix does not appear at all, and in e, f, and j it is to the right of the modal prefix in classifier position. In i it appears as shi- again, and, more important, the usual sh- deletion rule that applies in ∅/ł perfectives has not applied (presuming, of course, that this is a ∅-class verb).

These radical alternations, shi:sh:∅, plus the jump in position, pos. 6 when subject pronoun is filled and pos. 10 when it is empty, can be derived from a single base only by readjustment rules that truncate or insert a vowel or delete to the prefix. Such rules would be unprecedented.

Investigation of 'scold him' with twelve speakers reveals that it is being used with a great deal of variability. 19a, b, c, and j were consistently heard as above, but the following variants were recorded for the other forms in (19).

(20) d. hoshideeshkeeł
    e. hoshidííkeeł   hodííkeeł
    f. hoshidookeeł   hodookeeł
    g. hoshidiikeeł
    h. hoshidoohkeeł
    i. hoshííkeed

There is little pattern in the responses of the speakers questioned. In the futures most speakers, including William Morgan (personal communication), despite the dictionary entry, tend to treat the 'scold' prefix as a pos. 6 throughout where YM have it in classifier position or delete it entirely. The unusual perfective, 19i is the preferred form for most speakers rather than the more regular 20i.

Although there is widespread variation in 'scold', no consensus was reached as to the more conservative form. This variation indicates that speakers treat the 'scold' prefix as having no single, consistent underlying form.

4.112 Suppletive stem initial consonants

Most stem initial consonants in Navajo verbs are entirely regular. As was demonstrated in 2.71, stem initials undergo two phonological rules. Continuant obstruents are devoiced by a voiceless continuant or are affricated when next to d-. D- also glottalizes sonorants and turns '- to t'-. Non-continuant obstruents remain unchanged.

A number of verbs show alternations in the stem initial consonant that cannot be captured by these general rules. In this section I demonstrate that some of these suppletive verbs are being regularized.

The most conspicuous verbs with irregular stem initial consonants are 'sg S goes' and 'eat', which contain vowel initial stems. Their stem alternations can be explained in part by phonological rules, but some special markings are also required. For example, in the imperfective and perfective of 'sg S goes' (21) the gh- and y- stem initials and in the imperfective of 'eat' (22) the gh-, y-, and s- stem initials must be lexically marked.

(21) a. díshááh   I1
     b. dínááh   I2
     c. dighááh I3
     d. déyá   P1
     e. díníyá   P2
     f. deeyá   P3

(22) a. 'ashą́   I1
     b. 'íyą́   I2
     c. 'ayą́   I3
     d. 'iidą́ I1d
     e. 'ohsą́ I2d

Krauss has demonstrated that stem initials for 'sg S goes' correlate throughout Athapaskan and Eyak and that they reflect archaic vowel alternations in the proto-Athapaskan-Eyak classifiers (1969).

Some verb bases derived from 'sg S goes' that take a d- or ł- classifier, such as 'return' (23) and 'perform a ceremony' (24), have suppletive alternations in the perfective.

(23) a. nánishdááh I1
     b. nánisdzá   P1
     c. nádzá   P3

(24) a. nahółá   I2
     b. nahosésá   P1
     c. nahosiilzá P1d

Most of the bases that employ the 'sg S goes' and 'eat' stems are of very high frequency and are found with little variation. However, 'sg S goes' verbs with ł- classifier, like (24), are frequently heard with ł- in the perfective, nahosééłáá', nahosiilyáá' for 24b and c, where the irregular z- stem initial is dropped in favor of ł-. Most speakers regard this ł- stem as an innovation. William Morgan accepts only the z/s forms for 24b and c (personal communication).

The 'rope-like object' stem takes an irregular stem initial consonant, ly-, whenever d- classifier is next to the stem. This is evidenced in the 1d forms of 'roll a cigarette' (25) and 'carry a rope around' (26).

(25) a. diih yishłé   I1
    b. diih nilé   I2
    d. diih yiilyé   I1d
    d. diih yilá   P1
    e. diih yiilyá   P1d

(26) a. naashłé   I1
    b. nanilé   I2
    c. neiilyé   I1d
    d. nisélá   P1
    e. nisiilya   P1d

These ly- alternations seem to be invariable in the imperfectives, but some variation is detected in the perfectives. Of nine persons questioned, three gave diih yiidlá for 25e and nisiidlá for 26e. Similar variants recorded were ch'íniidlá for ch'íniilyá 'we carried a rope out' and ch'édlá for ch'élyá 'a rope was carried out'. However, the majority of speakers questioned these regularized stems. One person remarked that ch'íniidlá was "baby talk". Interestingly, in the Franciscan Fathers' 1912 dictionary variants are listed for 26e, nsílyă ∿ nsidlă (1912a:16). William Morgan's comment is that nisiidlá is just as acceptable as nis_ilyá but that in other forms such as ch'íniilyá, the regularized stem is unacceptable (personal communication). It is uncertain why one base should tolerate the regularization over another. Based on the Franciscan Fathers' data and Morgan's comment, it may be that older speakers are more tolerant of the regularization, nisiidlá, than are younger speakers.

A different sort of variation is present in other l- initial stems. In stems where l- is preceded by ∅ classifier and is followed by a nasal vowel or n- there is a tendency to reanalyze the stem initial l- as a classifier and the n- as a stem initial consonant. A frequent and perhaps preferred form for 'they look alike', 'ahinoolin is 'ahinoolnin. A few persons claim that they always use the ln- form here. On the other hand, the related verb nahalin 'it looks like', a very high frequency word, is not acceptable as *nahalnin. It is uncertain why the reanalysis should be confined to one base but not the other.

This l ∾ ln variation is found in the verb 'taste it'. Six of thirteen persons gave the perfective paradigm as the right-hand forms of (27).

(27) 1 sélįh   sélnih
      2 sínílįh   sínílnih
      3 yizlįh   yisnih
      1d siidlįh   siilnih
      2d soolįh   soołnih

The ln- paradigm is reinterpreted as having an l- classifier in 3 where s- voicing has not applied and in 2d where oh- reduction has not applied. However, the first person form is exceptional since the sh- pronoun has deleted next to the apparent l- classifier. It seems that the regularized sisnih has not yet become acceptable.

The imperfective paradigm of 'taste it' also shows this ln- reanalysis, yiishnih, yiilnih, yiyiilnih. This 1sg form is of interest because it is homophonous with yiishnih 'I am milking it'.[7]

In 2.71 I showed how the continuant devoicing rule has led us to assume that voiceless fricatives in stem initial position are voiced in underlying representation. An apparent exception to this is the verb 'be itchy', (28), which seems to contain a voiceless stem initial, h-.

(28) 1 yisxęs[8]

2 nihęs

3 yihęs

1d yiigęs

2d wohhęs

Reichard noted the idiosyncratic character of this stem initial h-. She provided a plausible explanation for it when she discovered a variant stem -kęs, yishkęs. It is a common fact that many Navajo speakers spirantize k- to a continuant x-, nix̱idégo' for niḵidégo' 'I fell and hit the ground'. Thus Reichard explained -hęs (or -xęs) as being derived from -kęs by spirantization (1945:162).

In investigating this verb with eleven speakers, no -kęs variant was found nor had anyone even heard it. This stem, it seems, has been reanalyzed completely as a x- initial. One speaker gave the paradigm with a ł- classfier (apparently still retaining the intransitive meaning), niłxęs, yiilghęs.

A few verbs with stem initial z- such as 'singe it' (29) and 'rip it' (30) have suppletive first dual and passive forms.

(29) 1 yiséés   (30) 1 'iisǫ́ǫ́s

2 nizéés   2 'anizǫ́ǫ́s

3 yizéés   3 'iizǫ́ǫ́s

1d yiiḏéés   1d 'iiḏǫ́ǫ́s

2d wohséés   2d 'oohsǫ́ǫ́s

ps bidi'ḏéés

I have detected a tendency to regularize the 1d and passive forms in these paradigms. For 29.1d seven of the fourteen persons questioned

accepted yiilzéés (three persons preferred this form), which is a
reanalysis of this stem with a ł- classifier. Four persons felt the
correct form to be yiidzéés, which is a regularization of the ∅-class
stem. Less variation was found for 'rip it'. One person preferred
'iilzǫ́ǫ́s, and another 'iidzǫ́ǫ́s for 30.1d. Generally speaking, the
suppletive forms for these verbs are holding up well, but for some
speakers there is a temptation to regularize them.

In Chapter Two I surveyed some of the confusion that has arisen
over the phoneme y-, which is phonetically identical to gh- before front
vowels. I showed in the analysis of the modes that /gh/ and /y/ are
readily distinguishable by morphophonemic rules. For example, in the
analysis of rule II-35, d- effect (2.71), it was shown that d+gh becomes
g- while d+y preglottalizes to 'y- like the other sonorants m- and n-.
However, there is more to be said about the stem initial y-, which poses
several phonological problems. Initially, a distinction must be made
between the y-'s that appear in vowel initial stems such as 'sg S goes'
(21) and 'eat' (22), which are secondary and are accounted for by
morphologically marked rules, and primary stem initial y-'s, which
follow two distinct morphophonemic patterns.

The most synchronically regular of the primary y-'s is exemplified
in only two verbs, -yói and -yóół, as is illustrated below in 'be good
at, excel' (31) and 'take a breath' (32).

(31)	1 honishyói	(32)	1 'iishyóół
	2 honíyói		2 'aniyóół
	3 hayói		3 'iiyóół
	1d honii'yói		1d 'ii'yóół
	2d honohyói		2d 'oohyóół

In these paradigms y- is shown to be distinctive from gh- by the non-application of continuant devoicing in 1sg and 2d and by the preglottalized 'y- in 1d (about which more will be said below).

The other y- initial paradigm is highly irregular synchronically. Haile referred to verbs such as 'be wise' (33) and 'drive (a small herd) about' (34) as 's-y-dz type' stems.

(33) 1 honisą́
     2 honíyą́
     3 hóyą́
     1d honiidzą́
     2d honohsą́

(34) 1 nanisood[9]
     2 naníyood
     3 neiniyood
     1d naniidzood
     2d nanohsood

The problem with these paradigms is the difficulty in reconciling the s:dz alternations in 1sg, 2d, and 1d and the y- in the other forms. On the surface the analysis is suspended between two possible underlying stem initials, y- and z-, and it might seem best to distinguish y-initials that undergo s:dz alternations from those that do not by a diacritic feature in the lexicon. Howren has proposed that a distinct phoneme, a front dorso-velar continuant gh^y- which corresponds to the PA stem initial consonant for these stems, underlies the s-y-dz verbs. This segment is deaffricated by d- and then merges with dz- by a readjustment rule. Howren makes no mention of the s- in 1sg or 2d (Howren, 1971:108). This analysis is on the right track but is in need of further amplification.

Sapir's view on the two y- paradigms is ironic from the point of view of current theory. He regarded the s-y-dz stems as regular and the y-'s that are preglottalized by d- effect as irregular.

> We should have expect *dzói in the d-modified forms of -yói but, for reasons which seem totally obscure at present, -yói here follows the analogy of stems with initial n and m . . . The process -dn-, -dm- → -'n-, -'m- may be considered true phonetic laws but -dy- → -'y- contravenes all known analogies,

> which suggest -dz- as the regular phonetic development. We
> shall therefore infer that 'y arose, not by the operation of
> a normal phonetic law, but by a peculiar type of morphophonemic
> analogy. Perhaps analogies of this sort have played a greater
> part in linguistic history than is generally suspected (1949:229).

The irony is that what was irregular to Sapir's comparative perspective on Athapaskan is regular in terms of current theory (i.e. y- groups with the other sonsorants in being preglottalized), and what Sapir treats as regular resists synchronic analysis.

What is left unstated in Sapir's comment is an explanation as to why the s-y-dz stems are historically regular. The explanation centers on the fact that two members of the PA front palatal series, *x^y- and *g^y-, have merged with s- and dz- in Navajo while the third member, *gh^y-, generally remains unchanged (i.e. it is usually a phonetic y-) (Hoijer, 1963).[10]

As Howren has surmised, it does appear that a distinct segment, the PA gh^y- (which is generally written by Athapaskanists as y-), underlies the s-y-dz stems. At an earlier point in time a Navajo verb with underlying gh^y- stem initial consonant such as (34) would have been as follows:

(35) 1 nanishx^{y}ood

    2 nanígh^{y}ood

    3 neinigh^{y}ood

  1d naniig^{y}ood

  2d nanohx^{y}ood.

The sh- and h- in 1sg and 2d would have devoiced gh^y- to x^y-. The d+gh^y sequence would have paralleled the d- effect rule that operates on d+gh to produce a dorso-palatal affricate, g^y-. The synchronically anomalous s- and dz- in the s-y-dz stem are the product of the sound mergers that have affected the secondarily derived x^y- and g^y-.

The question remains as to how these historical facts are to be treated in a synchronic grammar. The s-y-dz stem initials can be distinguished from the sonorant y-'s by adding a new phoneme, a front, dorso-palatal voiced fricative, gh^y- (that is orthographically just y-), to the obstruent system as we have done in Table 1. It is less certain whether $g^y \to dz$ and $x^y \to s$, the historical mergers, can then be treated as synchronic phonological rules.

What is most interesting is that both the obstruent initial y- and the sonorant initial y- paradigms are being used variably. In sampling s-y-dz stems regularization of the 1sg, 2d, and 1d forms was observed. Of ten persons asked, three said that nanishyood and nanii'yood were equally acceptable for 34.1 and 1d, and five persons said that nanohyood was acceptable for 34.2d. One of these people preferred the y- forms. For (33) of ten persons questioned three preferred sonorantized honishyą́, honii'yą́ for 33.1, 33.1d, and 33.2d, and two others accepted these as correct. Other regularized s-y-dz forms were neeshyoł, nii'yoł, noohyoł for neesoł, niidzoł, noohsoł 'be driving a small herd along'.

Variation detected in the verb 'dream' suggests that it too is an s-y-dz stem, but it seems to be further along toward being reanalyzed than are 'be wise' or 'drive a small herd about'. Sapir-Hoijer present the verb 'dream' with an s- in 1sg but with a gh- initial elsewhere as in the left-hand forms of (36) (SH:52). Young and Morgan present 'dream' as a regular gh- initial as in the right-hand forms below.

(36) 1 naiseeł   neishheeł

     2   neígheeł

     3 nayigheel   neigheeł

                1d   neigeeł
            2d naoheeł   naoheeł

In checking these forms with nine speakers, the gh- forms were given initially by six persons.[11] Two gave the 1sg, 1d, and 2d forms as neiseeł, neidzeeł, and naohseeł. Most speakers questioned said that s- was possible in both 1sg and 2d, and most identified it as an archaism. There was less support given for dz- in the 1d form. William Morgan (personal communication) said that s- is possible for the 1sg form only and that dz- is vaguely possible for 1d.

Thus it appears that 'dream' is an s-y-dz verb and that it has been undergoing reanalysis for some time, as is suggested by the 2d form given by Sapir-Hoijer. It is interesting to note that 'dream' is being reanalyzed as a gh- because of the front vowel e-, while 'drive a small herd about' and 'be wise' are treated as y- because of the back vowels o- and a-.

This tendency to regularize allomorphy in the s-y-dz stems is very likely a glimpse at the "peculiar type of morphophonemic analogy" noted by Sapir. Thus, the sonorant initials, -yóí and -yóół, are s-y-dz stems that have been reanalyzed by this regularization.

Significant variation was also found in the sonorant initial paradigms (including those that are variants to the s-y-dz initials). In the first dual pronoun instead of 'y- a new phoneme, an unaspirated dorso-palatal affricate, g^y-, was recorded. Of 29 persons sampled on 31.1d honii'yóí, nine reported it as honiig^{y}óí. Of 27 persons sampled on 32.1d 'ii'yóół, ten reported it as 'iig^{y}óół. Two of ten persons preferred g^y- for the 1d of s-y-dz verbs, naniig^{y}ood, honiig^{y}ǫ́. One of these two people treated the 1sg of these verbs as a sonorant y- initial while the other kept

it with the original s-. It was also observed that some persons used
g^y- with one verb but 'y- with another, indicating that the new phoneme
is being diffused gradually and unevenly through the lexicon.

This new sound implies that some speakers are treating y- as a
voiced, front dorso-palatal continuant, gh^y-. The regular d- effect
rule applies to gh^y- and makes it [-continuant] g^y-.[12] What is most
significant is that the g^y- phoneme in the regularized y- initials is a
return to the original front palatal spirant treatment of y-.

This investigation of the variation in the obstruent and sonorant
y- stem initials gives us further clues to the historical processes that
have affected these sounds. In order to regularize allomorphy, verbs
with obstruent y- initial, gh^y-, before back vowels, by analogy with
n- and m-, have taken on the morphophonemic trait of sonorants, a
preglottalized output from d- effect. The sonorantized y-'s may first
have been treated as in velar position, $\begin{bmatrix} -cor \\ -ant \end{bmatrix}$, although we have no
phonetic proof of this. There is now a tendency to return the rare
and unstable 'y- to dorso-palatal position, $\begin{bmatrix} +cor \\ -ant \end{bmatrix}$, the very position
that is the antecedent of all the y-'s, where it is once again treated
as an obstruent. Thus, the synchronic problem posed by the y- stem
initials is being attacked by the processes of change.

As we have just seen, there is a trend for obstruent gh^y- to
become sonorantized. There is evidence that sonorantization is affecting
one other Navajo phoneme. In our discussion of d- effect in 2.71 it
was noted that a few verbs before a stem vowel o- show a distinct velar
affricate, g^w-. In checking two g^w- verbs with nine persons, four gave
them with a preglottalized back glide, yii'wozh instead of yiig^{w}ozh 'we
are ticklish', na'ii'wo' instead of na'iig^{w}o' 'we fell over stiffly'.

It appears that the one environment where d+gh clearly produces an affricate (when gh- precedes o-), is being sonorantized to 'w-. Instead of becoming [-continuant], it becomes [-continuant, +glottalized]. No speakers were heard glottalizing gh- before a front vowel. It was noted that some speakers regularly use both sonorantized 'w- and desonorantized g^y-.

In this section I have demonstrated some of the variation in the use of verbs with irregular stem initial consonants. In most cases the variation reflects a tendency to regularize allomorphy in paradigms.

4.20 Variation Summary

Although this investigation of morphophonemic variation in Navajo has been limited in scope, it has provided perspective to the analysis of the verb prefix phonology. We see that some of the more exotic aspects of the synchronic grammar--the highly marked aspect+si paradigm, the perfective and progressive da- shifts, the unusual yi- doubling rule, the obscure hi- 'seriative' and si- 'destruct' prefixes, the suppletive stem initial consonants--are giving way to various types of change.

The motivations behind these changes have been given informal interpretation in terms of Kiparsky's substantive conditions on language change. A range of factors has been cited--rule loss, rule simplification, and reanalysis of underlying segments due to conditions on paradigm allomorphy, rule opacity, and the abstractness of underlying forms. Although the analyses I have presented are far from conclusive, they demonstrate that because of Navajo's abstract phonology and complex morphology, it will be an extremely rich source of information on linguistic change.

A highly interesting sociolinguistic survey could be constructed using as markers the variants discussed in this chapter plus a rule such as II-100, syllabic n-, which appears to be used variably by everyone and is keyed to speech rate as well as some of the more obvious regional dialect markers such as the assimilation of o- and the replacement of é- by í-. Once Navajo speaking linguists construct a survey that provides a proper conversational context for each marker, structured and spontaneous interviews can be conducted across a demographic sample of Navajo speakers and a great deal of data on Navajo linguistic diversity can be amassed. A variety of questions about the nature of Navajo linguistic variation can then come under closer scrutiny. 1) For example, certain markers on this survey should shed light on Wang's lexical diffusion hypothesis. The g^y- sound change can be easily checked for diffusion since it can occur in only a handful of morphemes. It should be possible to observe whether this change will become obligatory or whether it will lose momentum and die out. Perhaps the sociolinguistic factors that determine its fate can be isolated. 2) A broad geographic sample of these markers should clarify whether there is in fact a difference in the pattern of occurrence of what I have characterized as randomly distributed deep morphophonemic variation, such as the streamlining of progressive da- shift or the loss/extension of the oh- reduction rule, and what we think of as geographically stable dialect differences, such as the assimilation of o- to a- in eastern Navajo dialects. It could be that there are intermediate points on this scale. Such variation as is found in aspect+si paradigms has been present in Navajo for a long time and may be lexicalized into a number of regional patterns. 3) Geographic data on these markers should make it possible to determine whether use of the markers correlates with what is known about the geographical trends in Navajo language maintenance (Spolsky, 1971). Since there is a clear correlation between accessibility of a chapter area on the reservation to a school and to a large urbanized area and the amount of Navajo known by a Navajo six-year-old, we might expect at least some of these markers, such as the regularization of suppletive stem initials or the simplification of the da- shifts, to show the same geographic distribution. 4) There is already considerable empirical evidence to indicate that Navajo children use significantly more English loan words in their speech than was the case thirty years ago when proficiency in English was much more the exception than the rule (Holm, Holm, and Spolsky, 1971). A survey of these deeper grammatical changes across the generations, should reveal that the frequency of grammatical innovations increases in successively younger generations. Such data would give us a substantial look at the less conscious aspects of Navajo linguistic acculturation. 5) It would be intriguing to see if the late phonetic and variable process, II-100, syllabic n-, might function as an informality index like Labov's word final r-. Subjectively, it appears that as speech tempo increases, the incidence of syllabic n- increases. If this is indeed the case, we would have a basis for evaluating data on other types of linguistic diversity, regional dialect mixture and morphophonemic regularization, in terms of incidence per level of formality. 6) Further empirical research on Navajo linguistic variation should prove to be of practical importance to the growing movement toward bilingual schooling on the Reservation. Decisions in the writing of language materials can be clarified by an understanding of the dialect and grammatical differences across the Reservation. It is even possible that pedagogical materials can be developed to maintain such prized obscurities in the grammar as the progressive and perfective da- shifts, the suppletive stem initial consonants, the ni- replacement rule, etc.

4.30 Rule Summary

(5) aspect+si metathesis $\{^{di}_{ni}\} + si \rightarrow si + \{^{di}_{ni}\}$

condition: optional or dialect dependent for di-

(III-163r) si- deletion $si \rightarrow \emptyset$ / ASP+___+X+[

condition: optional if $X \rightarrow VC$

(III-192) ji+hi metathesis $ji + hi \rightarrow hi + ji$ / ___X+C_o[

condition: optional if $X \rightarrow V$

(12) hi- copying hi+(di)+X $\rightarrow$ hi+(di)+hi+X
                  1   2   3   1   2   1 3

Notes to Chapter Four

[1]Saville-Troike (1973) has suggested that certain changes in the VCV assimilation and strident assimilation rules can be surmised from archival data. Given the current flux in the use of these rules, such an assumption seems tenuous.

[2]I have not included variation in the use of stems, a topic that presupposes a better understanding of stem phonology than is now available. There are indications that this will be a productive area for the study of Navajo linguistic diversity. For example, with the prefix náhi- 'turn over' Young and Morgan present verbs with an unvaried stem set, -jįsh, jįsh, -jįsh; -ghał, -ghał, -ghał. A majority of younger speakers treat the perfectives of these verbs with a voiced stem final consonant (náhidéshjįzh, náhidéshghal), implying that the aspectual distinction that is conveyed by the non-varied stem set is being replaced by the more conventional stem alternations. Another good example of variation in the use of stems is in the unusual stem set, -tał, -táád, -tah, -ta', -táád 'unroll it', where the imperfective -táád resembles a perfective stem and the perfective -tah looks like an imperfective. It is possible to find a few persons who switch the imperfective and perfective stems, náoshtah instead of náoshtáád 'I am unrolling it', néiséłtáád instead of néiséłtah 'I unrolled it'.

[3]The metathesis of hi+si to si+hi is completely impossible since this would place a conjunct prefix before hi-, which is the environment for the loss of h-.

[4]Reichard and Bitanny make note of the variation in classifiers with ná- 'back', claiming that the classifier shift is more correct in the third person than in first person forms (1940:20-21).

[5]This fact was pointed out by Ken Hale (personal communication).

[6]This is added support for the claim that progressive strident assimilation is an early rule. See 2.75 and 3.534.

[7]Reichard has made brief reference to the existence of l ∿ ln doublets in Navajo (1951:140).

[8]Some persons render this verb with +ł+, yiisxęs, yiixęs.

[9]Certain apparent dz- initial stems are in fact derived from s-y-dz stems. For example, the verb 'talk him out of it' (literally 'drive it through him'), bighanisdzood I1, bighaineedzood P3, is clearly derived from the s-y-dz stem 'drive' with the addition of a d- classifier which causes the dz- to appear in all forms of the verb.

[10]However, upon analogy with the other sound mergers in the front palatal series, gh^y- becomes z- in some stems in some dialects. The most obvious example is the eastern Navajo zas 'snow' instead of yas, which is a PA stem initial *gh^y-. Hoijer has suggested that PA may have had two y- phonemes, a voiced palatal spirant, gh^y-, and a semi-vowel (1963:5fn). This merits further comparative study.

[11] Frequently the mysterious i- or yi- prefix present in the above paradigms is dropped, naaseeł, nanigheeł.

[12] This interpretation was made by Ken Hale (personal communication).

CHAPTER FIVE
CONCLUSION

In this study I have presented a fairly comprehensive analysis of the morphophonemic alternations in the prefix complex of the Navajo regular active verb. This analysis has contributed to a clearer notion of the basic paradigms and conjugation patterns in the Navajo verb. The underlying representations I have employed for the verb modes are considerably more concrete than those in Stanley 1969a.

The most significant contribution to Navajo phonology in this study is the # disjunct boundary. The disjunct boundary reflects a fundamental synchronic-diachronic distinction in the prefix complex and is central to a definition of the three mode variants and a full structural statement of the verb modes. With the help of the disjunct boundary, the basic verbal paradigms can be reduced from eleven to ten with the elimination of the phonologically predictable yi- imperfective. It is also the key to a number of important phonological rules such as II-11 ni- absorption, II-12 vowel deletion, and II-46 pepet vowel insertion. There is no doubt that the disjunct boundary will play a similarly important role in phonological descriptions of other Athapaskan languages.

A number of the phonological and derivational processes that have been discussed in this study are of general theoretical interest. 1) Vowel assimilation is a most complex topic, and the formulation presented in this work is the most complete to date (2.73). We saw that the central process, rule II-57, is the assimilation of i- to the height and backness of an adjacent vowel in the internal environment, $\underline{\quad} C_o [$. It is of special interest that the eastern dialect which assimilates o- to a- has generalized the i- assimilation to all high vowels. 2) The directionality of the strident assimilation processes is an interesting problem (2.75, 3.534). I have suggested that there are two separate rules, an early progressive strident assimilation rule and a later regressive rule. Perhaps this can be further refined into a single process. 3) The graded nature of the syllabic n- rule, II-100, is a test of phonological formalism (2.77). The features [+coronal, -continuant] are a target environment for syllabic n-; the further from this target, the less likely the rule is to operate. 4) It is an interesting fact that the two reduplication rules, III-19 yi- doubling and III-87 náá- reduplication, are both triggered by a vowel to the right of the prefix that is copied. 5) The alternations in high tones in the prefix complex can be predicted by positing certain inherently high tones and a series of rules that derive and alter tones. 6) The obscurity of Navajo phonology is epitomized by the hi- 'seriative' prefix which undergoes an array of amazingly complex phonological rules, all of which are triggered when hi- is preceded by a conjunct prefix. Even more surprising is the extension of two of the hi- 'seriative' rules to the unproductive si- 'destruct' prefix (3.6). 7) It appears that morphophonemic alternations in Navajo can be handled by the extrinsically ordered non-cyclic rules of the standard theory of generative phonology, i.e. without recourse to more powerful global rules. Certain conflicts in rule ordering within a paradigm have been noted (3.422 and 3.423) which deserve further consideration. 8) The introduction of da- plural into certain ni- and ghi- perfectives causes a shift to the si- perfective, a highly abstract paradigmatic alternation. This seems to be correlated in part with the "choice" of perfectives by productive derivational prefixes in pos. 1. Perfective da- shift promises to be a fruitful topic for future Navajo and Athapaskan research.

In addition, this analysis of the verb prefix morphophonemics has illuminated those areas of the verb, noted by Harris and Krauss, that resist synchronic analysis. I have noted the difficulty of deriving certain vowels, especially e-, which is almost always secondary yet is usually beyond explanation. The use of non-phonological readjustment rules to "force" a synchronic solution is most prevalent in the perfective mode for the classifier subdivisions and the unusual si- perfective alternations. Readjustment rules also play a prominant part in the derivation of the ni- imperfective, the progressive, and the +i+ aspect verbs. These areas of "resistance" are the points of tension between the synchronic and the diachronic grammar; they point the way toward a combined study of Navajo and comparative Athapaskan phonology.

Other questions for further research have been raised in this study. 1) In a sense, this analysis of the verb mode system is conservative since it is based on the outline of the Navajo verb as it was conceived to be more than thirty years ago by Sapir and Hoijer. Krauss has noted that we have yet to arrive at substantial definitions for 'mode' and 'aspect'. There are signs that the basic paradigmatic mode system may be somewhat simpler than we have assumed it to be (3.7). 2) In this study no attempt has been made to incorporate the several productive and semi-productive aspectual sub-systems in a systematic way. These include yí- 'tentative', o- imperfective, and the puzzling +i+ aspect. Just how do these aspects interact with mode? 3) A major topic for further study is to integrate the analysis of the prefix phonology and the stem phonology. Prefixes in at least three positions (1, 6, and 7) trigger variations in the stems. How should the aspectual stem variations be incorporated into the heretofore basically prefixal definition of the mode system? 4) The paradigmatic alternations in the verb prefix complex have been explored with rigor, but the derivational properties of the verb, as Krauss 1970 has noted, have received very little study to date. Three topics discussed in this study have potential for revealing insights into the processes of Navajo word formation: the distribution of adverbial prefixes in the progressive (3.41), perfective choice and perfective da- shift (3.55). 5) This study has been confined to the active verbs. There is considerable work to be done in Navajo neuter verb phonology where there is evidence of some unique phonological processes such as the non-application of the continuant devoicing rule (2.71) and the alternations involving the łi- 'inherent quality' prefix (3.125). 6) The study of the verb should be placed in a broader range of syntactic environments to elucidate issues such as the strength of the word initial verb boundary in prepounded and non-prepounded verb bases (2.6) and the effect of stem-suffixing enclitics on stem variation.

In this study I have also presented evidence that certain verb forms are being used variably. My intention was to isolate some of these structures and to give them preliminary documentation and informal analysis. It is of considerable significance that most of the variants discussed in Chapter Four occur in such highly marked verbs as the aspect+si paradigms, the progressive and perfective da- shifts, the hi- 'seriative' and si- 'destruct' verbs, verbs with suppletive stem initial consonants, etc. The variations suggest that some of the more obscure regions of the synchronic grammar are giving way to change. The study of Navajo linguistic variation has much to contribute to the theory of linguistic change. Also, the variations discussed in this study could form the basis of a highly interesting sociolinguistic study.

In concluding this work I should point out that the practical applications of the study of Navajo phonology, verb morphology, and linguistic diversity could easily be the subject of several dissertations. Navajo linguistics is (or should be) an integral part of the teacher training program for Navajo bilingual teachers. Navajo phonology is an ideal medium for teaching concepts of hypothesis building, rule generalization, etc. Several excellent materials for the introductory course in Navajo phonology for Navajos now exist (Hale, 1970, 1971, 1972d; Hale and Honie, 1972; Higgins, 1971). At a later stage in the Navajo linguistics program the study of Navajo linguistic diversity could provide training in dialectology and sociolinguistics as well as advanced phonology.

We have just begun to explore the ways in which Navajo linguistics can be incorporated into the bilingual curriculum. For example, verb paradigms can be used as a structural control in many types of pedagogical materials. It is possible to construct literacy materials based on verb paradigms that provide writing practice on the tone and vowel length distinctions and, at the same time, develop an awareness of the structure of the verb. A range of games based on the internal structure of the verb are possible. For instance, Hale (1973b) has outlined a verb prefix game based on the writing of the underlying forms of prefixes on chips or cards. At its most complex level, this prefix game could involve the full range of verb prefix phonological and morphological information. The curriculum potential of Navajo linguistics will surely develop as more Navajos become involved in the study of their language.

REFERENCES

Akmajian, Adrian, and Stephen Anderson

    1970 "On the use of the fourth person in Navajo, or Navajo made harder", *IJAL* 36, 1-8.

Cook, Eung-Do

    1971a "Vowels and tones in Sarcee", *Language* 47, 164-179.

    1971b "Phonological constraint and syntactic rule", *Linguistic Inquiry* 2, 465-478.

Franciscan Fathers

    1910 *Ethnologic dictionary of the Navajo language*, St. Michaels, Arizona.

    1912a *Vocabulary of the Navajo language* Vol. I, English-Navajo, St. Michaels, Arizona.

    1912b *Vocabulary of the Navajo language* Vol. II, Navajo-English St. Michaels, Arizona.

Golla, Victor K.

    1970 *Hupa grammar*, Unpublished Ph.D. dissertation, University of California at Berkeley.

Haile, Father Berard

    1941 *Learning Navaho* Vol. I, St. Michaels, Arizona.

    1942 *Learning Navaho* Vol. II, St. Michaels, Arizona.

    1947 *Learning Navaho* Vol. III, St. Michaels, Arizona.

    1948 *Learning Navaho* Vol. IV, St. Michaels, Arizona.

    1950 *A stem vocabulary of the Navaho language*, Navaho-English, St. Michaels, Arizona.

    1951 *A stem vocabulary of the Navaho language*, English-Navaho, St. Michaels, Arizona.

Hale, Ken

    1956 *The distribution of Class II prefixes in Navaho*, Unpublished M. A. thesis, Indiana University.

    1970 Navajo linguistics, Pt. I, *MS*, MIT.

    1971 Navajo linguistics, Pt. II, *MS*, MIT.

    1972a Letter to Jim Kari, April 26, 1972.

    1972b Letter to Jim Kari, May 25, 1972

    1972c Navajo linguistics, Pt. III, *MS*, MIT.

    1972d Navajo phonology problems: I-V, *MS*, MIT.

    1973a "A note on subject object inversion in Navajo", in *Issues in linguistics*, ed., B. Kachru, University of Illinois Press.

    1973b "Some comments on the role of American Indian linguistics in bilingual education", in *Bilingualism in the Southwest*, ed., Paul Turner, 203-227, University of Arizona Press.

Hale, Ken and Lorraine Honie

    1972 An introduction to the sound system of Navajo, Pt. I: Articulatory phonetics, *MS*, MIT.

Harris, Zellig

    1945 "Navaho phonology and Hoijer's analysis", *IJAL* 11, 239-246.

Harris, Zellig S. and Carl F. Voegelin

    1953 "Eliciting in linguistics", *Southwestern Journal of Anthropology* 9, 59-76.

Higgins, Roger

    1971 A dialogue on the Navajo classifier, *MS*, MIT.

Hoijer, Harry

    1945a "Navaho phonology", *University of New Mexico Publications in Anthropology* No.1.

Hoijer, Harry

    1945b "The Apachean verb I: verb structure and pronominal prefixes", *IJAL* 11, 193-203.

    1946a "The Apachean verb II: the prefixes for mode and tense", *IJAL* 12, 1-13.

    1946b "The Apachean verb III: the classifiers", *IJAL* 12, 51-59.

    1946c "Chiricahua Apache". *Linguistic structures of native America, Viking Fund for Anthropology* No. 6, 55-84.

    1948 "The Apachean verb IV: major form classes", *IJAL* 14, 247-59.

    1949 "The Apachean verb V: the theme and prefix complex", *IJAL* 15, 12-22.

    1953 "Review of Navaho grammar by Reichard", *IJAL* 19, 78-83.

    1963 "The Athapaskan languages", *University of California Publications in Linguistics* 29, 1-29.

    1964 "Cultural implications of some Navaho linguistic categories", in *Language in Culture and Society*, ed., Dell Hymes, 142-148, Harper and Row.

    1969 "Internal reconstruction in Navaho", *Word* 25, 155-160.

    1971 "Athapaskan morphology", *University of California Publications in Linguistics* 65, 113-147.

Holm, Agnes, Wayne Holm and Bernard Spolsky

    1971 "English loan words in the speech of six-year-old Navajo children", *Navajo Reading Study Progress Report* No. 16, The University of New Mexico.

Howren, Robert

    forthcoming "The phonology of Rae Dogrib", *Bulletin of the National Museum of Canada*.

    1971 "A formalization of the Athapaskan 'D-effect'", *IJAL* 39, 96-114.

Kari, James

    1972 Tanaina field notes, *MS*.

    1973 "Navajo language bibliography", *Navajo Reading Study Progress Report* No. 22, The University of New Mexico.

Kiparsky, Paul

    1968 "Linguistic universals and linguistic change", in *Universals in Linguistic Theory*, eds. E. Bach and R. Harms, 171-202, Holt, Rinehart and Winston.

    1971 "Historical linguistics", in *A Survey of Linguistic Science*, ed., W. O. Dingwall, 576-650, University of Maryland.

Kaufman, Ellen

    1972 Navajo spatial enclitics: a case for unbounded rightward movement, *MS*, MIT.

Krauss, Michael E.

    1965 "Eyak: A preliminary report", *Canadian Journal of Linguistics* 10, 167-187.

    1969 "On the classifiers in the Athapaskan, Eyak, and Tlingit verb", *IJAL Memoir* No. 24.

    1970 "Review of the phonology and morphology of the Navaho language by Sapir and Hoijer", *IJAL* 36, 220-228.

    forthcoming "Na-Dene", *Current Trends in Linguistics* 10.

Labov, William

    1972 "The internal evolution of linguistic rules", in *Linguistic Change and Generative Theory*, eds., R. Stockwell and R. Macaulay, 101-172, Indiana University Press.

Landar, Herbert J.

    1962 "Navaho optatives", *IJAL* 28, 9-13.

Li, Fang-Kuei

    1930 *Mattole, an Athapaskan Language*, The University of Chicago Press.

    1933 "Chipewyan consonants" Tsai Yuan Pei Anniversary Volume, *Bulletin of the History and Philology of the Academia Sinica* Suppl. Vol. 1, 429-467, Peiping.

    1946 "Chipewyan" *Linguistic structures of native America, Viking Fund Publications in Anthropology* No. 6, 398-423.

Ohannessian, Sirapi editor

    1969 *Conference on Navajo Orthography*, Center for Applied Linguistics, Washington, D. C.

Parrish, James E., Stephen Anderson, Adrian Akmajian, and Kenneth Hale

    1968 Remarks on pronominalization and the passive in Navaho, *MS*, MIT.

Perry, Edgar

    1972 *Western Apache dictionary*, White Mountain Apache Culture Center, Ft. Apache, Arizona.

Pike, Kenneth L. and Alton L. Becker

    1964 "Progressive neutralization in dimensions of Navaho stem matrices", *IJAL* 30, 144-154.

Reichard, Gladys A.

    1945 "Linguistic diversity among the Navaho Indians", *IJAL* 11, 156-68.

    1951 "Navaho grammar", *Publications of the American Ethnological Society* No. 21, New York: J. J. Augustin.

    n.d. A preliminary analysis of Navajo prefixes, Carbon copy of *MS*, Peabody Museum, Harvard University.

Reichard, Gladys and Adolph E. Bitanny

    1940 *Agentive and causative elements in Navajo*, New York: J. J. Augustin.

Sapir, Edward

    1925 "Pitch accent in Sarcee, an Athapaskan language", *Journal de la Société des Américanistes de Paris* 17, 185-205.

    1949 "Glottalized continuants in Navaho, Nootka, and Kwakiutl (with a note on Indo-European)", in *Selected Writings of Edward Sapir*, ed., D. Mandlebaum, 225-251, University of California Press.

Sapir, Edward and Harry Hoijer

    1967 "The phonology and morphology of the Navaho language", *University of California Publications in Linguistics* 50.

Saville, Muriel

    1968 *Navajo morphophonemics*, Unpublished Ph.D. dissertation, University of Texas.

Saville-Troike, Muriel

    1973 "Variation and change in Navajo: some preliminary notes", *Languages and Linguistics Working Papers* No. 7, Georgetown University Press.

Spolsky, Bernard

    1971 "Navajo language maintenance III: Accessibility of school and town as a factor in language shift", *Navajo Reading Study Progress Report* No. 14, The University of New Mexico.

Stanley, Richard

    1969a *Navaho phonology*, Unpublished Ph.D. dissertation, MIT.

    1969b "Review of the phonology and morphology of the Navaho language by Sapir and Hoijer", *Language* 45, 927-939.

    1971 *Boundaries in phonology*, Indiana University Linguistics Club.

Wang, William

    1969 "Competing changes as a cause of residue", *Language* 45, 9-25.

Werner Oswald

    1963 *A typological comparison of four Trader Navaho speakers*, Unpublished Ph.D. dissertation, Indiana University.

Witherspoon, Gary

    1971 "Navaho categories of objects at rest", *American Anthropologist*, 73, 110-127.

Young, Robert W.

    1940 Athapaskan vocabulary, MS.

    1973 Relative sequence of prefixes in the Navajo verb, MS, University of New Mexico.

Young, Robert W. and William Morgan

    1943 *The Navaho language*, Education Division, United States Indian Service, Phoenix, Arizona.

    1948 *The function and signification of certain Navaho particles*, Education Division, United States Indian Service, Phoenix, Arizona.

    1951 *A vocabulary of colloquial Navaho*, Education Division, United States Indian Service, Phoenix, Arizona.

THE LIBRARY
ST. MARY'S COLLEGE OF MARYLAND
ST. MARY'S CITY, MARYLAND 20686